Lecture Notes in Control and Information Sciences

Edited by A. V. Balakrishnan and M. Thoma

Vol. 1: Distributed Parameter Systems: Modelling and Identification
Proceedings of the IFIP Working Conference, Rome, Italy, June 21–26, 1976
Edited by A. Ruberti
V, 458 pages. 1978

Vol. 2: New Trends in Systems Analysis
International Symposium, Versailles, December 13–17, 1976
Edited by A. Bensoussan and J. L. Lions
VII, 759 pages. 1977

Vol. 3: Differential Games and Applications
Proceedings of a Workshop, Enschede, Netherlands, March 16–25, 1977
Edited by P. Hagedorn, H. W. Knobloch, and G. J. Olsder
XII, 236 pages. 1977

Vol. 4: M. A. Crane, A. J. Lemoine
An Introduction to the Regenerative Method for Simulation Analysis
VII, 111 pages. 1977

Vol. 5: David J. Clements, Brian D. O. Anderson
Singular Optimal Control: The Linear Quadratic Problem
V, 93 pages. 1978

Vol. 6: Optimization Techniques
Proceedings of the 8th IFIP Conference on Optimization Techniques, Würzburg, September 5–9, 1977
Part 1
Edited by J. Stoer
XIII, 528 pages. 1978

Vol. 7: Optimization Techniques
Proceedings of the 8th IFIP Conference on Optimization Techniques, Würzburg, September 5–9, 1977
Part 2
Edited by J. Stoer
XIII, 512 pages. 1978

Vol. 8: R. F. Curtain, A. J. Pritchard
Infinite Dimensional Linear Systems Theory
VII, 298 pages. 1978

Vol. 9: Y. M. El-Fattah, C. Foulard
Learning Systems:
Decision, Simulation, and Control
VII, 119 pages. 1978

Vol. 10: J. M. Maciejowski
The Modelling of Systems with Small Observation Sets
VII, 241 pages. 1978

Vol. 11: Y. Sawaragi, T. Soeda, S. Omatu
Modelling, Estimation, and Their Applications for Distributed Parameter Systems
VI, 269 pages. 1978

Vol. 12: I. Postlethwaite, A. G. J. McFarlane
A Complex Variable Approach to the Analysis of Linear Multivariable Feedback Systems
IV, 177 pages. 1979

Vol. 13: E. D. Sontag
Polynomial Response Maps
VIII, 168 pages. 1979

Vol. 14: International Symposium on Systems Optimization and Analysis
Rocquentcourt, December 11–13, 1978;
IRIA LABORIA
Edited by A. Bensoussan and J. Lions
VIII, 332 pages. 1979

Vol. 15: Semi-Infinite Programming
Proceedings of a Workshop, Bad Honnef, August 30 – September 1, 1978
V, 180 pages. 1979

Vol. 16: Stochastic Control Theory and Stochastic Differential Systems
Proceedings of a Workshop of the „Sonderforschungsbereich 72 der Deutschen Forschungsgemeinschaft an der Universität Bonn"
which took place in January 1979 at Bad Honnef
VIII, 615 pages. 1979

Vol. 17: O. I. Franksen, P. Falster, F. J. Evans
Qualitative Aspects of Large Scale Systems
Developing Design Rules Using APL
XII, 119 pages. 1979

Vol. 18: Modelling and Optimization of Complex Systems
Proceedings of the IFIP-TC 7 Working Conference
Novosibirsk, USSR, 3–9 July, 1978
Edited by G. I. Marchuk
VI, 293 pages. 1979

Vol. 19: Global and Large Scale System Models
Proceedings of the Center for Advanced Studies (CAS)
International Summer Seminar
Dubrovnik, Yugoslavia, August 21–26, 1978
Edited by B. Lazarević
VIII, 232 pages. 1979

Vol. 20: B. Egardt
Stability of Adaptive Controllers
V, 158 pages. 1979

Vol. 21: Martin B. Zarrop
Optimal Experiment Design for Dynamic System Identification
X, 197 pages. 1979

For further listing of published volumes please turn over to inside of back cover.

Lecture Notes in
Control and
Information Sciences

Edited by A.V. Balakrishnan and M. Thoma

56

Dines Chandra Saha
Ganti Prasada Rao

Identification of Continuous Dynamical Systems

The Poisson Moment Functional (PMF) Approach

Springer-Verlag Berlin Heidelberg GmbH

Authors
Dr. Dines Chandra Saha
Department of Electrical Engineering
Indian Institute of Technology
KHARAGPUR 721 302
India

Professor Ganti Prasada Rao
Lehrstuhl für Elektrische Steuerung und Regelung
Ruhr-Universität Bochum
4630 Bochum 1
Federal Republic of Germany

(on Sabbatical Leave from the
Department of Electrical Engineering
Indian Institute of Technology
KHARAGPUR 721 302
India)

AMS Subject Classification (1980): 93-xx

ISBN 978-3-540-12759-8 ISBN 978-3-540-38728-2 (eBook)
DOI 10.1007/978-3-540-38728-2

Originally published by Springer-Verlag Berlin Heidelberg New York Tokyo in 1983

TO

OUR FAMILIES

(DCS)

Rina
Aniruddha

(GPR)

Meenakshi
Nagalakshmi
Rajeswari
Venkata Lakshmi Narayana

About the authors

DINES CHANDRA SAHA was born at Nabagram, West Bengal, India, on the 20th August, 1943. He studied in the University of Calcutta, India, and received the B.Sc. (Honors in Physics), B. Tech., and M. Tech. degrees in Applied Physics in 1963, 1965 and 1966 respectively. He received the M.E.E. degree from Jadavpur University, Calcutta, in 1969 and the Ph.D. degree in engineering from the Indian Institute of Technology, Kharagpur, in 1981.

From 1967 to 1969 he was with the Department of Electrical Engineering Jadavpur University as a Technical Teacher Trainee. In June 1970 he joined the Department of Electrical Engineering, Indian Institute of Technology, Kharagpur, as a Lecturer. His research interests and publications are in the field of control systems engineering in general and system identification in particular.

GANTI PRASADA RAO was born in Seethanagaram, Andhra Pradesh, India, on the 25th August, 1942. He studied at the College of Engineering, Kakinada, and received the B.E. degree in Electrical Engineering from Andhra University, Waltair (India) in 1963 with first class and high honours. He received the M. Tech. (Control Systems Engineering) and Ph.D. Degrees in Electrical Engineering in 1965 and 1969 respectively, both from the Indian Institute of Technology (I.I.T.) Kharagpur.

From July 1969 to October 1971 he was with the Department of Electrical Engineering, PSG College of Technology, Coimbatore, as an Assistant Professor. In October 1971 he joined the Department of Electrical Engineering, I.I.T. Kharagpur as an Assistant Professor and became a Professor in May 1978. From May 1978 to August 1980, he was the Chairman of the Electrical Engineering Curriculum Development Cell at I.I.T. Kharagpur. From October 1975 to July 1976, he was with the Control Systems Center, UMIST, Manchester, England, as a Commonwealth Post doctoral Research Fellow. Presently he is with the Lehrstuhl für Elektrische Steuerung und Regelung, Ruhr-Universität Bochum, West Germany, as a Research Fellow of the Alexander von Humboldt Foundation.

He has research interests and publications in the areas of mathematical instruments, time-varying systems, parametric phenomena, system identification, applications of Walsh and related piecewise constant functions, and fuzzy logic control

Professor GANTI PRASADA RAO is a Senior Member of the IEEE and a Fellow of the Institution of Engineers (India).

P R E F A C E

In order to overcome the difficulties associated with the derivative measurement problem in continuous model identification (CMI), certain techniques have appeared in the literature around the early nineteen sixties. Some of these depend on off-line computation of certain definitie integrals. The Poisson moment functional (PMF) method appeared in the early nineteen seventies to render the technique on-line, by realising the necessary integrals as the physically measurable outputs at the various stages of a Poisson filter chain (PFC) system. The PMF method at that stage was in a form without adequate generality and was applicable to a limited class of continuous models. In the last few years, considerable work has been done in this area. The basic PMF method has been generalized. Conditions of identifiability have been established. Modifications of the general PMF algorithm to handle models containing unknown time delays and nonlinear elements have been suggested. Methods of structure identification have been reported. The PMF method in noisy situations has been assessed. Recently, Kalman filtering applied to the PFC is found to give excellent results in noisy situations, removing the earlier difficulties due to correlated noise at the various stages of the PFC. With its extension to MIMO models and to distributed parameter systems, the PMF method has attained a level of maturity and generality in CMI.

In this book the authors have attempted to put together the various developments in the PMF area in a comprehensive form. Relevant discussions on the relationship of the PMF method with certain other techniques are presented at appropriate places. The authors hope that this book will be of interest to those working in the area of CMI.

The authors are indebted to several colleagues for their assistance at various stages of preparation of this book. In particular, at the Indian Institute of Technology, Kharagpur, Professors C.N.Kaul (Mathematics) and N. Kesavamurthy (Electrical Engineering) reviewed the initial version of the manuscript and gave constructive comments. They are grateful to Professor H. Unbehauen, Lehrstuhl für Elektrische Steuerung und Regelung, Ruhr-Universität Bochum, for his interest, encouragement and advice throughout the preparation of the book. Ganti Prasada Rao gratefully acknowledges the support received from the Alexander von Humboldt Foundation which greatly helped in the realisation of this book. The authors are grateful to Frau H. Hupp, Frau P. Kiesel and Frau E. Schmitt for typewriting the text. They thank Frau M.-L. Schmücker and Frl. H. Vollbrecht for the figures. The several phases of research and writing took place in an excellent atmosphere of warmth, love and encouragement created by the authors' families. This book is dedicated to them.

Dr. Dines Chandra Saha
Department of Electrical
Engineering
Indian Institute of Technology
Kharagpur (WB) 721 302, India

Prof. Dr. Ganti Prasada Rao
Alexander von Humboldt
Research Fellow
Lehrstuhl für Elektrische
Steuerung und Regelung
Ruhr-Universität Bochum
4630 Bochum 1
Federal Republic of Germany
(on Sabbatical Leave from the
Department of Electrical
Engineering
IIT, Kharagpur 721 302, India)

May 1983

SPECIAL ACKNOWLEDGEMENT

The authors thank the publishers of the following journals, for permission to include in this book, considerable parts from references as detailed below:

1. IEEE Transactions on Automatic Control, Transactions on Industrial Electronics: References P.10, P.11, P.17.

2. Proceedings IEE: Reference P.14.

3. International Journal of Control (Taylor & Francis): References P.12, P.13, P.15, P.16, P.18, P.19, P.23.

4. International Journal of Systems Science (Taylor & Francis): Reference: P.24.

Dines Chandra Saha

and

Ganti Prasada Rao

CONTENTS

CHAPTER I

CONTINUOUS MODEL IDENTIFICATION (CMI)-INTRODUCTION

During the early period of development of automatic control techniques, system models were obtained with sinusoidal and transient stimuli from planned experiements in mind. The models were continuous time descriptions such as differential equations and transfer functions. Such modelling is natural since most physical systems are inherently continuous. With the advent of powerful digital computers, techniques based on discrete models have increased considerably tending to obscure parallel developments in continuous model identification (CMI) although most of the control concepts have their roots in the continuous time domain. Recently, Young [G 32] gave an excellent account of the situation in a unified framework in a survey paper. Many other surveys [G 2, G 3, G 5, G 8] and books [G 11, G 23] also cover the subject of CMI to some extent.

An important problem in CMI is due to the need to know the time derivatives of input-output data which, in practice invariably contains noise. CMI algorithms involving direct generation of the time-derivatives of process signals either physically or by computation, are good only in deterministic situations and remain satisfactory if the noise level in the measured input-output data is low (< 5 %, noise to signal ratio) [G 32]. This state of affairs has motivated many researchers in the early nineteen sixties to devise methods having considerable resistance to noise. The various approaches to the derivative measurement problem have been reviewed by Young [G 32]. Prasada Rao and Sivakumar [P 9] discussed the problem in a general framework unifying a class of techniques of CMI.

A continuous time SISO model is generally in the form

$$\sum_{k=o}^{N_2 \geq n} \sum_{i=o}^{N_2 \geq n} S_{f_i}(t, \tau_{f_k})\, U_{f_{i,k}} = \sum_{j=o}^{R_2 \geq m} \sum_{k=o}^{R_1 > m} S_{r_j}(t, \tau_{r_j})\, U_{r_{j,k}} \tag{1.1}$$

where $U_{f_{i,k}}$ and $U_{r_{j,k}}$ are the constant unknown parameters of the output and input sections respectively. S_{f_i} and S_{r_j} are members of the output and input signal families respectively. That is, if f(t) is the output signal, terms like $d^i f(t)/dt^i$, $t^i d^i f(t)/dt^i$, $[f(t)]^j$, $[f(t-\tau)]^j$, $t^j\ d^i f(t-\tau)/dt^i$, etc. may represent the form of the individual members of the output signal family. In actual practice, it is neither possible to directly observe some S_{f_i} and S_{r_j}, nor is it desirable to generate them directly using f(t) and r(t), owing to the derivative operations required therein. However, if we perform some linear dynamical operation on equation (1.1) on either side of it to transform S_{f_i} and S_{r_j} into some measurable terms denoted as, say, $\bar{S}_{f_i}$ and $\bar{S}_{r_j}$, then, we would avoid the undesirable direct derivative operations on f(t) and r(t). Thus

$$\bar{S}_{f_i} = \mathcal{L} S_{f_i} \quad ,$$

and

$$\bar{S}_{r_i} = \mathcal{L} S_{r_i} \quad ,$$

where $\mathcal{L}$ represents a low-pass linear dynamic operator. This has been the basis for a class of CMI methods.

Shinbrot's technique [P 22] of 'method functions' (or 'modulating functions'), involves a linear operation wherein the terms S_{f_i} and S_{r_j} are first multiplied by well behaved and suitably chosen known functions and then integrated over the period of available data. Perdreauville and Goodson [P 8] use method (or modulating) functions in two dimensions in identifying the parameters of systems characteriszed by partial differential equations. The offline computation of the integrals may be avoided by choosing method (or modulating) functions that stem from the impulse response functions of linear time invariant dynamical instruments or filters. The required values of the definite integrals may be 'measured'. The convolution integrals may be measured as the outputs at the various stages of a set of filter chains. The Poisson moment functional (PMF) method, with which this book is mainly concerned, employs such a filter chain, each element of which has transfer function of the form $1/(s+\lambda)$, $\lambda \geq 0$. The method of integrals (P1, P2, P8, P22) is the special case of $\lambda = 0$. The method of state variable filters [G 32] and the so called linear filter method [G 22] and the related techniques surveyed by Unbehauen et al [G 29] belong to this category. The method of moments, of the impulse response function, discussed by Bolch [G 6] in identifying time-invariant systems is close in spirit to the PMF technique.

In recent years techniques of CMI using Walsh functions and block-pulse functions have appeared in the literature. In these methods, the process signals are first converted into respective spectral components. When the spectra of input-output signals are inserted in the differential equations describing the models, their calculus is reduced to an elegant algebra, approximate in the sense of least squares. The resulting algebraic equations may be solved for the unknown parameters. The basic technique [W 2, W 9] is extended to handle continuous time models of several kinds [W 3, W 4, W 6, W 10 - W 14]. The algorithms are all reviewed and recently improved by Prasada Rao and Palanisamy [W 8]. For a unified and comprehensive account of the various applications, including CMI, of Walsh and block pulse functions, the reader may see the recent monograph: 'Piecewise constant orthogonal (basis) functions (PCBF) and their application to systems and control' by Prasada Rao [W 7].

In a way, the PCBF method of CMI may be viewed as a method function approach. Each basis function may be considered as a method function. The piecewise constant property and the orthogonal nature of the sets of Walsh functions and block pulse functions offer a number of advantages making the approach quite attractive in practice.

In the following chapters, we discuss the so called Poisson moment functional (PMF) method and its several variants and applications in a generalised treatment. The mathematical basis of the PMF method may be traced into the theory of generalised functions or distributions. In Chapter II, signal characterisation in terms of distributions is discussed. Chapters II-IX deal with the various problems of CMI in lumped systems. Chapter X presents the concept of multi-dimensional distributions and illustrates its use in the problem of parameter identification in distributed parameter systems.

CHAPTER II

SIGNAL CHARACTERIZATION IN TERMS OF DISTRIBUTIONS

2.1. Introduction

The main task in an identification problem is to process the input-output (I/O) data from an active operating record over a given interval of time. The process signals may be characterized basically by two different approaches. One method, frequently employed, is to treat the process signals as functions in the ordinary sense. The concept of ordinary functions has a numerical character so familiar to all that we are inclined to depend on it inspite of its several limitations. There exists another method in which the process signals are treated as distributions or generalised functions. The latter characterization is superior due to its unlimited 'differentiability'. The familiar numerical character of ordinary functions has to be sacrificed in order to gain advantage of making all continuous functions limitlessly 'differentiable'. The concept of generalised functions is orginally due to Dirac. Schwartz [P 20] established the necessary mathematical foundations, formalism and justification for generalised functions. Temple [G 27] gave a lucid theory of generalised functions and showed how these functions can be handled with considerable ease and simplicity and that certain fundamental theorems are remarkably free from the harassing restrictions which are necessary in the theory of ordinary functions. On the basis of generalised functions, Green and Messel [P 6] discussed the use of higher order time derivatives of Dirac delta function $\delta(t)$ in a series expansion of a function. It is well known that $\delta(t)$ cannot be treated as an ordinary function with the familiar numerical characterization with a definite value for every value of t. It should rather be treated as a distribution or generalised function.

2.2. The Poisson Moment Functional (PMF) Approach

A signal $f(t)$, $t \in (o,t_o)$ is treated as a distribution or a generalised function and expanded about a time t_o in the following exponentially weighted series, as initially suggested by Fairman and Shen [P 5]:

$$f(t) = \sum_{k=o}^{\infty} M_k\{f(t)\}\exp[-\lambda(t-t_o)]\delta^{(k)}(t-t_o) \quad , \tag{2.1}$$

where $\delta^{(k)}(t-t_o)$ is the k-th generalised time derivative of an impulse distribution occuring at $t = t_o$.

$$M_k\{f(t)\} \triangleq f_k^o = \int_0^{t_o} f(t)\; p_k(t_o-t)\; dt \quad , \tag{2.2}$$

$$p_k(t_o) \triangleq p_k^o = \frac{t_o^k}{k!} \exp(-\lambda\, t_o) \quad , \tag{2.3}$$

and λ is a positive real number. p_k^o is termed as the k-th order Poisson pulse function at t_o and f_k^o is called the k-th Poisson Moment Functional (PMF) of f(t) about $t = t_o$. f_k^o can be viewed as the output due to an input f(t), at $t = t_o$, of the (k+1)-th stage of a cascaded filter with identical stages, each element of which has a transfer function $\frac{1}{s+\lambda}$ as indicated in Fig. 2.1. Such a filter chain is known as a Poisson filter chain (PFC).

Some attractive features of the PMF characterization are:

a) The PMF transformation converts a process differential equation into an algebraic equation without any approximation. This is not so in other methods such as discretization of continuous models, numerical approximation methods, Walsh function methods [G 13, G 14, G 24, G 25, P 12] etc., where the process of reduction from continuous calculus to discrete algebra involves some approximation.

b) Noise accentuating derivative operations are efficiently avoided.

c) The integrals required in the determination of PMF's need not be computed off-line. They can be 'measured' physically as well-behaved output signals at $t = t_o$ of the various stages of a PFC excited by f(t).

d) The PMF characterization has unlimited differentiability.

e) There exists a regular pattern of relations between PMF's of the functions and their derivatives.

2.3. Some fundamental PMF relations including the effects of initial conditions

a) Consider

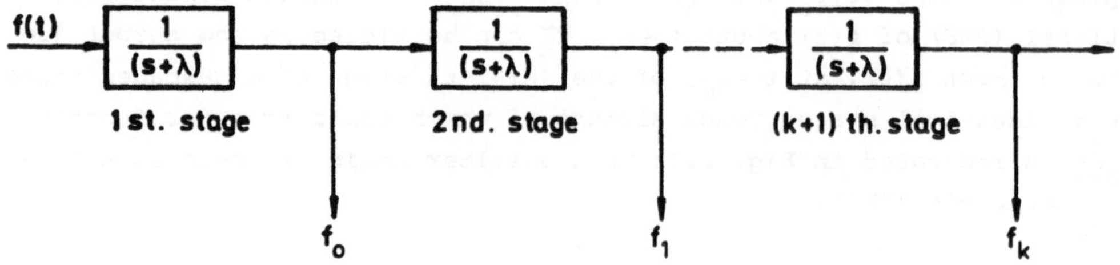

Fig. 2.1: A Poisson filter chain (PFC).

$$M_k\{\frac{df(t)}{dt}\} \triangleq M_k\{f^{(1)}(t)\}$$
$$\triangleq \int_o^{t_o} \frac{(t_o-t)^k}{k!} e^{-\lambda(t_o-t)} f^{(1)}(t)\, dt \quad .$$

Integrating by parts, the R.H.S. of the above equation may be written as

$$\frac{(t_o-t)^k}{k!} e^{-\lambda(t_o-t)} f(t) \Big|_o^{t_o} - \int_o^{t_o} \Big[-\frac{(t_o-t)^{k-1}}{(k-1)!} e^{-\lambda(t_o-t)}$$
$$+ \lambda \frac{(t_o-t)^k}{k!} e^{-\lambda(t_o-t)} \Big] f(t)\, dt \quad .$$

Thus we get

$$M_k\{f^{(1)}(t)\} = f^o_{k-1} - \lambda f^o_k - p^o_k f^{(o)}(o) \quad . \tag{2.4}$$

Here $f^{(o)}(o)$ denotes the value of the function $f(t)$ at $t=o$.

b) Consider

$$M_k\{\frac{d^2f(t)}{dt^2}\} \triangleq M_k\{f^{(2)}(t)\}$$
$$\triangleq \int_o^{t_o} \frac{(t_o-t)^k}{k!} e^{-\lambda(t_o-t)} f^{(2)}(t)\, dt \quad .$$

Integrating by parts, the R.H.S. of above equation may be written as

$$\frac{(t_o-t)^k}{k!} e^{-\lambda(t_o-t)} f^{(1)}(t) \Big|_o^{t_o} - \int_o^{t_o} \Big[-\frac{(t_o-t)^{k-1}}{(k-1)!} e^{-\lambda(t_o-t)}$$
$$+ \lambda \frac{(t_o-t)^k}{k!} e^{-\lambda(t_o-t)} \Big] f^{(1)}(t)\, dt \quad .$$

Therefore,

$$M_k\{f^{(2)}(t)\} = -p^o_k f^{(1)}(o) + M_{k-1}\{f^{(1)}(t)\} - \lambda M_k\{f^{(1)}(t)\}$$
$$= f^o_{k-2} - 2\lambda f^o_{k-1} + \lambda^2 f^o_k - (p^o_{k-1} - \lambda p^o_k) f^{(o)}(o)$$
$$- p^o_k f^{(1)}(o) \quad . \tag{2.5}$$

c) Consider the evaluation of

$$M_k\{t\, f(t)\} \triangleq \int_0^{t_o} \left[\frac{t(t_o-t)^k}{k!} e^{-\lambda(t_o-t)}\right] f(t)\, dt$$

$$= -\int_0^{t_o} (t_o-t) \frac{(t_o-t)^k}{k!} e^{-\lambda(t_o-t)} f(t)\, dt$$

$$+ t_o \int_0^{t_o} \frac{(t_o-t)^k}{k!} e^{-\lambda(t_o-t)} f(t)\, dt$$

$$= t_o\, f_k^o - (k+1)\, f_{k+1}^o \quad . \tag{2.6}$$

d) Consider

$$M_k\{t\, f^{(1)}(t)\} \triangleq \int_0^{t_o} \left[\frac{t(t_o-t)^k}{k!} e^{-\lambda(t_o-t)}\right] f^{(1)}(t)\, dt \quad .$$

Integrating by parts,

$$\frac{t(t_o-t)^k}{k!} e^{-\lambda(t_o-t)} f(t) \Bigg|_0^{t_o} - \int_0^{t_o} \frac{d}{dt} \left[\frac{t(t_o-t)^k}{k!} e^{-\lambda(t_o-t)}\right] f(t)\, dt$$

$$= -\int_0^{t_o} \left[\frac{(t_o-t)^k}{k!} e^{-\lambda(t_o-t)} - \frac{t(t_o-t)^{k-1}}{(k-1)!} e^{-\lambda(t_o-t)}\right.$$

$$\left. + \lambda \frac{t(t_o-t)^k}{k!} e^{-\lambda(t_o-t)}\right] f(t)\, dt \quad .$$

Simplifying and rearranging, we get

$$M_k\{t\, f^{(1)}(t)\} \triangleq t_o\, f_{k-1}^o - \{\lambda\, t_o + (k+1)\} f_k^o + \lambda(k+1) f_{k+1}^o \, . \tag{2.7}$$

e) Lastly, consider

$$M_k\{t\, f^{(2)}(t)\} \triangleq \int_0^{t_o} \left[\frac{t(t_o-t)^k}{k!} e^{-\lambda(t_o-t)}\right] f^{(2)}(t)\, dt \quad .$$

Integrating by parts, the R.H.S. of the above equation may be written as

$$\frac{t(t_o-t)^k}{k!} e^{-\lambda(t_o-t)} f^{(1)}(t) \Bigg|_0^{t_o} - \int_0^{t_o} \frac{d}{dt} \left[\frac{t(t_o-t)^k}{k!} e^{-\lambda(t_o-t)}\right] f^{(1)}(t)\, dt$$

$$= - \int_o^{t_o} \frac{d}{dt} \left[t \, \frac{(t_o - t)^k}{k!} \, e^{-\lambda (t_o - t)} \right] f^{(1)}(t) \, dt$$

$$= - \{ \frac{d}{dt} \left[t \, \frac{(t_o - t)^k}{k!} \, e^{-\lambda (t_o - t)} \right] f(t) \} \Big|_o^{t_o}$$

$$+ \int_o^{t_o} \frac{d^2}{dt^2} \left[t \, \frac{(t_o - t)^k}{k!} \, e^{-\lambda (t_o - t)} \right] f(t) \, dt \quad .$$

Simplifying and rearranging, we get

$$M_k\{t \, f^{(2)}(t)\} = t_o \, f^o_{k-2} - \{2 \lambda t_o + (k+1)\} \, f^o_{k-1}$$

$$+\{\lambda^2 t_o + 2 \lambda (k+1)\} \, f^o_k - \lambda^2 (k+1) \, f^o_{k+1} + p^o_k \, f^{(o)}(o) \quad . \tag{2.8}$$

Notice here that the PMF's of terms multiplied by t require one higher order PMF of the function f(t).

In this way we can express PMF's of the terms of the form $[t^i \, d^j f(t)/dt^j]$ about t_o as a linear combination of the various PMF's of f(t) itself about t_o. The factors of weightage depend on k, t_o and λ.

2.4. Development of transformation matrices in a general format

In order to aid the understanding of the development of a general form, consider, first, the following three relationships that exist among f(t) and its PMF's f_o, f_1 and f_2:

$$\frac{df_o(t)}{dt} + \lambda \, f_o(t) = f(t)$$

$$\frac{df_1(t)}{dt} + \lambda \, f_1(t) = f_o(t)$$

$$\frac{df_2(t)}{dt} + \lambda \, f_2(t) = f_1(t) \quad .$$

Here f_o, f_1 and f_2 are written as functions of time for the purpose of describing the PFC in state space form. The above equations may be written as

$$\frac{dF}{dt} = (\Delta_{(3x3)} - \lambda \, I_{(3x3)}) \, F + Q_{(1x3)} f(t) \quad , \tag{2.9}$$

where $F = [f_o(t),\ f_1(t),\ f_2(t)]^T$,

$$\Delta_{(3x3)} = \begin{bmatrix} 0 & 0 & 0 \\ 1 & 0 & 0 \\ 0 & 1 & 0 \end{bmatrix} ,$$

$$Q_{(3x1)} = [1,\ 0,\ 0]^T ,$$

and $I_{(3x3)}$ is an identity matrix.

The fundamental relations shown in equations (2.2 - 2.9) may now be arranged in a format whose convenience will be evident in PMF transfomations of process differential equations of lumped linear systems. We first consider PMF transformation of a set of terms with $k = 2$ for illustration about $t = t_o$, which may be arranged in the vector form as follows:

$$M_2[f^{(2)}(t),\ f^{(1)}(t),\ f(t)]^T$$

$$= \begin{bmatrix} f_o^o - 2\lambda f_1^o + \lambda^2 f_2^o - (p_1^o - \lambda\ p_2^o)\ f^{(o)}(o) - p_2 f^{(1)}(o) \\ f_1^o - \lambda\ f_2^o - p_2^o\ f^{(o)}(o) \\ f_2^o \end{bmatrix} . \qquad (2.10)$$

Similarly,

$$M_2[t\ (f^{(2)}(t),\ f^{(1)}(t),\ f(t))]^T$$

$$= \begin{bmatrix} t_o f_o^o - (2\lambda t_o + 3)\ f_1^o + \lambda(\lambda t_o + 6)\ f_2^o - 3\lambda^2 f_3^o + p_2^o\ f^{(o)}(o) \\ t_o f_1^o - (\lambda\ t_o + 3)\ f_2^o + 3\lambda f_3^o \\ t_o f_2^o - 3\ f_3^o \end{bmatrix} . \qquad (2.11)$$

The state space description for the PFC and the PMF relations arranged in the vector form become convenient while dealing with the general models of lumped linear systems. We will now present the general format considering a q-th order PFC excited by f(t).

The state space description of PFC is written as

$$\frac{dF}{dt} = DF + Q\ f(t) \quad , \quad D = \Delta - \lambda\ I \quad , \qquad (2.12)$$

where F is a q-vector of PMF's (as functions of time) of order 0, 1, 2, ... (q-1). Δ, Q and I are matrices of appropriate dimensions. Let F^o denote the state (output) of the PFC at $t = t_o$ given by

$$F^o = [f_o^o, f_1^o, \ldots\ldots, f_{q-1}^o]^T \quad . \tag{2.13}$$

If f(t) and its derivatives are zero for $t < 0$, it is possible to show that (see Appendix 2.6) the PMF transformation of the general term about t_o:

$$M_k[t^j(f^{(n)}(t), f^{(n-1)}(t), \ldots\ldots, f(t))]^T$$
$$= \mathcal{F}_{k,j}^o - (-1)^j S_{f,j} \mathcal{P}_{k,o}^o \quad , \tag{2.14}$$

where

$$\mathcal{F}_{k,j}^o = \mathcal{J}_{k,j}^o \mathcal{F}^o \quad , \tag{2.15}$$

$$\mathcal{J}_{k,j}^o = [Q^T \nabla^j T_k^o] \otimes I_{(n+1) \times (n+1)} \quad , \tag{2.16a}$$

$$S_{f,j} = S_{f,o} H^j \quad , \tag{2.16b}$$

$$S_{f,o} = \sum_{i=o}^{n} \nabla^{i-1}{}_{(n+1) \times (n+1)} f^{(i)}(o) \quad , \tag{2.16c}$$

$$H = \left[\sum_{i=1}^{n+1} (n-i+1) \Delta^{i-1}_{(n+1) \times (n+1)} \nabla^n_{(n+1) \times (n+1)} \Delta^{n-i+1}_{(n+1) \times (n+1)} \right] \tag{2.17}$$

$$\nabla_{(n+1) \times (n+1)} \quad ,$$

$$\mathcal{P}_{k,o}^o = [p_k^{(n)}, p_k^{(n-1)}, \ldots\ldots, p_k^{(o)}]^T$$
$$= \Gamma^{(k-n)} p^o \quad . \tag{2.18}$$

$p_k^{(n)}$ is the k-th PMF of $d^n\delta(t)/dt^n$ about $t = t_o$.

$$p^o = [p_o^o, p_1^o, \ldots\ldots, p_{q-1}^o]^T \quad . \tag{2.19}$$

It is important to note that since H is nilpotent with index n, $S_{f,i}$ becomes null for $i \geq n$.

The matrices T_k^o, ∇ and $\mathcal{F}^o$ in the above are given by

$$T_k^o = \sum_{i=1}^{j+1} \nabla^{j-i+1}_{(j+1)\times(j+1)} \Delta^{j}_{(j+1)\times(j+1)} \tau_k^{o\,i-1} , \tag{2.20}$$

$$\tau_k^o = t_o I_{(j+1)\times(j+1)} - \left[\sum_{i=1}^{j} (k+i) \Delta^{i-1}_{(j+1)\times(j+1)} \nabla^{j}_{(j+1)\times(j+1)} \Delta^{j-i+1}_{(j+1)\times(j+1)}\right] \cdot \nabla_{(j+1)\times(j+1)} , \tag{2.21}$$

$$\nabla = \Delta^T , \tag{2.22}$$

$$\mathcal{F}^o = \left[\mathcal{F}^{o\,T}_{k,o} \,\vdots\, \mathcal{F}^{o\,T}_{k+1,o} \,\vdots\, \ldots\ldots \,\vdots\, \mathcal{F}^{o\,T}_{k+m,o}\right]^T , \tag{2.23}$$

$$\mathcal{F}^o_{k+i,o} \triangleq \left[f^{(n)}_{k+i}, f^{(n-1)}_{k+i}, \ldots, f^{(o)}_{k+i}\right]^T$$

$$= \Gamma^{(k+i-n)} F^o, \text{ (See Appendix 2.6)} . \tag{2.24}$$

$f^{(n)}_{k+i}$ is the (k+i)-th PMF of $f^{(n)}(t)$ about $t = t_o$.

The matrix $\Gamma^{(k-n)}$ may be formed as:

$$\Gamma^{(k-n)}_{(n+1)xq} = [\underbrace{0}_{\substack{k-n\\ \text{cols.}}} \,\vdots\, \underbrace{\gamma}_{\substack{n+1\\ \text{cols.}}} \,\vdots\, \underbrace{0}_{\substack{q-k-1\\ \text{cols.}}}] , \tag{2.25}$$

$$\gamma_{(n+1)x(n+1)} = \sum_{i=1}^{n+1} \Delta^{i-1}_{(n+1)x(n+1)} Q_{(n+1)x1} [\Delta_{(n+1)x(n+1)} Q_{(n+1)x1}]^T (\Delta_{(n+1)x(n+1)} - \lambda I_{(n+1)x(n+1)})^{n-i+1} . \tag{2.26}$$

It is also possible to show that

$$\Gamma^{(k-n)}_{(n+1)xq} = \Gamma^{(k=n)}_{(n+1)xq} (\Delta^T_{q\,x\,q})^{k-n} . \tag{2.27}$$

The Kronecker product

$$X \otimes Y = \begin{bmatrix} x_{11}\,Y & x_{12}\,Y \ldots\ldots \\ x_{21}\,Y & x_{22}\,Y \ldots\ldots \\ \ldots\ldots & \ldots\ldots \\ \ldots\ldots & \ldots\ldots \end{bmatrix} . \tag{2.28}$$

For illustration, let us develop equations (2.10) and (2.11) using formula (2.14). In those cases $k = 2$, $n = 2$ and $j = 0$ and 1. We choose $q = 4$, since PMF transformation of the second derivative of the function requires f_o, f_1, f_2 and the PMF transformation of the terms multiplied by t requires one more higher order PMF of f(t) i.e. f_3. Therefore,

$$F^o = [f_o^o,\ f_1^o,\ f_2^o,\ f_3^o]^T \quad ,$$

$$P^o = [p_o^o,\ p_1^o,\ p_2^o,\ p_3^o]^T \quad ,$$

$$\gamma = \sum_{i=1}^{3} \Delta^{i-1}_{(3x3)}\ Q_{(3x1)}\ [\Delta^2_{(3x3)}\ Q_{(3x1)}]^T\ (\Delta_{(3x3)} - \lambda\, I_{(3x3)})^{3-i}$$

$$= \begin{bmatrix} 1 & -2\lambda & \lambda^2 \\ 0 & 1 & -\lambda \\ 0 & 0 & 1 \end{bmatrix} \quad ,$$

$$\Gamma^{(o)} = \begin{bmatrix} 1 & -2\lambda & \lambda^2 & 0 \\ 0 & 1 & -\lambda & 0 \\ 0 & 0 & 1 & 0 \end{bmatrix} \quad ,$$

$$\Gamma^{(1)} = \begin{bmatrix} 0 & 1 & -2\lambda & \lambda^2 \\ 0 & 0 & 1 & -\lambda \\ 0 & 0 & 0 & 1 \end{bmatrix} \quad ,$$

$$\mathcal{F}^o_{2,o} = [f_2^{(2)},\ f_2^{(1)},\ f_2^{(o)}]^T \quad ,$$

$$= \Gamma^{(o)}\ F^o \quad ,$$

$$= [(f_o^o - 2\lambda f_1^o + \lambda^2 f_2^o),\ (f_1^o - \lambda f_2^o),\ f_2^o]^T \quad ,$$

$$\mathcal{F}^o_{3,o} = [f_3^{(2)},\ f_3^{(1)},\ f_3^{(o)}]^T \quad ,$$

$$= \Gamma^{(1)}\ F^o \quad ,$$

$$= [(f_1^o - 2\lambda f_2^o + \lambda^2 f_3^o),\ (f_2^o - \lambda f_3^o),\ f_3^o]^T \quad ,$$

$$\mathcal{F}^o = [(f_o^o - 2\lambda f_1^o + \lambda^2 f_2^o),\ (f_1^o - \lambda f_2^o),\ f_2^o \quad ,$$

$$(f_1^o - 2\lambda f_2^o + \lambda^2 f_3^o),\ (f_2^o - \lambda f_3^o),\ f_3^o]^T \quad ,$$

$$\mathcal{P}^{o}_{2,o} = \Gamma^{(o)}\ p^{o}$$

$$= [(p^{o}_{o} - 2\lambda p^{o}_{1} + \lambda^{2} p^{o}_{2}), (p^{o}_{1} - \lambda\ p^{o}_{2}),\ p^{o}_{2}]^{T} \quad ,$$

$$H = \left[\sum_{i=1}^{3} (3-i)\ \Delta^{i-1}_{(3x3)}\ \nabla^{2}_{(3x3)}\ \Delta_{(3x3)}\right] \cdot \nabla_{(3x3)}$$

$$= \begin{bmatrix} 0 & 2 & 0 \\ 0 & 0 & 1 \\ 0 & 0 & 0 \end{bmatrix} \quad ,$$

$$S_{f,o} = \sum_{i=o}^{2} \nabla^{i+1}_{(3x3)}\ f^{(i)}(o)$$

$$= \begin{bmatrix} 0 & f^{(o)}(o) & f^{(1)}(o) \\ 0 & 0 & f^{(o)}(o) \\ 0 & 0 & 0 \end{bmatrix} \quad ,$$

$$S_{f,1} = S_{f,o}\ H$$

$$= \begin{bmatrix} 0 & 0 & f^{(o)}(o) \\ 0 & 0 & 0 \\ 0 & 0 & 0 \end{bmatrix} \quad ,$$

$$\tau^{o}_{2} = t_{o}\ I_{(2x2)} - 3\ \Delta^{o}_{(2x2)}\ \nabla_{(2x2)}\ \Delta_{(2x2)}\ \nabla_{(2x2)}$$

$$= \begin{bmatrix} t_{o} & -3 \\ 0 & t_{o} \end{bmatrix} \quad ,$$

$$T^{o}_{2} = \sum_{i=1}^{2} \nabla^{2-i}_{(2x2)}\ \Delta_{(2x2)}\ {\tau^{o}_{2}}^{i-1}$$

$$= \begin{bmatrix} 1 & 0 \\ t_{o} & -3 \end{bmatrix}$$

$$\mathcal{J}^{o}_{2,o} = \left[Q^{T}_{(2x1)}\ \nabla^{o}_{(2x2)}\ T^{o}_{2}\right] \otimes I_{(3x3)}$$

$$= \begin{bmatrix} 1 & 0 & 0 & 0 & 0 & 0 \\ 0 & 1 & 0 & 0 & 0 & 0 \\ 0 & 0 & 1 & 0 & 0 & 0 \end{bmatrix} ,$$

$$\mathcal{J}^{o}_{2,1} = \left[Q^{T}_{(2x1)}\ \nabla_{(2x2)}\ T^{o}_{2}\right] \otimes I_{(3x3)}$$

$$= \begin{bmatrix} t_o & 0 & 0 & -3 & 0 & 0 \\ 0 & t_o & 0 & 0 & -3 & 0 \\ 0 & 0 & t_o & 0 & 0 & -3 \end{bmatrix} ,$$

$$\mathcal{F}^{o}_{2,o} = \mathcal{J}^{o}_{2,o}\mathcal{F}^{o}$$

$$= [(f^{o}_{o} - 2\lambda f^{o}_{1} + \lambda^2 f^{o}_{2}), (f^{o}_{1} - \lambda f^{o}_{2}), f^{o}_{2}]^{T} ,$$

$$\mathcal{F}^{o}_{2,1} = \mathcal{J}^{o}_{2,1}\mathcal{F}^{o}$$

$$= [\{t_o(f^{o}_{o} - 2\lambda f^{o}_{1} + \lambda^2 f^{o}_{2}) - 3(f^{o}_{1} - 2\lambda f^{o}_{2} + \lambda^2 f^{o}_{3})\} ,$$

$$\{t_o(f^{o}_{1} - \lambda f^{o}_{2}) - 3(f^{o}_{2} - \lambda f^{o}_{3})\}, \{t_o f^{o}_{2} - 3 f^{o}_{3}\}]^{T}.$$

Therefore, using formula (2.14)

$$M_2\ [f^{(2)}(t), f^{(1)}(t), f(t)]^{T}$$

$$= \mathcal{F}^{o}_{2,o} - s_{f,o}\mathcal{P}^{o}_{2,o}$$

$$= \begin{bmatrix} f^{o}_{o} - 2\lambda f^{o}_{1} + \lambda^2 f^{o}_{2} - (p^{o}_{1} - \lambda p^{o}_{2})\ f^{(o)}(o) - p^{o}_{2}\ f^{(1)}(o) \\ f^{o}_{1} - \lambda f^{o}_{2} - p^{o}_{2}\ f^{(o)}(o) \\ f^{o}_{2} \end{bmatrix} ,$$

and

$$M_2\ [t(f^{(2)}(t), f^{(1)}(t), f(t))]^{T}$$

$$= \mathcal{F}^{o}_{2,1} + S_{f,1}\mathcal{P}^{o}_{2,o}$$

$$= \begin{bmatrix} t_o f_o^o - (2\lambda t_o + 3)\ f_1^o + \lambda(\lambda\ t_o + 6)\ f_2^o - 3\ \lambda^2 f_3^o + p_2^o f^{(o)}(o) \\ t_o f_1^o - (\lambda\ t_o + 3)\ f_2^o + 3\lambda f_3^o \\ t_o f_2^o - 3\ f_3^o \end{bmatrix} ,$$

which are same as equations (2.10) and (2.11).

In order to practically implement the general formula (2.14), it now remains to insert appropriate numerical values in the F^o vector. The elements of this vector are regularly ordered PMF's which can either be obtained by physical measurement on an analog PFC or computed digitially by a suitable numerical integration technique. The elements of the vector P^o are computed from the relation for p_k^o.

2.5. Discussion

The following are certain useful features of the formula (2.14):

(i) It is based on PMF relationships of functions and their derivatives including the effect of initial conditions. This feature renders the present approach applicable to the practical situation in which process data is frequently available on an arbitrary but active interval of time.

(ii) The PFC is characterized by a system in state variable form. The various PMF's are ordered and the set is treated as the state variable of the PFC model.

(iii) The vector term

$$[t^j(f^{(n)}(t),\ f^{(n-1)}(t), \ldots\ldots, f^{(o)}(t))]^T ,$$

for which the k-th PMF transformation formula is given in equation (2.14) has the virtue that with it as the general term, a large class of linear lumped models, both time-invariant and time-varying, may be developed by choosing n, and varying j as required, giving each term an appropriate vector weightage. For instance, if we consider a general n-th order time-invariant model, we set j = o and write

$$[f^{(n)}(t),\ f^{(n-1)}(t), \ldots\ldots, f^{(o)}(t)][a_o,\ a_1, \ldots\ldots a_n]^T$$

$$= [r^{(n)}(t),\ r^{(n-1)}(t), \ldots\ldots, r^{(o)}(t)][b_o,\ b_1, \ldots\ldots b_n]^T \quad ,$$

where the vectors $[a_o, a_1, \ldots\ldots, a_n]^T$ and $[b_o, b_1, \ldots\ldots, b_n]^T$ represent the sets of parameters in the model.

In the case of a time-varying process, we represent the time varying parameters as polynomials in t. Consequently, the two sides of the model equation may be represented by weighted sum of terms in the form given in equation (2.14).

(iv) Formulae (2.14 - 2.28) may be embedded in an elegant computer programme package which invites n, λ and F^o as the inputs to give the PMF of the general term. Ultimately, the PMF transformation of linear lumped model equations requires repeated application of this routine.

2.6. Appendix

PMF's of terms of the form: $t^j \dfrac{d^i f(t)}{dt^i}$ including the effects of initial conditions.

If F(s) is the Laplace transform of f(t), the Laplace transform of the output of the Poisson filter chain at the (k+1)-th stage for an input $[f^{(n)}(t), \ldots\ldots, f^{(o)}(t)]^T$ including the effect of initial conditions, is given by

$$\frac{\Psi(t)}{(s+\lambda)^{k+1}}(F(s) - S_{f,o}) = G_o(s), \text{ say,}$$

where

$$\Psi(s) = [s^n,\ s^{n-1}, \ldots\ldots, 1]^T$$

and $S_{f,o}$ is given by (2.16b).

Next, for an input $\{t[f^{(n)}(t),\ f^{(n-1)}(t), \ldots\ldots, f^{(o)}(t)]^T\}$, the Laplace transform of the output of the Poisson filter chain at the (k+1)-th stage is obtained as

$$\frac{1}{(s+\lambda)^{k+1}}\{-\frac{d}{ds}G_o(s)\} = -\frac{d}{ds}\{\frac{G_o(s)}{(s+\lambda)^{k+1}}\} - (k+1)\frac{G_o(s)}{(s+\lambda)^{k+2}} \quad .$$

This may be written as

$$-\frac{d}{ds}\{\frac{F(s)\Psi(s)}{(s+\lambda)^{k+1}}\} - (k+1)\frac{F(s)\Psi(s)}{(s+\lambda)^{k+2}} + S_{f,o}\, H\Psi(s) = G_1(s), \text{ say,}$$

where H is given by (2.17). Now the PMF transformation about t_o of the terms of our interest are given by

$$M_k\{[f^{(n)}(t),\ f^{(n-1)}(t),\ \ldots,\ f^{(o)}(t)]^T\} = \mathcal{L}^{-1}\, G_o(s)\Big|_{t=t_o}$$

$$= \mathcal{F}^o_{k,o} - S_{f,o}\mathcal{P}^o_{k,o}$$

$$= \mathcal{J}^{o^T}_{k,o}\mathcal{F}^o - S_{f,o}\mathcal{P}^o_{k,o} \quad .$$

$$M_k\{t[f^{(n)}(t),\ f^{(n-1)}(t),\ \ldots,\ f^{(o)}(t)]^T\} = \mathcal{L}^{-1}\, G_1(s)\Big|_{t=t_o}$$

$$= \mathcal{F}^o_{k,1} + S_{f,o}\, H\mathcal{P}^o_{k,o}$$

$$= t_o\mathcal{F}^o_{k,o} - (k+1)\mathcal{F}^o_{k+1,o} + S_{f,o}\, H\mathcal{P}^o_{k,o}$$

$$= \mathcal{J}^{o^T}_{k,1}\mathcal{F}^o + S_{f,o}\, H\mathcal{P}^o_{k,o} \quad .$$

On similar lines

$$M_k\{t^j[f^{(n)}(t),\ f^{(n-1)}(t),\ \ldots,\ f^{(o)}(t)]^T\}$$

$$= \mathcal{F}^o_{k,j} - (-1)^j\, S_{f,o}\, H^j\mathcal{P}^o_{k,o}$$

$$= \mathcal{J}^{o^T}_{k,j}\mathcal{F}^o - (-1)^j\, S_{f,o}\, H^j\mathcal{P}^o_{k,o} \quad ,$$

where $\mathcal{F}^o_{k,j}, \mathcal{J}^o_{k,j}, \mathcal{P}^o_{k,o}$ and $\mathcal{F}^o$ are given by (2.15), (2.16), (2.18) and (2.23) respectively.

PMF's of derivatives in terms of those of the functions themselves

If the vector $[f^{(n)}(t),\ f^{(n-1)}(t),\ \ldots\ldots,\ f^{(o)}(t)]^T$ is let into the Poisson filter chain, the Laplace transform of the corresponding filter output at the (k+1)-th stage is $F(s)\ \Psi(s)/(s+\lambda)^{k+1}$, if the initial conditions are ignored. Then,

$$\mathcal{L}^{-1}\frac{F(s)\Psi(s)}{(s+\lambda)^{k+1}} = [(f^o_{k-n} - \dots (-1)^n\lambda^n f^o_k), \dots ,$$

$$(f^o_{k-2} - 2\lambda f^o_{k-1} + \lambda^2 f^o_k),\ (f^o_{k-1} - \lambda f^o_k),\ f^o_k]^T$$

$$= \gamma[f^o_{k-n}, \dots , f^o_k]^T , \tag{2.29}$$

where γ is given by (2.26). If we consider a q-vector $F^o = [f^o_o, f^o_1, \dots , f^o_{q-1}]^T$ in our treatment, we should have correspondingly, $M_k\{[f^{(n)}(t), f^{(n-1)}(t), \dots , f^{(o)}(t)]^T\} \triangleq \mathcal{F}^o_{k,o} = \Gamma^{(k-n)} F^o$. Equation (2.29) is thus rewritten with enlarged matrices to suit F^o by converting γ to $\Gamma^{(k-n)}$ by a process of augmentation with zero columns as indicated in (2.25).

CHAPTER III

A GENERAL ALGORITHM FOR PARAMETER IDENTIFICATION IN LUMPED LINEAR CONTINUOUS SYSTEMS - THE POISSON MOMENT FUNCTIONAL (PMF) APPROACH [P 17]

3.1. Introduction

This chapter is concerned with the problem of parameter identification in linear lumped continuous models in the general form:

$$\sum_{i=o}^{n} \sum_{j=o}^{m} a_{i,j} \, t^j \, \frac{d^{n-i} f(t)}{dt^{n-i}} = \sum_{i=o}^{n} \sum_{j=o}^{m} b_{i,j} \, t^j \, \frac{d^{n-i} r(t)}{dt^{n-i}} \quad , \quad (3.1)$$

from active record of f(t) and r(t) over an arbitrary period of time. When equation (3.1) is PMF transformed, it is reduced to an algebraic equation without any approximation while noise accentuating derivative operations are totally avoided. By varying k, the order of PMF transformation, or t_o, the instant about which the impulse distribution is considered, or both, we may develop a set of linear algebraic equations, which when solved, would yield the model parameters $a_{i,j}$, $b_{i,j}$ along with certain terms involving the unknown initial conditions. The flexible approach to the formation of simultaneous algebraic equations is illustrated with respect to two border situations. In Section 3.2 the role of PMF's of the process signals in the identification problem is illustrated in detail with reference to a second order time varying model. Section 3.3 generalizes the approach with PMF transformation about a single instant of time and Section 3.4 deals with algorithms employing minimal order PMF's taken about several instants of time. The general algorithms presented in Section 3.3a and 3.4a are reduced, under certain conditions, to simpler forms in which they become applicable to time-invariant models with unknown initial conditions or with initial conditions known a priori to be zero. These special cases are discussed in Sections 3.3b, 3.3c, 3.3d, 3.4b, 3.4c, and 3.4d.

3.2. Parameter identification in lumped linear systems

In order to illustrate the role of PMF transformation discussed in Chapter II in problems of parameter identification in lumped linear models, let us consider the following problem:

"Given f(t) and r(t) along with all the related PMF's over an arbitrary but active interval of time (O,T), determine the parameters of a system modelled by

$$(1 + a_{o,1}t)\ \frac{d^2f(t)}{dt^2} + (a_{1,o} + a_{1,1}t)\ \frac{df(t)}{dt} + (a_{2,o} + a_{2,1}t)\ f(t)$$

$$= (b_{2,o} + b_{2,1}t)\ r(t)"\quad .$$

To set up a procedure to solve this problem, we first take the k-th PMF transformation of the model equation about $t_o \in (O,T)$ as

$$[f_{k-2}^o - 2\lambda f_{k-1}^o + \lambda^2 f_k^o - (p_{k-1}^o - \lambda p_k^o)\ f^{(o)}(o) - p_k^o\ f^{(1)}(o)]$$

$$+ a_{o,1}[t_o\ f_{k-2}^o - \{2\lambda t_o + (k+1)\}\ f_{k-1}^o + \lambda\{\lambda t_o + 2(k+1)\}\ f_k^o$$

$$- \lambda^2(k+1)\ f_{k+1}^o + p_k^o\ f^{(o)}(o)] + a_{1,o}\ [f_{k-1}^o - \lambda\ f_k^o - p_k^o\ f_{(o)}^{(o)}]$$

$$+ a_{1,1}[t_o\ f_{k-1}^o - \{\lambda t_o + (k+1)\}\ f_k^o + \lambda(k+1)\ f_{k+1}^o] + a_{2,o}\ f_k^o$$

$$+ a_{2,1}\{t_o\ f_k^o - (k+1)\ f_{k+1}^o\}$$

$$= b_{2,o}\ r_k^o + b_{2,1}\{t_o\ r_k^o - (k+1)\ r_{k+1}^o\}\quad .$$

This may be arranged and written in the form:

$$[-(f_{k-1}^o - \lambda\ f_k^o),\ -f_k^o,\ -\{t_o f_{k-2}^o - (2\lambda t_o + \overline{k+1})\ f_{k-1}^o$$

$$+ \lambda(\lambda\ t_o + 2\ \overline{k+1})\ f_k^o - \lambda^2(k+1)\ f_{k+1}^o\}\quad ,$$

$$-\{t_o f_{k-1}^o - (\lambda\ t_o + k+1)\ f_k^o + \lambda(k+1)\ f_{k+1}^o\}\quad ,$$

$$-\{t_o f_k^o - (k+1)\ f_{k+1}^o\},\ r_k^o,\ \{t_o\ r_k^o - (k+1)\ r_{k+1}^o\}\quad ,$$

$$(p_{k-1}^o - \lambda\ p_k^o),\ p_k^o]$$

$$[a_{1,o},\ a_{2,o},\ a_{o,1},\ a_{1,1},\ a_{2,1},\ b_{2,o},\ b_{2,1},\ \theta_{1,o},\ \theta_{2,o}]^T$$

$$= [f_{k-2}^o - 2\lambda f_{k-1}^o + \lambda^2 f_k^o]\quad ,$$

where $\theta_{1,o} = f^{(o)}(o)$ and $\theta_{2,o} = \{(a_{1,o} - a_{o,1})\ f^{(o)}(o) + f^{(1)}(o)\}$.

To evaluate the 9 unknowns (seven essential model parameters and two related to the unknown initial conditions), we require 9 simultaneous equations. These may be formed by following two methods:

Method 1:

In this method we use PMF's about a single instant of time $t_o \in (0,T)$ with $k = 2,3,\ldots,10$. The resulting set of 9 equations may be ultimately written in the form:

$$\Phi U = C \quad ,$$

where Φ, the information matrix, consists of elements which are known in terms of PMF's of process signals, Poisson pulse functions, the Poisson filter constant λ, and the time instant t_o about which PMF transformations are taken; C consists of elements in terms of PMF's of the process output and λ. The vector of unknowns U will be obtained as

$$U = \Phi^{-1} C \quad .$$

The matrix Φ may be partitioned as

$$\Phi = [\,\Phi_F \,\vdots\, \Phi_R \,\vdots\, \Phi_P] \quad ,$$

where the block suffixes F, R and P indicate that the blocks are related to the PMF's of f(t), r(t) and Poisson pulse functions.

In the present problem,

$$\Phi_P = \begin{bmatrix} (p_1^o - \lambda\, p_2^o) & p_2^o \\ (p_2^o - \lambda\, p_3^o) & p_3^o \\ \vdots & \vdots \\ (p_9^o - \lambda\, p_{10}^o) & p_{10}^o \end{bmatrix} ,$$

$$\Phi_R = \begin{bmatrix} r_2^o & (t_o r_2^o - 3r_3^o) \\ r_3^o & (t_o r_3^o - 4r_4^o) \\ \vdots & \vdots \\ r_{10}^o & (t_o r_{10}^o - 11r_{11}^o) \end{bmatrix} ,$$

and

$$
\Phi_F = \begin{bmatrix}
-(f_1^o-\lambda f_2^o), -f_2^o, -\{t_o f_o^o-(2\lambda t_o+3)f_1^o+(\lambda^2 t_o+6\lambda)f_2^o-3\lambda^2 f_3^o\}, -\{t_o f_1^o-(\lambda t_o+3)f_2^o+3\lambda f_3^o\}, \\
-(t_o f_2^o-3f_3^o) \\
-(f_2^o-\lambda f_3^o), -f_3^o, -\{t_o f_1^o-(2\lambda t_o+4)f_2^o+(\lambda^2 t_o+8\lambda)f_3^o-4\lambda^2 f_4^o\}, -\{t_o f_2^o-(\lambda t_o+4)f_3^o+4\lambda f_4^o\}, \\
-(t_o f_3^o-4f_4^o) \\
\vdots \\
-(f_9^o-\lambda f_{10}^o), -f_{10}^o, -\{t_o f_8^o-(2\lambda t_o+11)f_9^o+(\lambda^2 t_o+22\lambda)f_{10}^o-11\lambda^2 f_{11}^o\}, -\{t_o f_9^o-(\lambda t_o+11) \\
f_{10}^o+11\lambda f_{11}^o\}, -(t_o f_{10}^o-11f_{11}^o)
\end{bmatrix} .
$$

The 9-vector C is obtained as

$$
C = [(f_o^o - 2\lambda f_1^o + \lambda^2 f_2^o),\ (f_1^o - 2\lambda f_2^o + \lambda^2 f_3^o),\ \ldots\ldots \\
\ldots\ldots\ (f_8^o - 2\lambda f_9^o + \lambda^2 f_{10}^o)]^T .
$$

The vector of unknowns is given by

$$
U = [a_{1,o},\ a_{2,o},\ a_{o,1},\ a_{1,1},\ a_{2,1},\ b_{2,o},\ b_{2,1},\ \theta_{1,o},\ \theta_{2,o}]^T .
$$

<u>Corollary 1</u>

If it is known a priori that the system is time invariant, then the matrix Φ and vectors C and U will be reduced in dimension (since $a_{o,1} = a_{1,1} = a_{2,1} = b_{2,1} = 0$) and become

$$
\Phi = \left[\begin{array}{cc|c|cc}
-(f_1^o-\lambda f_2^o) & -f_2^o & r_2^o & (p_1^o-\lambda p_2^o) & p_2^o \\
-(f_2^o-\lambda f_3^o) & -f_3^o & r_3^o & (p_2^o-\lambda p_3^o) & p_3^o \\
\vdots & \vdots & \vdots & \vdots & \vdots \\
-(f_5^o-\ f_6^o) & -f_6^o & r_6^o & (p_5^o-\ p_6^o) & p_6^o
\end{array}\right]
$$

$$
= [\Phi_F \,\vdots\, \Phi_R \,\vdots\, \Phi_P] ,
$$

$$
C = [(f_o^o - 2\lambda f_1^o + \lambda^2 f_2^o),\ (f_1^o - 2\lambda f_2^o + \lambda^2 f_3^o), \ldots,\ (f_4^o - 2\lambda f_5^o + \lambda^2 f_6^o)]^T ,
$$

$$U = [a_{1,o}, a_{2,o}, b_{2,o}, \theta_{1,o}, \theta_{2,o}]^T \quad .$$

Corollary 2

If the initial conditions are further known a priori to be all zero in the above, then it becomes a case of transfer function synthesis. In this situation Φ, C and U become

$$\Phi = \begin{bmatrix} -(f_1^o - \lambda f_2^o) & -f_2^o & r_2^o \\ -(f_2^o - \lambda f_3^o) & -f_3^o & r_3^o \\ -(f_3^o - \lambda f_4^o) & -f_4^o & r_4^o \end{bmatrix} ,$$

$$C = [(f_o^o - 2\lambda f_1^o + \lambda^2 f_2^o), (f_1^o - 2\lambda f_2^o + \lambda^2 f_3^o), (f_2^o - 2\lambda f_3^o + \lambda^2 f_4^o)]^T ,$$

$$U = [a_{1,o}, a_{2,o}, b_{2,o}]^T \quad .$$

Method 2:

In order to determine the 9 unknowns we can alternatively form 9 simultaneous equations by choosing k = 2 at 9 different instants of time, $t_i \in (0,T)$; i = 1,2,...9. We then get

$$\hat{\Phi}_P = \begin{bmatrix} (p_1^1 - \lambda p_2^1) & p_2^1 \\ (p_1^2 - \lambda p_2^2) & p_2^2 \\ \vdots & \vdots \\ (p_1^9 - \lambda p_2^9) & p_2^9 \end{bmatrix} ,$$

$$\hat{\Phi}_R = \begin{bmatrix} r_2^1 & (t_1 r_2^1 - 3\, r_3^1) \\ r_2^2 & (t_2 r_2^2 - 3\, r_3^2) \\ \vdots & \vdots \\ r_2^9 & (t_9 r_2^9 - 3\, r_3^9) \end{bmatrix} ,$$

and

$$\hat{C} = [(f_o^1 - 2\lambda f_1^1 + \lambda^2 f_2^1),\ (f_o^2 - 2\lambda f_1^2 + \lambda^2 f_2^2),\ \ldots\ldots (f_o^9 - 2\lambda f_1^9 + \lambda^2 f_2^9)]^T \quad .$$

These can be written in the form

$$\hat{\Phi}\, U = \hat{C} \quad ,$$

$$\hat{\Phi}_F = \begin{bmatrix} -(f_1^1-\lambda f_2^1), -f_2^1, -\{t_1 f_1^1-(2\lambda t_1+3) f_1^1+(\lambda^2 t_1+6\lambda) f_2^1-3\lambda^2 f_3^1\}, -\{t_1 f_1^1-(\lambda t_1+3) f_2^1+3\lambda f_3^1\}, \\ -(t_1 f_2^1-3f_3^1) \\ -(f_1^2-\lambda f_2^2), -f_2^2, -\{t_2 f_1^2-(2\lambda t_2+3) f_1^2+(\lambda^2 t_1+6\lambda) f_2^2-3\lambda^2 f_3^2\}, -\{t_2 f_1^2-(\lambda t_2+3) f_2^2+3\lambda f_3^2\}, \\ -(t_2 f_2^2-3f_3^2) \\ \vdots \qquad \vdots \qquad \vdots \qquad \vdots \qquad \vdots \\ -(f_1^9-\lambda f_2^9), -f_2^9, -\{t_9 f_1^9-(2\lambda t_9+3) f_1^9+(\lambda^2 t_9+6\lambda) f_2^9-3\lambda^2 f_3^9\}, -\{t_9 f_1^9-(\lambda t_9+3) f_2^9+3\lambda f_3^9\}, \\ -(t_9 f_2^9-3f_3^9) \end{bmatrix} ,$$

where

$$\hat{\Phi} = [\ \hat{\Phi}_F \ \vdots\ \hat{\Phi}_R \ \vdots\ \hat{\Phi}_P] \quad ,$$

and the unknowns are determined as

$$U = \hat{\Phi}^{-1}\, \hat{C} \quad .$$

The time invariant case and the case of transfer function synthesis may be treated in a similar manner as discussed in corollaries of Method 1.

Fig. 3.1 indicates the set up for identification.

3.3. Generalisation of Method 1

The algorithms with PMF's taken about a single instant of time will now be generalized to treat models described by equation (3.1). The development is based on the formula (2.14).

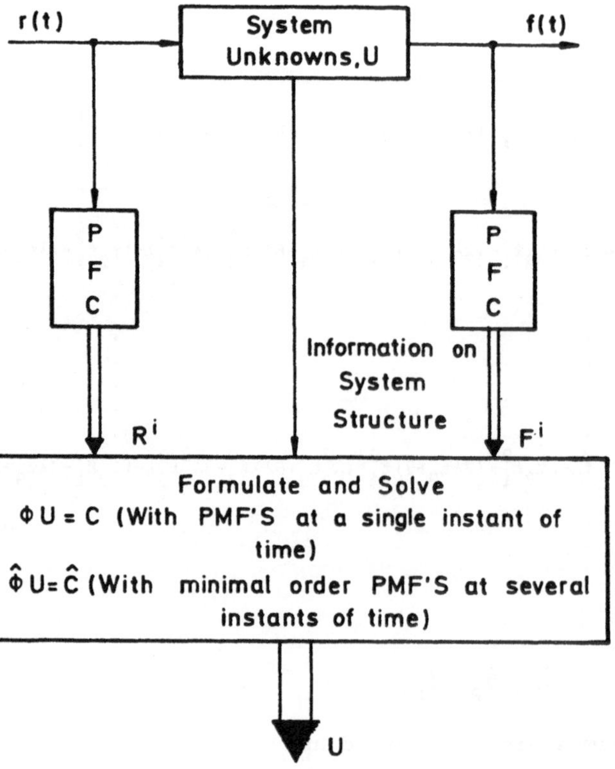

Fig. 3.1: Parameter identification in lumped systems - The PMF approach

3.3a. System model in the general form of equation (3.1) and initial conditions unknown [P 15, P 17]

In the general time-varying model the initial conditions $\{f^{(i)}(o),\ r^{(i)}(o)\ :\ i = 1,2,\ldots,(n-1)\}$, and the constant parameters $\{a_{i,j},\ b_{i,j}\ :\ i = 0,1,2,\ldots,n;\ j = 0,1,2,\ldots,m\}$ are unknowns to be determined. Without loss of generality we consider $a_{o,o} = 1$. For a proper system $b_{i,j} = 0$ for $i = 0$. Although $f^{(o)}(o)$ and $r^{(o)}(o)$ are known from actual data, we will ignore this fact and treat these as unknowns along with the others for reasons to be discussed later. We consider a column vector of unknowns arranged as

$$U = [\bar{A}_o^T \,\vdots\, A_1^T \,\vdots\, \ldots \,\vdots\, A_m^T \,\vdots\, \bar{B}_o^T \,\vdots\, \bar{B}_1^T \,\vdots\, \ldots \,\vdots\, \bar{B}_m^T \,\vdots\, \bar{\theta}^T]^T \tag{3.2}$$

$$\left.\begin{aligned} A_o &= [0,\ a_{1,o},\ a_{2,o},\ \ldots\ldots,\ a_{n,o}]^T, \\ A_j &= [a_{o,j},\ a_{1,j},\ \ldots\ldots,\ a_{n,j}]^T, \quad j \neq 0 \\ B_j &= [0,\ b_{1,j},\ b_{2,j},\ \ldots\ldots,\ b_{n,j}]^T, \quad \text{for all } j \\ \text{and} \quad \theta &= [0,\ \theta_{1,o},\ \theta_{2,o},\ \ldots\ldots,\ \theta_{n,o}]^T . \end{aligned}\right\} \tag{3.3}$$

The bar on any vector signifies that its first element is removed. The (n+1)-vector θ is composed of elements which happen to be combinations of the unknown initial conditions fused into n distinct unknowns which will ultimately be obtained along with other parameters. In fact, (see Appendix 3.6)

$$\begin{aligned} \theta &= [(Q^T + A_o^T)\ S_{f,o} - A_1^T\ S_{f,1} + \ldots + (-1)^m\ A_m^T\ S_{f,m}]^T \\ &\quad - [B_o^T\ S_{r,o} - B_1^T\ S_{r,1} + \ldots + (-1)^m\ B_m^T\ S_{r,m}]^T . \end{aligned} \tag{3.4}$$

The matrix $S_{r,i}$ corresponds to $r(t)$. The inclusion of $r^{(n-1)}(o)$ as a dummy in $S_{r,o}$ is only to preserve structural identity with $S_{f,o}$.

Since the first elements of the vectors A_o, B_j and θ are zero, the actual number of unknowns will be $M = (2n+1)m + 3n$. The length of the vectors F^o, R^o and P^o will each be $q = 2(n+1)m + 4n$. We successively take the k-th PMF transformation about t_o of equation (3.1) with $k = n$, $(n+1), \ldots \{(2n+1)m + 4(n-1)\}$ and form a set of linear equations as

$$\Phi\ U = C, \tag{3.5}$$

where

$$\Phi = [\Phi_F \mid \Phi_R \mid \Phi_P] \quad , \tag{3.6}$$

$$\Phi_F = \begin{bmatrix} \bar{\Phi}_{F_{1,1}} & \Phi_{F_{1,2}} & \cdots\cdots & \Phi_{F_{1,m+1}} \\ \bar{\Phi}_{F_{2,1}} & \Phi_{F_{2,2}} & \cdots\cdots & \Phi_{F_{2,m+1}} \\ \vdots & \vdots & \cdots\cdots & \vdots \\ \bar{\Phi}_{F_{M,1}} & \Phi_{F_{M,2}} & \cdots\cdots & \Phi_{F_{M,m+1}} \end{bmatrix} \quad , \tag{3.7}$$

$$\Phi_R = \begin{bmatrix} \bar{\Phi}_{R_{1,1}} & \bar{\Phi}_{R_{1,2}} & \cdots\cdots & \bar{\Phi}_{R_{1,m+1}} \\ \bar{\Phi}_{R_{2,1}} & \bar{\Phi}_{R_{2,2}} & \cdots\cdots & \bar{\Phi}_{R_{2,m+1}} \\ \vdots & \vdots & \cdots\cdots & \vdots \\ \bar{\Phi}_{R_{M,1}} & \bar{\Phi}_{R_{M,2}} & \cdots\cdots & \bar{\Phi}_{R_{M,m+1}} \end{bmatrix} \quad , \tag{3.8}$$

$$\Phi_P = [\bar{\Phi}^T_{P_1} \mid \bar{\Phi}^T_{P_2} \mid \cdots\cdots \mid \bar{\Phi}^T_{P_M}]^T , \tag{3.9}$$

$$\left.\begin{aligned} \Phi_{F_{i,j}} &= -F^{o^T} E^{(i-1)} \mathcal{J}^o_{k,j} , \\ \Phi_{R_{i,j}} &= R^{o^T} E^{(i-1)} \mathcal{J}^o_{k,j} , \\ \Phi_{P_i} &= P^{o^T} E^{(i-1)} \mathcal{J}^o_{k,1} , \end{aligned}\right\} \quad \begin{aligned} i &= 1,2,\ldots, M \\ j &= 1,2,\ldots, (m+1) \\ k &= (n-1) + i \end{aligned} \tag{3.10}$$

$$\left.\begin{aligned} E^{(i)} &= \Delta^i_{(q \times q)} E^{(o)} , \\ E^{(o)} &= [\Gamma^{(o)^T} \mid \Gamma^{(1)^T} \mid \cdots\cdots \mid \Gamma^{(m)^T}] \end{aligned}\right\} . \tag{3.11}$$

The bar on any matrix signifies that its first column is removed.

The M-vector C is

$$C = [Q^T \Gamma^{(o)} F^o \mid Q^T \Gamma^{(1)} F^o \mid \cdots\cdots \mid Q^T \Gamma^{(M-1)} F^o]^T . \tag{3.12}$$

The vector of unknowns U may now be obtained as

$$U = \Phi^{-1} C \quad . \tag{3.13}$$

Example 3.1:

Consider for illustration the system model:

$$(1 + a_{o,1}t) \frac{df(t)}{dt} + (a_{1,o} + a_{1,1}t)\ f(t) = (b_{1,o} + b_{1,1}t)\ r(t) \quad . \tag{3.14}$$

With reference to the general model (3.1), this corresponds to the case wherein $n = 1$, $m = 1$, $M = 6$, and $q = 8$. Here

$$A_o = [0,\ a_{1,o}]^T \ , \qquad A_1 = [a_{o,1},\ a_{1,1}]^T \ ,$$

$$B_o = [0,\ b_{1,o}]^T \ , \qquad B_1 = [0,\ \ b_{1,1}]^T \ ,$$

$$S_{f,o} = \begin{bmatrix} 0 & f^{(o)}(o) \\ 0 & 0 \end{bmatrix} , \quad S_{f,1} = \begin{bmatrix} 0 & 0 \\ 0 & 0 \end{bmatrix} ,$$

$$\Theta = [0,\ f^{(o)}(o)]^T \triangleq [0,\ \ \theta_{1,o}]^T \ ,$$

$$U = [\bar{A}_o^T \mid A_1^T \mid \bar{B}_o^T \mid \bar{B}_1^T \mid \bar{\Theta}^T]^T$$

$$= [a_{1,o},\ a_{o,1},\ a_{1,1},\ b_{1,o},\ b_{1,1},\ \theta_{1,o}]^T$$

$$F^o = [f_o^o,\ f_1^o, \ldots\ldots, f_7^o]^T \ ,$$

$$R^o = [r_o^o,\ r_1^o, \ldots\ldots, r_7^o]^T \ ,$$

$$P^o = [p_o^o,\ p_1^o, \ldots\ldots, p_7^o]^T \ ,$$

$$\Gamma^{(o)} = \begin{bmatrix} 1 & -\lambda & 0 & \ldots\ldots & 0 \\ 0 & 1 & 0 & \underbrace{\ldots\ldots}_{6\ \text{zeros}} & 0 \end{bmatrix} ,$$

$$\Gamma^{(1)} = \begin{bmatrix} 0 & 1 & -\lambda & 0 & \ldots\ldots & 0 \\ 0 & 0 & 1 & 0 & \underbrace{\ldots\ldots}_{5\ \text{zeros}} & 0 \end{bmatrix} , \quad \text{and so on.}$$

$$E^{(o)} = \begin{bmatrix} 1 & 0 & 0 & 0 \\ -\lambda & 1 & 1 & 0 \\ 0 & 0 & -\lambda & 1 \\ 0 & 0 & 0 & 0 \\ \vdots & \vdots & \vdots & \vdots \\ 0 & 0 & 0 & 0 \end{bmatrix} \left.\vphantom{\begin{matrix}0\\ \vdots \\ 0\end{matrix}}\right\} \text{5 zeros}$$

$$E^{(1)} = \begin{bmatrix} 0 & 0 & 0 & 0 \\ 1 & 0 & 0 & 0 \\ -\lambda & 1 & 1 & 0 \\ 0 & 0 & -\lambda & 1 \\ 0 & 0 & 0 & 0 \\ \vdots & \vdots & \vdots & \vdots \\ 0 & 0 & 0 & 0 \end{bmatrix} \left.\vphantom{\begin{matrix}0\\ \vdots \\ 0\end{matrix}}\right\} \text{4 zeros}$$

and so on.

$$T_k^o = \begin{bmatrix} 1 & 0 \\ t_o & -(k+1) \end{bmatrix} ,$$

$$\mathcal{J}_{k,1}^o = \begin{bmatrix} 1 \\ 0 \end{bmatrix} \otimes I_{(2x2)} = \begin{bmatrix} 1 & 0 \\ 0 & 1 \\ 0 & 0 \\ 0 & 0 \end{bmatrix} ,$$

$$\mathcal{J}_{k,2}^o = \begin{bmatrix} t_o \\ -(k+1) \end{bmatrix} \otimes I_{(2x2)} = \begin{bmatrix} t_o & 0 \\ 0 & t_o \\ -(k+1) & 0 \\ 0 & -(k+1) \end{bmatrix} .$$

Now,

$$\Phi_{P_1} = [p_o^o, p_1^o, \ldots\ldots, p_7^o] \begin{bmatrix} 1 & 0 & 0 & 0 \\ -\lambda & 1 & 1 & 0 \\ 0 & 0 & -\lambda & 1 \\ 0 & 0 & 0 & 0 \\ 0 & 0 & 0 & 0 \\ 0 & 0 & 0 & 0 \\ 0 & 0 & 0 & 0 \\ 0 & 0 & 0 & 0 \end{bmatrix} \begin{bmatrix} 1 & 0 \\ 0 & 1 \\ 0 & 0 \\ 0 & 0 \end{bmatrix}$$

$$= [(p_o^o - \lambda p_1^o),\ p_1^o] \ .$$

Similarly,

$$\Phi_{P_2} = [(p_1^o - \lambda p_2^o),\ p_2^o] \ ,$$

$$\ldots \qquad \ldots\ldots \qquad \ldots$$

$$\Phi_{P_6} = [(p_5^o - \lambda p_6^o),\ p_6^o] \ .$$

Therefore,

$$\Phi_P = [\bar{\Phi}_{P_1}^T \mid \bar{\Phi}_{P_2}^T \mid \ldots\ldots \mid \bar{\Phi}_{P_6}^T]^T$$

$$= [p_1^o, p_2^o, \ldots\ldots, p_6^o]^T \ .$$

Next, since in this case k = i

$$\Phi_{F_{1,1}} = -[f_o^o, f_1^o, \ldots, f_7^o] \begin{bmatrix} 1 & 0 & 0 & 0 \\ -\lambda & 1 & 1 & 0 \\ 0 & 0 & -\lambda & 1 \\ 0 & 0 & 0 & 0 \\ 0 & 0 & 0 & 0 \\ 0 & 0 & 0 & 0 \\ 0 & 0 & 0 & 0 \\ 0 & 0 & 0 & 0 \end{bmatrix} \begin{bmatrix} 1 & 0 \\ 0 & 1 \\ 0 & 0 \\ 0 & 0 \end{bmatrix}$$

$$= -[(f_o^o - \lambda f_1^o),\ f_1^o]$$

$$\Phi_{F_{1,2}} = -[f_o^o,\ f_1^o, \ldots, f_7^o] \begin{bmatrix} 1 & 0 & 0 & 0 \\ -\lambda & 1 & 1 & 0 \\ 0 & 0 & -\lambda & 1 \\ 0 & 0 & 0 & 0 \\ 0 & 0 & 0 & 0 \\ 0 & 0 & 0 & 0 \\ 0 & 0 & 0 & 0 \\ 0 & 0 & 0 & 0 \end{bmatrix} \begin{bmatrix} t_o & 0 \\ 0 & t_o \\ -(k+1) & 0 \\ 0 & -(k+1) \end{bmatrix}$$

$$= -[\{t_o f_o^o - (\lambda t_o + 2)\ f_1^o + 2\lambda f_2^o\},\ (t_o f_1^o - 2\ f_2^o)] \quad .$$

Proceeding in this manner, we obtain $\Phi_{F_{2,1}}$, $\Phi_{F_{3,1}}$, $\Phi_{F_{4,1}}$, $\Phi_{F_{5,1}}$, $\Phi_{F_{6,1}}$, $\Phi_{F_{2,2}}$, $\Phi_{F_{3,2}}$, $\Phi_{F_{4,2}}$, $\Phi_{F_{5,2}}$ and $\Phi_{F_{6,2}}$.

Inserting these in equation (3.7),

$$\Phi_F = \begin{bmatrix} -f_1^o & -\{t_o f_o^o - (\lambda t_o + 2)\ f_1^o + 2\lambda f_2^o\} & -(t_o f_1^o - 2f_2^o) \\ -f_2^o & -\{t_o f_1^o - (\lambda t_o + 3)\ f_2^o + 3\lambda f_3^o\} & -(t_o f_2^o - 3f_3^o) \\ \cdot & \cdot & \cdot \\ \cdot & \cdot & \cdot \\ \cdot & \cdot & \cdot \\ -f_6^o & -\{t_o f_5^o - (\lambda t_o + 7)\ f_6^o + 7\lambda f_7^o\} & -(t_o f_6^o - 7f_7^o) \end{bmatrix} \quad .$$

Similarly, we use equation (3.8) to get

$$\Phi_R = \begin{bmatrix} r_1^o & (t_o r_1^o - 2r_2^o) \\ r_2^o & (t_o r_2^o - 3r_3^o) \\ \cdot & \cdot \\ \cdot & \cdot \\ \cdot & \cdot \\ r_6^o & (t_o r_6^o - 7r_7^o) \end{bmatrix} \quad .$$

Inserting Φ_F, Φ_R and Φ_P in equation (3.6) we get Φ. Finally, equation (3.5) may be completed by writing the M-vector C as

$$C = [(f_o^o - \lambda f_1^o),\ (f_1^o - \lambda f_2^o), \ldots\ldots, (f_5^o - \lambda f_6^o)]^T \quad .$$

The vector of unknowns U may now be computed from equation (3.13).

In a process modelled by equation (3.14) consider f(t) and r(t) over an interval (0, 1.5 sec). The PMF's about $t_o = 1.5$ sec with $\lambda = 1$ are obtained to form the following:

$$F^o = [0.19263842D\ 01,\quad 0.10349684D\ 01,$$
$$0.39670042D\ 00,\quad 0.11976823D\ 00,$$
$$0.29961129D{-}01,\quad 0.64099301D{-}02,$$
$$0.11989059D{-}02,\quad 0.19927461D{-}03]^T\ ,$$

$$R^o = [0.13960539D\ 01,\quad 0.13786061D\ 01,$$
$$0.77331537D\ 00,\quad 0.30873157D\ 00,$$
$$0.96310359D{-}01,\quad 0.24725837D{-}01,$$
$$0.54009184D{-}02,\quad 0.10274031D{-}02]^T\ .$$

The vector P^o comprises of elements which are known as:

$$p_i^o = \frac{(1.5)^i}{i!}\, e^{-1.5}\ , \quad i = 0,1,\ldots\ldots, 7\ .$$

Using the above numerical data we form the matrix Φ and vector C and obtain the unknowns U using equation (3.13) as:

$$U = [0.5,\ -0.5,\ 0.0,\ 1.0,\ 0.0,\ 0.0]^T\ .$$

The vector of actual unknowns is

$$[\tfrac{1}{2},\ -\tfrac{1}{2},\ 0,\ 1,\ 0,\ 0]^T\ ,$$

which corresponds to the model

$$(1-\tfrac{1}{2}t)\,\frac{df(t)}{dt} + \frac{1}{2}\,f(t) = r(t)$$

simulated with

$$r(t) = -(t-2)^3 \text{ and } f(t) = (t-2)^3 - 4(t-2), \quad \text{with } f(t)$$

at the beginning of the interval (0,1.5 sec) having zero value.

Example 3.2:

Consider the system modelled by equation (3.14) with different input-output data. The PMF's of f(t) and r(t) about t = 1.5 sec. with $\lambda = 1$, are obtained as follows:

$$F^o = [0.86148384D\ 00,\ 0.30982430D\ 00,\ 0.89327551D{-}01,\ 0.21544973D{-}01,\ 0.44722187D{-}02,\ 0.81534034D{-}03,\ 0.13256847D{-}03,\ 0.19454764D{-}04]^T ,$$

$$R^o = [0.77686984D\ 00,\ 0.44217460D\ 00,\ 0.19115317D\ 00,\ 0.65642454D{-}01,\ 0.18575936D{-}01,\ 0.44559808D{-}02,\ 0.92599191D{-}03,\ 0.16956573D{-}03]^T .$$

The vector P^o will be the same as in Example 3.1. With these the matrix Φ and vector C are obtained. Then using equation (3.13), we have

$$U = [0.00000037,\ -0.00000014,\ 1.99999981,\ 4.00000002,\ 0.00000000,\ 0.00000000]^T .$$

The vector of actual unknowns is

$$[0,\ 0,\ 2,\ 4,\ 0,\ 0]^T ,$$

which corresponds to the system

$$\frac{df(t)}{dt} + 2t\ f(t) = 4t\ r(t) \quad ,$$

simulated by

$$r(t) = 1 \text{ and } f(t) = 2(1 - e^{-t^2}) \quad .$$

The data considered here is over (0, 1.5 sec.) with f(t) at the beginning of the interval having zero value.

Example 3.3:

Consider a second order TVP system modelled by the equation (illustrated in Section 3.2)

$$(1 + a_{o,1}t)\ \frac{d^2f(t)}{dt^2} + (a_{1,o} + a_{1,1}t)\ \frac{df(t)}{dt} + (a_{2,o} + a_{2,1}t)\ f(t)$$

$$= (b_{2,o} + b_{2,1}t)\ r(t) \quad .$$

The process signals f(t) and r(t) over an interval (0, 1.8 sec.) are used. The PMF's about t_o = 1.8 sec. with λ = 1 are obtained as follows:

$$F^o = [0.13525785D\ 02,\quad 0.34242724D\ 01,\quad 0.80339308D\ 00,$$
$$0.17390941D\ 00,\quad 0.34684557D-01,\quad 0.63780048D-02,$$
$$0.10836329D-02,\quad 0.17060007D-03,\quad 0.24968340D-04,$$
$$0.34086183D-05,\quad 0.43550605D-06,\quad 0.52243496D-07]^T\ ,$$

$$R^o = [0.56147975D\ 02,\quad 0.29753800D\ 02,\quad 0.75352211D\ 01,$$
$$0.23867547D\ 01,\quad 0.67530202D\ 00,\quad 0.17057378D\ 00,$$
$$0.38618474D-01,\quad 0.78843798D-02,\quad 0.14611923D-03,$$
$$0.24742597D-03,\quad 0.38515178D-04,\quad 0.55423185D-05]^T\ .$$

The vector P^o comprises of elements which are known as:

$$p_i^o = \frac{(1.8)^i}{i!}\, e^{-1.8}, \quad i = 0,1, \ldots\ldots, 11\ .$$

Using the above PMF's the matrix Φ and vector C are obtained. Finally the vector of unknowns U is got using equation (3.13) which gives

$$U = [-2.24010241,\quad 0.54088233,\quad 0.26286125,$$
$$-0.47976893,\ -0.10406163,\quad 0.33334211,$$
$$0.00748083,\quad 0.00000013,\ -0.00000465]^T\ .$$

The actual vector of unknowns is

$$[-\tfrac{7}{3},\ \tfrac{2}{3},\ \tfrac{1}{3},\ -\tfrac{2}{3},\ 0,\ \tfrac{1}{3},\ 0,\ 0,\ 0]^T\ ,$$

which corresponds to the model

$$(1 + \tfrac{1}{3}\, t)\ \frac{d^2 f(t)}{dt^2} - (\tfrac{7}{3} + \tfrac{2}{3}\, t)\ \frac{df(t)}{dt} + \tfrac{2}{3}\, f(t) = \tfrac{1}{3}\, r(t)\quad .$$

The process is simulated with

$$r(t) = (3 + t)^2\, e^t$$

and

$$f(t) = \tfrac{7}{4} + \tfrac{1}{4}\, t - (t + 4)\, e^t + \tfrac{9}{4}\, e^{2t}\quad ,$$

with f(t) at the beginning of the interval (0,1.8 sec.) having zero value.

3.3b. Time-invariant model with unknown initial conditions [P 13]

This refers to the particular case of Section 3.3a with $m=0$. In this situation the equations (3.7) and (3.8) reduce to the special case with

$$\Phi_F = [\bar{\Phi}^T_{F_{1,1}} \,\vdots\, \bar{\Phi}^T_{F_{2,1}} \,\vdots\, \cdots\cdots \,\vdots\, \bar{\Phi}^T_{F_{M,1}}]^T \,,$$
$$\Phi_R = [\bar{\Phi}^T_{R_{1,1}} \,\vdots\, \bar{\Phi}^T_{R_{2,1}} \,\vdots\, \cdots\cdots \,\vdots\, \bar{\Phi}^T_{R_{M,1}}]^T \,, \tag{3.15}$$

and Φ_p is the same as in Section 3.3a with an appropriately reduced dimension.

In this case the vector of unknown is

$$U = [\bar{A}^T_o \,\vdots\, \bar{B}^T_o \,\vdots\, \bar{\theta}^T]^T$$
$$= [a_{1,o}, a_{2,o}, \ldots, a_{n,o}, b_{1,o}, b_{2,o}, \ldots, b_{n,o}, \theta_{1,o}, \theta_{2,o}, \ldots, \theta_{n,o}]^T \,.$$

The vector Θ will be reduced to

$$\Theta = [(Q^T + A^T_o)\, S_{f,o} - B^T_o\, S_{r,o}]^T \;;$$

also

$$C = [Q^T\, \Gamma^{(o)}\, F^o \,\vdots\, Q^T\, \Gamma^{(1)}\, F^o \,\vdots\, \cdots\cdots \,\vdots\, Q^T\, \Gamma^{(3n-1)}\, F^o]^T \,.$$

Example 3.4:

Consider for illustration the system model:

$$\frac{d^2 f(t)}{dt^2} + a_{1,o}\frac{df(t)}{dt} + a_{2,o}\, f(t) = b_{1,o}\frac{dr(t)}{dt} + b_{2,o}\, r(t)\,. \tag{3.16}$$

Here $n = 2$, $M = 6$, $q = 8$. The PMF's of $f(t)$ and $r(t)$ over (0,1.5 sec.) with $\lambda = 1$ lead to

$$F^o = [0.57226066D-01,\ 0.16288184D-01,\ 0.39358871D-02,\ 0.82406097D-03,\ 0.15198072D-03,\ 0.25023889D-04,\ 0.37191585D-05,\ 0.50354753D-06]^T \,,$$

$$R^o = [0.72313016D\ 00,\quad 0.23095556D\ 00,$$
$$0.89802391D\text{-}01,\quad 0.24159937D\text{-}01,$$
$$0.55840005D\text{-}02,\quad 0.11280197D\text{-}02,$$
$$0.20202777D\text{-}03,\quad 0.32462039D\text{-}04]^T\ ,$$

$$P^o = [0.22313016D\ 00,\quad 0.33469524D\ 00,$$
$$0.25102143D\ 00,\quad 0.12551072D\ 00,$$
$$0.47066518D\text{-}01,\quad 0.14119955D\text{-}01,$$
$$0.35299889D\text{-}02,\quad 0.75642618D\text{-}03]^T\ .$$

Using the above PMF's the matrix Φ and vector C may be obtained. Finally the vector of unknowns is determined as

$$U = [4.00000030,\quad 3.00000009,\quad 0.00000007,$$
$$1.00000006,\quad 0.00000003,\quad 0.00000011]^T\ .$$

The vector of actual unknowns is

$$[4,\ 3,\ 0,\ 1,\ 0,\ 0]^T\ .$$

The process is simulated with r(t) = t and f(t) at the beginning of the interval having zero value.

Example 3.5:

Input-output data generated by the model

$$\frac{df(t)}{dt} + af(t) = br(t)$$

with a = 4, b = 4 and r(t) as a unit step at t = 0, is employed in the identification algorithm.

The present algorithm is applied to data in the interval $t \in (0,1.5\text{ sec.})$ and $t \in (0.2,\ 1.5\text{ sec.})$ and the vectors of unknowns obtained using equation (3.13) are as follows:

$$[1.00000091,\quad 3.99998378,\quad 0.00000000]^T\ ,$$

and

$$[4.00001120,\quad 4.00003460,\quad 0.55066931]^T\ .$$

The actual values of the initial states are f(o) = 0.0 and f(0.2) = 0.55071035.

3.3c. Transfer function synthesis [P 12] (i.e. under the condition that all initial conditions are known a priori to be zero)

The case of parameter identification in linear time invariant models with all initial conditions known a priori to be zero will refer to the special case where Θ becomes a vector known to be null. Equation (3.6) under this condition will be reduced to

$$\Phi = [\Phi_F \,\vdots\, \Phi_R] \;, \tag{3.17}$$

while Φ_F and Φ_R are the same as Section 3.3b.

The vector of unknowns will merely be

$$U = [\bar{A}_o^T \,\vdots\, \bar{B}_o^T]^T \;.$$

Example 3.6:

Consider the model of Example 3.5 when all initial conditions are known a priori to be zero. The PMF vectors of f(t) and r(t) about t_o = 1 sec. with λ = 1 are obtained as follows:

$$F^o = [0.51561170, \quad 0.18074620, \quad 0.04694130]^T \;,$$

$$R^o = [0.63213000, \quad 0.26426000, \quad 0.08032500]^T \;.$$

With these PMF values, the unknown parameter vector is obtained using equation (3.13), as:

$$[4.00008260, \quad 4.00008360]^T \;.$$

3.3d. State Equation Synthesis [P 12]

Suppose we are interested in realizing the following system

$$\dot{X} = AX$$

from its zero input response data: $X(t)$, $t \in (0,t_f)$; when X is an n-vector and A is a constant square matrix.

At the outset, we represent the system (3.17) in its equivalent zero state form:

$$\dot{X} = AX + Y\,\delta(t) \;,$$

where

$$Y\,\delta(t) = \delta(t)\,[x_1(0),\, x_2(0),\, \ldots,\, x_n(0)]^T$$
$$\triangleq [y_1,\, y_2,\, \ldots,\, y_n]^T$$

and $\delta(t)$ is an unit impule function at $t = 0$.

We take the PMF's of the state vector $X(t)$ and define

$$\chi_{k-1} \triangleq \begin{bmatrix} x^o_{1,k+1} & x^o_{1,k} & \cdots\cdots & x^o_{1,k+n-2} \\ x^o_{2,k+1} & x^o_{2,k} & \cdots\cdots & x^o_{2,k+n-2} \\ \vdots & \vdots & & \vdots \\ x^o_{n,k+1} & x^o_{n,k} & \cdots\cdots & x^o_{n,k+n-2} \end{bmatrix}, \tag{3.18}$$

$$\chi_{k} \triangleq \begin{bmatrix} x^o_{1,k} & x^o_{1,k+1} & \cdots\cdots & x^o_{1,k+n-1} \\ x^o_{2,k} & x^o_{2,k+1} & \cdots\cdots & x^o_{2,k+n-1} \\ \vdots & \vdots & & \vdots \\ x^o_{n,k} & x^o_{n,k+1} & \cdots\cdots & x^o_{n,k+n-1} \end{bmatrix}, \tag{3.19}$$

and

$$Y_{k} \triangleq \begin{bmatrix} y^o_{1,k} & y^o_{1,k+1} & \cdots\cdots & y^o_{1,k+n-1} \\ y^o_{2,k} & y^o_{2,k+1} & \cdots\cdots & y^o_{2,k+n-1} \\ \vdots & \vdots & & \vdots \\ y^o_{n,k} & y^o_{n,k+1} & \cdots\cdots & y^o_{n,k+n-1} \end{bmatrix}, \tag{3.20}$$

and $x_{i,j}$ and $y_{i,j}$ are the j-th PMF's of $x_i(t)$ and $y_i(t)$ respectively. Using equation (3.20), (3.19), (3.18) and (3.17) and rearranging

$$A = [\chi_{k-1} - Y_k - \lambda\,\chi_k]\,\chi_k^{-1}\ . \tag{3.21}$$

<u>Example 3.7:</u>

The zero input response of a system with $x_1(0) = x_2(0) = 1.0$ is given in terms of the PMF's with $\lambda = 1$ and $k = 1$ about $t_o = 1$ sec. as

$$x_{1,0}^{o} = 0.6385490, \quad x_{2,0}^{o} = -17346100,$$

$$x_{1,1}^{o} = 0.28114850, \quad x_{2,1}^{o} = -0.01047850,$$

$$x_{1,2}^{o} = 0.08673050, \quad x_{2,2}^{o} = 0.01047850.$$

From the above data about $t_o = 1$ sec., we have

$$y_{1,1}^{o} = y_{2,1}^{o} = 0.36787900,$$

$$y_{1,2}^{o} = y_{2,2}^{o} = 0.18393950.$$

Equation (3.21) with these gives

$$A = \begin{bmatrix} 0 & 1 \\ -2 & -3 \end{bmatrix} .$$

The data actually belongs to a system with matrix A same as above.

3.4. Generalization of Method 2

The algorithm with minimal order PMF's taken about several instants of time will now be generalized to treat models described by equation (3.1).

3.4a. System model in the general form (3.1) and initial conditions unknown [P 15, P 17]

Equation (3.5) may be formed in an alternative method in which PMF's of order 0,1, ..., (n+m), about several instants of time depending upon the number of unknowns, are used. F^i, R^i and P^i each will be a $q = (n+m+1)$-vector comprising of PMF's about t_i. Taking the n-th order PMF's about t_i, $i = 1,2, \ldots, M$ on both sides of equation (3.1), we get similar to equation (3.5) an equation of the form:

$$\hat{\Phi}\, U = \hat{C} \quad , \tag{3.22}$$

where

$$\hat{\Phi} = [\hat{\Phi}_F \,\vdots\, \hat{\Phi}_R \,\vdots\, \hat{\Phi}_P] \quad , \tag{3.23}$$

$$\hat{\Phi}_F = \left[\begin{array}{c|c|c|c} \bar{\hat{\Phi}}_{F_{1,1}} & \bar{\hat{\Phi}}_{F_{1,2}} & \cdots\cdots & \bar{\hat{\Phi}}_{F_{1,m+1}} \\ \hline \bar{\hat{\Phi}}_{F_{2,1}} & \bar{\hat{\Phi}}_{F_{2,2}} & \cdots\cdots & \bar{\hat{\Phi}}_{F_{2,m+1}} \\ \hline \vdots & \vdots & \cdots\cdots & \vdots \\ \hline \bar{\hat{\Phi}}_{F_{M,1}} & \bar{\hat{\Phi}}_{F_{M,2}} & \cdots\cdots & \bar{\hat{\Phi}}_{F_{M,m+1}} \end{array}\right] , \tag{3.24}$$

$$\hat{\Phi}_R = \left[\begin{array}{c|c|c|c} \bar{\hat{\Phi}}_{R_{1,1}} & \bar{\hat{\Phi}}_{R_{1,2}} & \cdots\cdots & \bar{\hat{\Phi}}_{R_{1,,+1}} \\ \hline \bar{\hat{\Phi}}_{R_{2,1}} & \bar{\hat{\Phi}}_{R_{2,2}} & \cdots\cdots & \bar{\hat{\Phi}}_{R_{2,m+1}} \\ \hline \vdots & \vdots & \cdots\cdots & \vdots \\ \hline \bar{\hat{\Phi}}_{R_{M,1}} & \bar{\hat{\Phi}}_{R_{M,2}} & \cdots\cdots & \bar{\hat{\Phi}}_{R_{M,m+1}} \end{array}\right] , \tag{3.25}$$

$$\hat{\Phi}_P = [\Phi^T_{P_1} \;\vdots\; \hat{\Phi}^T_{P_2} \;\vdots\; \cdots\cdots \;\vdots\; \hat{\Phi}^T_{P_M} \;]^T \tag{3.26}$$

$$\left.\begin{array}{lcl} \hat{\Phi}_{F_{i,j}} & = & -F^{i^T} \, E^{(o)} \, \mathcal{J}^i_{k,j} \\ \hat{\Phi}_{R_{i,j}} & = & R^{i^T} \, E^{(o)} \, \mathcal{J}^i_{k,j} \\ \hat{\Phi}_{P_i} & = & P^{i^T} \, E^{(o)} \, \mathcal{J}^i_{k,1} \end{array}\right\} \begin{array}{l} i = 1,2, \ldots, M \\ \\ j = 1,2, \ldots, (m+1) \end{array} \tag{3.27}$$

The M-vector $\hat{C}$ is

$$\hat{C} = [Q^T \, \Gamma^{(o)} \, F^1 \,\vdots\, Q^T \, \Gamma^{(o)} \, F^2 \,\vdots\, \cdots\cdots \,\vdots\, Q^T \, \Gamma^{(o)} \, F^M]^T . \tag{3.28}$$

The vector of unknowns is the same as in equation (3.2) and may now be obtained as

$$U = \hat{\Phi}^{-1} \, \hat{C} \, . \tag{3.29}$$

<u>Example 3.8:</u>

Consider for illustration the system modelled by equation (3.14). In this case $n = 1$, $m = 1$, $M = 6$ and $q = n+m+1 = 3$. The PMF transformation for $k = n$ of the model about t_i; $i = 1,2, \ldots, M$ leads to

$$F^i = [f_o^i,\ f_1^i,\ f_2^i]^T ,$$

$$R^i = [r_o^i,\ r_1^i,\ r_2^i]^T ,$$

$$P^i = [p_o^i,\ p_1^i,\ p_2^i]^T ,$$

$$\Gamma^{(o)} = \begin{bmatrix} 1 & -\lambda & 0 \\ 0 & 1 & 0 \end{bmatrix} ,$$

$$\Gamma^{(1)} = \begin{bmatrix} 0 & 1 & -\lambda \\ 0 & 0 & 1 \end{bmatrix} ,$$

$$E^{(o)} = \begin{bmatrix} 1 & 0 & 0 & 0 \\ -\lambda & 1 & 1 & 0 \\ 0 & 0 & -\lambda & 1 \end{bmatrix} ,$$

$$\hat{\Phi}_{F_{1,1}} = -[(f_o^1 - \lambda f_1^1),\ f_1^1] ,$$

$$\hat{\Phi}_{F_{1,2}} = -[\{t_1 f_o^1 - (\lambda t_1 + 2)\ f_1^1 + 2\lambda f_2^1\},\ (t_1 f_1^1 - 2\ f_2^1)] ,$$

$$\cdots \qquad \cdots \qquad \cdots$$

$$\hat{\Phi}_{F_{6,1}} = -[(f_o^6 - \lambda f_1^6),\ f_1^6] ,$$

$$\hat{\Phi}_{F_{6,2}} = -[\{t_6 f_o^6 - (\lambda t_6 + 2)\ f_1^6 + 2\lambda f_2^6\},\ (t_6 f_1^6 - 2\ f_2^6)] .$$

Similarly,

$$\hat{\Phi}_{R_{1,1}} = [(r_o^1 - \lambda r_1^1),\ r_1^1] ,$$

$$\hat{\Phi}_{R_{1,2}} = [\{(t_1 r_o^1 - (\lambda t_1 + 2)\ r_1^1 + 2\lambda r_2^1\},\ (t_1 r_1^1 - 2\ r_2^1)] ,$$

$$\cdots \qquad \cdots \qquad \cdots$$

$$\hat{\Phi}_{R_{6,1}} = [(r_o^6 - \lambda r_1^6),\ r_1^6] ,$$

$$\hat{\Phi}_{R_{6,2}} = [\{(t_6 r_o^6 - (\lambda t_6 + 2)\ r_1^6 + 2\lambda r_2^6\},\ (t_6 r_1^6 - 2\ r_2^6)] ,$$

and

$$\hat{\Phi}_{P_1} = [(p_o^1 - \lambda p_1^1),\ p_1^1] ,$$

$$\cdots\cdot \qquad \cdots\cdot \qquad \cdots\cdot$$

$$\hat{\Phi}_{P_6} = [(p_o^6 - \lambda p_1^6),\ p_1^6] \quad .$$

Substituting these in equations (3.24), (3.25), (3.26) and (3.23) we get $\hat{\Phi}$.

The vector $\hat{C}$ is given by

$$\hat{C} = [(f_o^1 - \lambda f_1^1),\ (f_o^2 - \lambda f_1^2),\ \ldots\ldots,\ (f_o^6 - \lambda f_1^6)]^T \quad .$$

The vector of unknowns may be obtained using equation (3.29).

In the process modelled by equation (3.14) in Example 3.1, the PMF's of f(t) and r(t) about 0.25 sec., 0.5 sec., 0.75 sec., 1.0 sec., 1.25 sec. and 1.5 sec., with $\lambda = 1$ are obtained. The vector P^i with elements corresponding to different time instants is also obtained to form the following.

$$\hat{\Phi} = \begin{bmatrix} -0.16689603\mathrm{D}{-01} & -0.15010080\mathrm{D}{-01} & -0.20970534\mathrm{D}{-02} & 0.18609552\mathrm{D}\ 00 & 0.15137402\mathrm{D}{-01} & 0.19470020\mathrm{D}\ 00 \\ -0.10622871\mathrm{D}\ 00 & -0.83172047\mathrm{D}{-01} & -0.26769101\mathrm{D}{-01} & 0.55009677\mathrm{D}\ 00 & 0.86702566\mathrm{D}{-01} & 0.30326533\mathrm{D}\ 00 \\ -0.28288079\mathrm{D}\ 00 & -0.18301917\mathrm{D}\ 00 & -0.10689829\mathrm{D}\ 00 & 0.90795539\mathrm{D}\ 00 & 0.20616245\mathrm{D}\ 00 & 0.35437491\mathrm{D}\ 00 \\ -0.52370300\mathrm{D}\ 00 & -0.25468265\mathrm{D}\ 00 & -0.26277683\mathrm{D}\ 00 & 0.11756726\mathrm{D}\ 01 & 0.33847188\mathrm{D}\ 00 & 0.36787944\mathrm{D}\ 00 \\ -0.78889546\mathrm{D}\ 00 & -0.23169230\mathrm{D}\ 00 & -0.49020393\mathrm{D}\ 00 & 0.13294558\mathrm{D}\ 01 & 0.45008388\mathrm{D}\ 00 & 0.35813100\mathrm{D}\ 00 \\ -0.10349684\mathrm{D}{-01} & -0.60587635\mathrm{D}{-01} & -0.75905178\mathrm{D}\ 00 & 0.13786061\mathrm{D}\ 01 & 0.52127847\mathrm{D}\ 00 & 0.33469524\mathrm{D}\ 00 \end{bmatrix}$$

$$\hat{C} = [0.18525576\mathrm{D}\ 00,\ 0.53856844\mathrm{D}\ 00,\ 0.85802458\mathrm{D}\ 00,\ 0.10411625\mathrm{D}\ 01,\ 0.10508543\mathrm{D}\ 01,\ 0.89141575\mathrm{D}\ 00]^T,$$

leading to

$$U = [0.50000000,\ -0.50000000,\ 0.00000000,\ 1.00000000,\ 0.00000000,\ 0.00000000]^T \ .$$

Example 3.9:

Consider the same first order model with input-output data as in Example 3.2. The PMF's of f(t) and r(t) about $t_i = 0.25$, 0.5, 0.75, 1.0, 1.25 and 1.5 sec. with $\lambda = 1$ are as follows:

$F^1 = [0.96121954D-02, \quad 0.58232220D-03, \quad 0.28496663D-04]^T,$

$F^2 = [0.6844663D-01, \quad 0.81378975D-03, \quad 0.78501636D-03]^T,$

$F^3 = [0.19864072D\ 00, \quad 0.35144251D-01, \quad 0.50451925D-02]^T,$

$F^4 = [0.39266624D\ 00, \quad 0.92694798D-01, \quad 0.17701936D-01]^T,$

$F^5 = [0.62389025D\ 00, \quad 0.18529671D\ 00, \quad 0.44318239D-01]^T,$

$F^6 = [0.86148384D\ 00, \quad 0.30982430D\ 00, \quad 0.89327551D-01]^T,$

$R^1 = [0.22119922D\ 00, \quad 0.26499021D-01, \quad 0.21614967D-02]^T,$

$R^2 = [0.39346934D\ 00, \quad 0.90204010D-01, \quad 0.14387678D-01]^T,$

$R^3 = [0.52763345D\ 00, \quad 0.17335853D-00, \quad 0.40505440D-01]^T,$

$R^4 = [0.63212056D\ 00, \quad 0.26424112D-00, \quad 0.80301397D-01]^T,$

$R^5 = [0.71349520D\ 00, \quad 0.35536421D-00, \quad 0.13153233D\ 00]^T,$

$R^6 = [0.77686984D\ 00, \quad 0.44217460D\ 00, \quad 0.19115317D\ 00]^T.$

The elements of the vector P^i for the purpose of constructing the matrix $\hat{\Phi}$ are also obtained as:

$p_1^1 = 0.19470020D\ 00, \quad p_1^2 = 0.30326533D\ 00,$

$p_1^3 = 0.35427491D\ 00, \quad p_1^4 = 0.36787944D\ 00,$

$p_1^5 = 0.35813100D\ 00, \quad p_1^6 = 0.33469524D\ 00.$

Using the above, the matrix $\hat{\Phi}$ and vector $\hat{C}$ are formed and the equation (3.29) leads to the vector of unknowns as

$$U = [0.00000000,\ 0.00000000,\ 2.00000000,\ 4.00000000,\ 0.00000000,\ 0.00000000]^T.$$

Example 3.10:

Consider the process modelled as in Example 3.3. The PMF's of f(t) and r(t) about $t_i' = 0.2, 0.4, 0.6, 0.8, 1.0, 1.2, 1.4, 1.6$ and 1.8 sec. with $\lambda = 1$ are obtained as follows:

$$F^1 = [0.45907324D{-}02,\ 0.21474196D{-}03,\ 0.82118160D{-}05,\ 0.26501863D{-}06]^T,$$

$$F^2 = [0.42517524D{-}01,\ 0.37222230D{-}02,\ 0.27188466D{-}03,\ 0.16971258D{-}04]^T,$$

$$F^3 = [0.16754124D\ 00,\ 0.20597656D{-}01,\ 0.21535303D{-}02,\ 0.19478708D{-}03]^T,$$

$$F^4 = [0.46752908D{-}00,\ 0.71796190D{-}01,\ 0.95439390D{-}02,\ 0.11107552D{-}02]^T,$$

$$F^5 = [0.10836881D\ 01,\ 0.19504248D\ 00,\ 0.30887429D{-}01,\ 0.43322373D{-}02]^T,$$

$$F^6 = [0.22398090D\ 01,\ 0.45401451D\ 00,\ 0.82195854D{-}01,\ 0.13326486D{-}01]^T,$$

$$F^7 = [0.42865959D\ 01,\ 0.95248355D\ 00,\ 0.19161462D\ 00,\ 0.34886776D{-}01]^T,$$

$$F^8 = [0.77686908D\ 01,\ 0.18559125D\ 01,\ 0.40637673D\ 00,\ 0.81336059D{-}01]^T,$$

$$F^9 = [0.13525785D\ 02,\ 0.34242724D\ 01,\ 0.80339308D\ 00,\ 0.17390941D\ 00]^T,$$

$$R^1 = [0.19438135D\ 01,\ 0.17732560D\ 00,\ 0.11282304D{-}01,\ 0.54849490D{-}03]^T,$$

$$R^2 = [0.42810608D\ 01,\ 0.70917954D\ 00,\ 0.85747210D{-}01,\ 0.80829907D{-}02]^T,$$

$$R^3 = [0.71994079D\ 01,\ 0.16195498D\ 01,\ 0.27795960D\ 00,\ 0.37992043D{-}01]^T,$$

$$R^4 = [0.10935944D\ 02,\ \ 0.29665024D\ 01,\ \ 0.64008685D\ 00,\ \ 0.11243221D\ 00]^T ,$$

$$R^5 = [0.15793653D\ 02,\ \ 0.48464468D\ 01,\ \ 0.12288773D\ 01,\ \ 0.25932313D\ 00]^T ,$$

$$R^6 = [0.22162334D\ 02,\ \ 0.74010130D\ 01,\ \ 0.21123630D\ 01,\ \ 0.51277091D\ 00]^T ,$$

$$R^7 = [0.30545256D\ 02,\ \ 0.10826990D\ 02,\ \ 0.33769286D\ 01,\ \ 0.91463552D\ 00]^T ,$$

$$R^8 = [0.41593203D\ 02,\ \ 0.15389959D\ 02,\ \ 0.51351625D\ 01,\ \ 0.15171737D\ 01]^T ,$$

$$R^9 = [0.56147975D\ 02,\ \ 0.21442474D\ 02,\ \ 0.75352211D\ 01,\ \ 0.23867547D\ 01]^T .$$

The vectors P^i with elements coresponding to different instants of time are also obtained as follows:

$$P^1 = [0.81873075D\ 00,\ \ 0.16374615D\ 00,\ \ 0.16374615D\text{-}01]^T ,$$
$$P^2 = [0.67032005D\ 00,\ \ 0.26812802D\ 00,\ \ 0.53625604D\text{-}01]^T ,$$
$$P^3 = [0.54881164D\ 00,\ \ 0.32928698D\ 00,\ \ 0.98786094D\text{-}01]^T ,$$
$$P^4 = [0.44932896D\ 00,\ \ 0.35946317D\ 00,\ \ 0.14378527D\ 00]^T ,$$
$$P^5 = [0.36787944D\ 00,\ \ 0.36787944D\ 00,\ \ 0.18393972D\ 00]^T ,$$
$$P^6 = [0.30119421D\ 00,\ \ 0.36143305D\ 00,\ \ 0.21685983D\ 00]^T ,$$
$$P^7 = [0.24659696D\ 00,\ \ 0.34523575D\ 00,\ \ 0.24166502D\ 00]^T ,$$
$$P^8 = [0.20189652D\ 00,\ \ 0.32303443D\ 00,\ \ 0.25842754D\ 00]^T ,$$
$$P^9 = [0.16529889D\ 00,\ \ 0.29753800D\ 00,\ \ 0.26778420D\ 00]^T .$$

With the above PMF vectors the matrix $\hat{\Phi}$ and vector $\hat{C}$ are formed and the vector of unknowns is obtained as

$$U = [-2.33333330,\ \ 0.66666660,\ \ 0.33333330,\ \ -0.66666657,\ -0.00000006,\ \ 0.33333333,\ \ 0.00000000,\ \ 0.00000000,\ \ 0.00000000]^T .$$

3.4b. Time-invariant model with unknown initial conditions [P 13]

This refers to the particular case of Section 3.4a with m = 0. In this situation, equations (3.24) and (3.25) reduce to the special case

$$\hat{\Phi}_F = [\bar{\hat{\Phi}}^T_{F_{1,1}} \mid \bar{\hat{\Phi}}^T_{F_{2,1}} \mid \ldots\ldots \mid \bar{\hat{\Phi}}^T_{F_{M,1}}]^T \quad ,$$
$$\hat{\Phi}_R = [\bar{\hat{\Phi}}^T_{R_{1,1}} \mid \bar{\hat{\Phi}}^T_{R_{2,1}} \mid \ldots\ldots \mid \bar{\hat{\Phi}}^T_{R_{M,1}}]^T \quad . \qquad (3.30)$$

$\hat{\Phi}_P$ and $\hat{C}$ are as in Section 3.4a and U is as in Section 3.3b. With these we form (3.22) and solve for U.

Example 3.11:

Consider the model of Example 3.4 in Section 6.3b. Here n = 2, q = 3 and M = 6. The PMF's of f(t) and r(t) about t_i = 0.25, 0.5, 0.75, 1.0, 1.25, 1.5 sec. with λ = 1 and P^i's lead to form the following.

$$\hat{\Phi} = \begin{bmatrix} -0.61013692D{-}05 & -0.26500591D{-}06 & 0.21614967D{-}02 & 0.14026522D{-}03 & 0.17036267D\ 00 & 0.24337524D{-}01 \\ -0.14734966D{-}03 & -0.13334083D{-}04 & 0.14387678D{-}01 & 0.19389713D{-}02 & 0.22744900D\ 00 & 0.75816332D{-}01 \\ -0.84996912D{-}03 & -0.12015047D{-}03 & 0.40505440D{-}01 & 0.85025803D{-}02 & 0.22142182D\ 00 & 0.13285309D\ 00 \\ -0.27374416D{-}02 & -0.53711309D{-}03 & 0.80301397D{-}01 & 0.23336926D{-}01 & 0.18393972D\ 00 & 0.18393972D\ 00 \\ -0.64219054D{-}02 & -0.16391040D{-}02 & 0.13153233D\ 00 & 0.49608255D{-}01 & 0.13429912D\ 00 & 0.22383187D\ 00 \\ -0.12352297D{-}01 & -0.39358871D{-}02 & 0.19115317D\ 00 & 0.89802391D{-}01 & 0.83673810D{-}01 & 0.25102143D\ 00 \end{bmatrix}$$

$\hat{C}$ = [0.11507199D-03, 0.13095856D-02, 0.47422756D-02, 0.10775852D-01, 0.19003359D-01, 0.28585585D-01]^T, leading to

U = [4.00000000, 3.00000000, 0.00000008, 1.00000000, 0.00000003, 0.00000011]^T.

Example 3.12:

The present algorithm is applied to the process modelled as in Example 3.5. The process data is taken in two intervals of time, $t \in (0, 1 \cdot 5$ sec.) and $t \in (0.2, 1.5$ sec.). The PMF's of order 0 and 1 with $\lambda = 1$ about $t_i = 0.5, 1.0$ and 1.5 sec. are used.

The vectors of unknowns obtained using equation (3.29) are as follows:

$$[3.99999980, \quad 3.99999982, \quad 0.00000000]^T$$

and

$$[3.99999106, \quad 3.99999989, \quad 0.55067139]^T .$$

3.4c. Transfer function synthesis [P 12]

This situation is as in Section 3.3c. Equation (3.23) will be reduced to the form:

$$\hat{\Phi} = [\hat{\Phi}_F \mid \hat{\Phi}_R]$$

where $\hat{\Phi}_F$ and $\hat{\Phi}_R$ are as in Section 3.4b. The vector of unknowns will be as in Section 3.3c.

Example 3.13:

Consider the process modelled as in Example 3.5 when all initial conditions are known a priori to be zero. The PMF vectors of f(t) and r(t) are obtained at two time instants:

$$t_1 = 0.5 \text{ sec. and } t_2 = 1.0 \text{ sec.}$$

$$F^1 = [0.23640360, \quad 0.04147010]^T ,$$

$$F^2 = [0.51561170, \quad 0.18047620]^T ,$$

$$R^1 = [0.39346900, \quad 0.09020350]^T ,$$

$$R^2 = [0.63212100, \quad 0.26426000]^T .$$

Using the above we form the matrix $\hat{\Phi}$ and vector $\hat{C}$ and the vector of unknown parameters is obtained as

$$[4.00006230, \quad 4.00006660]^T .$$

3.4d. State equation synthesis [P 12]

In the alternative method, we may take PMF's of the process signals about an appropriate number of instants of time as detailed in the following. We define

$$\hat{X}_{k-1} \triangleq \begin{bmatrix} x^1_{1,k-1} & x^2_{2,k-1} & \cdots\cdots & x^n_{1,k-1} \\ x^1_{2,k-1} & x^2_{2,k-1} & \cdots\cdots & x^n_{2,k-1} \\ \vdots & \vdots & & \vdots \\ x^1_{n,k-1} & x^2_{n,k-1} & \cdots\cdots & x^n_{n,k-1} \end{bmatrix}, \qquad (3.31)$$

$$\hat{X}_{k} \triangleq \begin{bmatrix} x^1_{1,k} & x^2_{1,k} & \cdots\cdots & x^n_{1,k} \\ x^1_{2,k} & x^2_{2,k} & \cdots\cdots & x^n_{2,k} \\ \vdots & \vdots & & \vdots \\ x^1_{n,k} & x^2_{n,k} & \cdots\cdots & x^n_{n,k} \end{bmatrix}, \qquad (3.32)$$

$$\hat{Y}_{k} \triangleq \begin{bmatrix} y^1_{1,k} & y^2_{1,k} & \cdots\cdots & y^n_{1,k} \\ y^1_{2,k} & y^2_{2,k} & \cdots\cdots & y^n_{2,k} \\ \vdots & \vdots & & \vdots \\ y^1_{n,k} & y^2_{n,k} & \cdots\cdots & y^n_{n,k} \end{bmatrix}, \qquad (3.33)$$

and $x^j_{i,k}$ and $y^j_{i,k}$ are k-th PMF's about $t = t_j$ of $x_i(t)$ and $y_i(t)$ respectively. Using equations (3.31), (3.32) and (3.33) in equation (3.17), we get

$$A = [\hat{X}_{k-1} - \hat{Y}_k - \lambda\ \hat{X}_k]\ \hat{X}_k^{-1}\ . \qquad (3.34)$$

Example 3.14:

Consider the system of Example 3.7 with the following PMF's with $\lambda = 1$ about $t_1 = 0.5$ sec. and $t_2 = 1.0$ sec.

$$x^1_{1,o} = 0.43249250, \quad x^1_{1,1} = 0.09822210,$$

$$x^1_{2,o} = 0.04481150, \quad x^1_{2,1} = 0.03100480,$$

$$y^1_{1,1} = y^1_{2,1} = 0.30326550,$$

$$x^2_{1,o} = 0.63854900, \quad x^2_{1,1} = 0.28114850,$$

$$x^2_{2,o} = -0.17346100, \quad x^2_{2,1} = -0.01047850,$$

$$y^2_{1,1} = y^2_{2,1} = 0.36787900.$$

Substituting these in equations (3.31), (3.32) and (3.33) and using equation (3.34) we obtain

$$A = \begin{bmatrix} 0.00001124 & 1.00001040 \\ -0.20000152 & -3.00002830 \end{bmatrix} .$$

3.5. Discussion

A general algorithm for parameter identification in lumped linear SISO models presented here employs Poisson moment functionals of the process signals. The emphasis of the PMF approach in this chapter has been limited to a simple illustration of state equation synthesis to suggest that straightforward extension of the method to more general state space description is possible on similar lines.

The present algorithm deliberately ignores a priori knowledge of f(t) and r(t) at t = 0, and treats them as unknowns along with the other initial conditions. Had these been considered known, their direct presence in Φ, C or $\hat{\Phi}$, $\hat{C}$ would lead to noise corruption of the results to a greater degree than when their knowledge is ignored.

3.6. Appendix

Development of Θ.

Equation (3.1) may be arranged as

$$\sum_{j=o}^{m} (-A_j^T\{t^j[f^{(n)}(t),\ f^{(n-1)}(t),\ldots,f^{(o)}(t)]^T\} + B_j^T\{t^j[f^{(n)}(t),\ f^{(n-1)}(t),\ldots,f^{(o)}(t)]^T\}) ,$$
$$= Q^T[f^{(n)}(t),\ f^{(n-1)}(t),\ldots,f^{(o)}(t)]^T \quad .$$

Taking the k-th PMF's on either side of this equation, we get

$$\sum_{j=o}^{m} \{-A_j^T[\mathcal{F}_{k,j}^{o} - (-1)^j\ S_{f,o}\ H^j\mathcal{P}_{k,o}^{o}] + B_j^T[\mathcal{R}_{k,j}^{o} - (-1)^j\ S_{r,o}\ H^j\mathcal{P}_{k,o}^{o}]\}$$
$$= Q^T\ \mathcal{F}_{k,o}^{o} - S_{f,o}\mathcal{P}_{k,o}^{o} \quad ,$$

where $\mathcal{R}_{k,j}^{o}$ corresponds to r(t). Re-arranging the terms,

$$\sum_{j=o}^{m} [-A_j^T\mathcal{F}_{k,j}^{o} + B_j^T\mathcal{R}_{k,j}^{o}] + [Q^T\ S_{f,o} + \sum_{j=o}^{m}\{(-1)^j\ A_j^T\ S_{f,o}\ H^j - (-1)^j\ B_j^T\ S_{r,o}\ H^j\}]\mathcal{P}_{k,o}^{o}$$
$$= Q^T\mathcal{F}_{k,o}^{o} \quad .$$

This may be written as

$$\sum_{j=o}^{m} [-A_j^T\mathcal{F}_{k,j}^{o} + B_j^T\mathcal{R}_{k,j}^{o}] + \Theta^T\mathcal{P}_{k,o}^{o} = Q^T\mathcal{F}_{k,o}^{o} \quad ,$$

where

$$\Theta^T = [Q^T\ S_{f,o} + \sum_{j=o}^{m}\{(-1)^j\ A_j^T\ S_{f,o}\ H^j - (-1)^j\ B_j^T\ S_{r,o}\ H^j\}]$$

and may be written as (3.4).

CHAPTER IV

TRANSFER FUNCTION MATRIX (TFM) IDENTIFICATION IN MULTIPLE INPUT MULTIPLE OUTPUT (MIMO) CONTINUOUS SYSTEMS - [P 18]

4.1. Introduction

This chapter presents a direct algorithm for parameter identification in the transfer function matrix (TFM) of a multi-input multi-output (MIMO) system from the observations of the process signals over a finite, arbitrary, but active interval of time. The method is a straightforward extension of the PMF approach developed in earlier chapters. The effect of initial conditions of the process is practically very important and is suitably included in the present formulation.

Section 4.2 formulates the problem of TFM identification in general. Section 4.3 then presents the PMF method. Here again two types of algorithm are discussed. One is based on PMF's taken about a single instant of time and the other on PMF's taken about several instants of time. The two algorithms are clearly illustrated with the help of examples.

4.2. Transfer function matrix identification [P 7, P 18]

Consider a continuous linear time invariant MIMO system characterised by

$$\sum_{j=0}^{n_i} a_j^i \frac{d^{n_i-j} f_i(t)}{dt^{n_i-j}} = \sum_{l=1}^{M} \sum_{j=0}^{n_i} b_{l,j}^i \frac{d^{n_i-j} r_l(t)}{dt^{n_i-j}}, \quad i = 1,2,\ldots,N \qquad (4.1)$$

where $f_i(t)$ and $r_l(t)$ are the i-th output and l-th input respectively. Laplace transform of equation (4.1) gives

$$F(s) = H(s)\; R(s), \qquad (4.2)$$

where

$$F(s) = \mathcal{L}[f_1(t),\; f_2(t),\; \ldots,\; f_N(t)]^T,$$

$$R(s) = \mathcal{L}[r_1(t),\; r_2(t),\; \ldots,\; r_M(t)]^T,$$

$$H(s) = \begin{bmatrix} \frac{Z_{11}(s)}{D_1(s)} & \frac{Z_{12}(s)}{D_1(s)} & \cdots & \frac{Z_{1M}(s)}{D_1(s)} \\ \frac{Z_{21}(s)}{D_2(s)} & \frac{Z_{22}(s)}{D_2(s)} & \cdots & \frac{Z_{2M}(s)}{D_2(s)} \\ \cdots & \cdots & \cdots & \cdots \\ \frac{Z_{N1}(s)}{D_N(s)} & \frac{Z_{N2}(s)}{D_N(s)} & \cdots & \frac{Z_{NM}(s)}{D_N(s)} \end{bmatrix} \tag{4.3}$$

$$D_i(s) = \sum_{j=0}^{n_i} a_j^i \, s^{(n_i-j)}, \quad a_o^i = 1$$

and

$$Z_{il}(s) = \sum_{j=0}^{n_i} b_{l,j}^i \, s^{(n_i-j)}, \quad b_{l,0}^i = 0.$$

$D_i(s)$ equals the least common denominator of the i-th row of H(s) having degree n_i.

System identification requires the determination of $\{a_j^i, b_{l,j}^i\}$, $j = 1,2,\ldots,n_i$; $i = 1,2,\ldots,N$; $l = 1,2,\ldots,M$; using arbitrary (but active) lengths of input-output data. In this situation, the initial conditions form a set of additional unknowns to be determined simultaneously with the essential system parameters. Although the initial conditions $f_i^{(0)}(0)$, $r_l^{(0)}(0)$ are actually known, we would deliberately ignore this information and include them in the set of unknowns for reasons given in Section 4.5.

4.3. TFM identification by PMF method

4.3.(a) Parameter identification with PMF's taken about a single instant of time

We consider the equation governing the i-th output and identify the a's and the b's in the corresponding row of the TMF and repeat the same procedure for all the rows. We simplify the notation in the development of the identification algorithm by dropping the row index 'i' from the subscripts and superscripts. That is,

$f_i(t) = f(t)$, $n_i = n$, $m_i = m$, $a_j^i = a_j$, $b_{l,j}^i = b_{l,j}$ and so on.

Consequently, the initial conditions

$$\{f^{(j)}(0),\ r_l^{(j)}(0)\},\ j = 0,1,2,\ldots(n-1);\ l = 1,2,\ldots,M$$

and the parameters a_j, $b_{l,j}$ are labelled as the unknowns in the i-th row. We form a column-vector of these unknowns as:

$$U = [a^T \mid b_1^T \mid \ldots \mid b_M^T \mid \theta^T]^T, \tag{4.4}$$

where

$$a = [a_1,\ a_2,\ \ldots,\ a_n]^T,$$

$$b_l = [b_{l,1},\ b_{l,2},\ \ldots,\ b_{l,n}]^T,$$

$$\Theta = [\theta_1,\ \theta_2,\ \ldots,\ \theta_n]^T.$$

The j-th element of Θ is the (j+1)-th element of

$$[1 \mid a]\ S_f - \sum_{l=1}^{M} [0 \mid b_l]\ S_{r_l}.$$

S_{r_l} corresponds to $r_l(t)$.

The actual number of unknowns is $m = n\ (M+2)$. We consider PMF vectors F^o, R_l^o and P^o, each of length $q = n_{max}(M+3)$, where $n_{max} = \max_i\{n_i\}$. We successively take the k-th PMF transformation about t_o of the i-th equation in (4.1) with $k = n_{max}, n_{max}+1, \ldots, (n_{max} + m-1)$ and form a set of linear equations in the form

$$\Phi\ U = C, \tag{4.5}$$

where

$$\Phi = \left[\begin{array}{c|c|c|c|c} \Phi_{F,1} & \Phi_{R_1,1} & \cdots & \Phi_{R_M,1} & \Phi_{P,1} \\ \hline \Phi_{F,2} & \Phi_{R_1,2} & \cdots & \Phi_{R_M,2} & \Phi_{P,2} \\ \hline \cdots & \cdots & \cdots & \cdots & \cdots \\ \hline \Phi_{F,m} & \Phi_{R_1,m} & \cdots & \Phi_{R_M,m} & \Phi_{P,m} \end{array}\right], \tag{4.6}$$

$$C = [Q^T\ \Gamma^{(0)}\ F^o \mid Q^T\ \Gamma^{(1)}\ F^o \mid \dots \mid Q^T\ \Gamma^{(m-1)}\ F^o]^T. \qquad (4.7)$$

The submatrices in the above are given by

$$\Phi_{F,j} = -F^{o^T}\ \Gamma^{(j-1)^T}\ D^n,$$

$$\Phi_{R_1,j} = R_1^{o^T}\ \Gamma^{(j-1)^T}\ D^n,$$

$$\Phi_{P,j} = P^{o^T}\ \Gamma^{(j-1)^T}\ D^n,$$

where

$$R_1^o = [r_{1,0}^o,\ r_{1,1}^o,\ \dots,\ r_{1,q-1}^o]^T,$$

$$D^n_{(n_{max}+1)\times n} = \begin{bmatrix} \dots\dots 0 \dots\dots \\ I_{(n\times n)} \end{bmatrix},$$

and Q and Γ are formed with $n = n_{max}$.

<u>Example 4.1:</u> Consider for illustration the 2-input - 1-output model

$$\frac{d^2f(t)}{dt^2} + a_1\ \frac{df(t)}{dt} + a_2\ f(t) = b_{1,1}\ \frac{dr_1(t)}{dt} + b_{1,2}\ r_1(t)$$

$$+ b_{2,1}\ \frac{dr_2(t)}{dt} + b_{2,2}\ r_2(t). \qquad (4.8)$$

The corresponding TFM is given by

$$H(s) = \left[\frac{b_{1,1}s + b_{1,2}}{s^2 + a_1s + a_2},\ \frac{b_{2,1}s + b_{2,2}}{s^2 + a_1s + a_2}\right]. \qquad (4.9)$$

In this model $M = 2$, $n_{max} = 2$, so total number of unknowns, $m = 2(2+2) = 8$. We consider $q = 2(2+3) = 10$. Hence,

$$F^o = [f_0^o,\ \ f_1^o,\ \dots,\ f_9^o]^T$$

$$R_1^o = [r_{1,0}^o,\ r_{1,1}^o,\ \dots,\ r_{1,9}^o]^T,$$

$$R_2^o = [r_{2,0}^o,\ r_{2,1}^o,\ \dots,\ r_{2,9}^o]^T,$$

$$P^o = [p_0^o,\ \ p_1^o,\ \dots,\ p_9^o]^T,$$

$$\Gamma^{(0)} = \begin{bmatrix} 1 & -2\lambda & \lambda^2 & 0 & \cdots & 0 \\ 0 & 1 & -\lambda & 0 & \cdots & 0 \\ 0 & 0 & 1 & \underbrace{0 & \cdots & 0}_{7\text{ zeros}} \end{bmatrix},$$

$$\Gamma^{(7)} = \begin{bmatrix} 0 & \cdots & 0 & 1 & -2\lambda & \lambda^2 \\ 0 & \cdots & 0 & 0 & 1 & -\lambda \\ \underbrace{0 & \cdots & 0}_{7\text{ zeros}} & 0 & 0 & 1 \end{bmatrix},$$

$$D^{(2)} = \begin{bmatrix} 0 & 0 \\ 1 & 0 \\ 0 & 1 \end{bmatrix}, \ \Delta = \begin{bmatrix} 0 & 0 & 0 \\ 1 & 0 & 0 \\ 0 & 1 & 0 \end{bmatrix}, \ Q = [1, 0, 0, 0]^T,$$

$$S_f = \begin{bmatrix} 0 & f^{(o)}(0) & f^{(1)}(0) \\ 0 & 0 & f^{(o)}(0) \\ 0 & 0 & 0 \end{bmatrix},$$

$$S_{r_1} = \begin{bmatrix} 0 & r_1^{(o)}(0) & r_1^{(1)}(0) \\ 0 & 0 & r_1^{(o)}(0) \\ 0 & 0 & 0 \end{bmatrix},$$

$$S_{r_2} = \begin{bmatrix} 0 & r_2^{(o)}(0) & r_2^{(1)}(0) \\ 0 & 0 & r_2^{(o)}(0) \\ 0 & 0 & 0 \end{bmatrix},$$

$$\phi_{F,1} = [-(f_1^o - \lambda f_2^o), -f_2^o], \ \ldots, \ \phi_{F,8} = [-(f_8^o - \lambda f_9^o), -f_9^o],$$

$$\phi_{R_1,1} = [(r_{1,1}^o - \lambda r_{1,2}^o), r_{1,2}^o], \ldots, \ \phi_{R_{1,8}} = [(r_{1,8}^o - \lambda r_{1,9}^o), r_{1,9}^o],$$

$$\phi_{R_{2,1}} = [(r_{2,1}^o - \lambda r_{2,2}^o), r_{2,2}^o], \ldots, \ \phi_{R_{2,8}} = [(r_{2,8}^o - \lambda r_{2,9}^o), r_{2,9}^o],$$

$$\phi_{P,1} = [(p_1^o - \lambda p_2^o),\ p_2^o],\ \ldots,\ \phi_{P,8} = [(p_8^o - \lambda p_9^o),\ p_9^o].$$

Inserting these submatrices in equation (4.6), we obtain

$$\Phi = \begin{bmatrix} -(f_1^o-\lambda f_2^o) & -f_2^o & (r_{1,1}^o-\lambda r_{1,2}^o) & r_{1,2}^o & (r_{2,1}^o-\lambda r_{2,2}^o) & r_{2,2}^o & (p_1^o-\lambda p_2^o) & p_2^o \\ -(f_2^o-\lambda f_3^o) & -f_3^o & (r_{1,2}^o-\lambda r_{1,3}^o) & r_{1,3}^o & (r_{2,2}^o-\lambda r_{2,3}^o) & r_{2,3}^o & (p_2^o-\lambda p_3^o) & p_3^o \\ -(f_3^o-\lambda f_4^o) & -f_4^o & (r_{1,3}^o-\lambda r_{1,4}^o) & r_{1,4}^o & (r_{2,3}^o-\lambda r_{2,4}^o) & r_{2,4}^o & (p_3^o-\lambda p_4^o) & p_4^o \\ -(f_4^o-\lambda f_5^o) & -f_5^o & (r_{1,4}^o-\lambda r_{1,5}^o) & r_{1,5}^o & (r_{2,4}^o-\lambda r_{2,5}^o) & r_{2,5}^o & (p_4^o-\lambda p_5^o) & p_5^o \\ -(f_5^o-\lambda f_6^o) & -f_6^o & (r_{1,5}^o-\lambda r_{1,6}^o) & r_{1,6}^o & (r_{2,5}^o-\lambda r_{2,6}^o) & r_{2,6}^o & (p_5^o-\lambda p_6^o) & p_6^o \\ -(f_6^o-\lambda f_7^o) & -f_7^o & (r_{1,6}^o-\lambda r_{1,7}^o) & r_{1,7}^o & (r_{2,6}^o-\lambda r_{2,7}^o) & r_{2,7}^o & (p_6^o-\lambda p_7^o) & p_7^o \\ -(f_7^o-\lambda f_8^o) & -f_8^o & (r_{1,7}^o-\lambda r_{1,8}^o) & r_{1,8}^o & (r_{2,7}^o-\lambda r_{2,8}^o) & r_{2,8}^o & (p_7^o-\lambda p_8^o) & p_8^o \\ -(f_8^o-\lambda f_9^o) & -f_9^o & (r_{1,8}^o-\lambda r_{1,9}^o) & r_{1,9}^o & (r_{2,8}^o-\lambda r_{2,9}^o) & r_{2,9}^o & (p_8^o-\lambda p_9^o) & p_9^o \end{bmatrix}.$$

The vector C may be obtained as

$$C = [(f_0^o-2\lambda f_1^o+\lambda^2 f_2^o),\ (f_1^o-2\lambda f_2^o+\lambda^2 f_3^o),\ (f_2^o-2\lambda f_3^o+\lambda^2 f_4^o),$$
$$(f_3^o-2\lambda f_4^o+\lambda^2 f_5^o),\ (f_4^o-2\lambda f_5^o+\lambda^2 f_6^o),\ (f_5^o-2\lambda f_6^o+\lambda^2 f_7^o),$$
$$(f_6^o-2\lambda f_7^o+\lambda^2 f_8^o),\ (f_7^o-2\lambda f_8^o+\lambda^2 f_9^o)]^T.$$

Here, the vector of the unknowns to be identified is

$$U = [a_1,\ a_2,\ b_{1,1},\ b_{1,2},\ b_{2,1},\ b_{2,2},\ \theta_1,\ \theta_2]^T.$$

The vector of unknowns may now be obtained as

$$U = \Phi^{-1} C. \tag{4.10}$$

In the process modelled by equation (4.8), consider $f(t)$, $r_1(t)$ and $r_2(t)$ over an interval (0, 1.6 sec). The PMF's about $t_o = 1.6$ sec with $\lambda = 1$ are obtained to form the following 10-vectors:

F_1^o = [0.18130959D 00, 0.47870044D-01, 0.11080454D-01,
0.22736134D-02, 0.41781900D-03, 0.69397431D-04,
0.10502166D-04, 0.14583433D-05, 0.18697092D-06,
0.22252853D-07]^T

R_1^o = [0.20456318D 00, 0.53287167D-01, 0.12197105D-01,
0.24795096D-02, 0.45210362D-03, 0.74595901D-04,
0.11225125D-04, 0.15511438D-05, 0.19802654D-06,
0.23481209D-07]^T

R_2^o = [0.80189652D 00, 0.32682746D 00, 0.11018595D 00,
0.31372467D-01, 0.76901893D-02, 0.16498982D-02,
0.31413695D-03, 0.53696735D-04, 0.83208637D-05,
0.11785719D-05]^T.

The vector P^o comprises of elements:

$$p_k^o = \frac{(1.6)^k}{k!} e^{-1.6}, \quad k=0,1,\ldots,9.$$

The (8x8) matrix Φ is given by

$$\Phi = \begin{bmatrix}
-0.36789591D{-}01 & -0.11080454D{-}01 & 0.41090063D{-}01 & 0.12197105D{-}01 \\
0.21664151D\ 00 & 0.11018595D\ 00 & 0.64606886D{-}01 & 0.25842754D\ 00^{*} \\
-0.88068404D{-}02 & -0.22736134D{-}02 & 0.97175953D{-}02 & 0.24795096D{-}02 \\
0.78813487D{-}01 & 0.31372467D{-}01 & 0.12059952D\ 00 & 0.13782802D\ 00 \\
-0.18557944D{-}02 & -0.41781900D{-}03 & 0.20274059D{-}02 & 0.45210362D{-}03 \\
0.23682278D{-}01 & 0.76901893D{-}02 & 0.82696814D{-}01 & 0.55131209D{-}01 \\
-0.34842157D{-}03 & -0.69397431D{-}04 & 0.37750772D{-}03 & 0.74595901D{-}04 \\
0.60402911D{-}02 & 0.16498982D{-}02 & 0.37489222D{-}01 & 0.17641987D{-}01 \\
-0.58895265D{-}04 & -0.10502166D{-}04 & 0.63370776D{-}04 & 0.11225125D{-}04 \\
0.13357613D{-}02 & 0.31413695D{-}03 & 0.12937457D{-}01 & 0.47045299D{-}02 \\
-0.90438226D{-}05 & -0.14583433D{-}05 & 0.96739810D{-}05 & 0.15511438D{-}05 \\
0.26044015D{-}03 & 0.53696795D{-}04 & 0.36292087D{-}02 & 0.10753211D{-}02 \\
-0.12713724D{-}05 & -0.18697092D{-}06 & 0.13531173D{-}05 & 0.19802654D{-}06 \\
0.45375931D{-}04 & 0.83208637D{-}05 & 0.86025689D{-}03 & 0.21506422D{-}03 \\
-0.16471807D{-}06 & -0.22252853D{-}07 & 0.17454533D{-}06 & 0.23481209D{-}07 \\
0.71422918D{-}05 & 0.11785719D{-}05 & 0.17683058D{-}03 & 0.38233639D{-}04
\end{bmatrix}.$$

*The 2nd, 4th, ... lines are extensions of the 1st, 3rd, ... rows.

The 8-vector C, is given by

$$C = [0.96649957D{-}01,\ 0.27982750D{-}01,\ 0.69510460D{-}02,\ 0.15073728D{-}02,$$
$$0.28952631D{-}03,\ 0.49851442D{-}04,\ 0.77724502D{-}05,\ 0.11066543D{-}05]^T.$$

Solving equation (4.10) with these, the TFM is found to be

$$H(s) = \left[\frac{0.99826129s + 0.49703136}{s^2 + 1.49830691s + 0.49595748},\ \frac{-0.00000059s + 1.00000629}{s^2 + 1.49830691s + 0.49595748}\right].$$

In fact, the actual TFM from which the output signal is generated is taken as

$$H(s) = \left[\frac{s + 0.5}{s^2 + 1.5s + 0.5}\ \frac{1}{s^2 + 1.5s + 0.5}\right].$$

The θ's obtained here correspond to the initial conditions which happen to be all zero in the simulated model. Having thus included their effects in the general algorithm we ultimately accept the parameters of the TFM only.

In the simulation of the above process, $r_1(t) = t^3/6$, $r_2(t) = t$, and $f(t) = t^3/6 - t^2/2 + 3t - 7 + 8\exp(-0.5t) - \exp(-t)$.

4.3.(b) Parameter Identification with minimal number of PMF's about several instants of time

Equation of the type (4.5) may be formed in an alternative method in which PMF's of order $0,1,\ldots,n_{max}$, about several instants of time depending upon the actual number of unknowns, are used. F^j, R_l^j and P^j each will be a $q = (n_{max}+1)$-vector comprising of PMF's about t_j. Taking the n_{max}-th PMF's about t_j: $j = 1,2,\ldots,m$ on both sides of the i-th equation in (4.1) we get

$$\hat{\Phi}\, U = \hat{C}, \tag{4.11}$$

where

$$\hat{\Phi} = \left[\begin{array}{c|c|c|c|c} \hat{\Phi}_{F,1} & \hat{\Phi}_{R_1,1} & \cdots & \hat{\Phi}_{R_M,1} & \hat{\Phi}_{P,1} \\ \hline \hat{\Phi}_{F,2} & \hat{\Phi}_{R_1,2} & \cdots & \hat{\Phi}_{R_M,2} & \hat{\Phi}_{P,2} \\ \hline \cdots & \cdots & \cdots & \cdots & \cdots \\ \hline \hat{\Phi}_{F,m} & \hat{\Phi}_{R_1,m} & \cdots & \hat{\Phi}_{R_M,m} & \hat{\Phi}_{P,m} \end{array}\right] \tag{4.12}$$

$$\hat{C} = [Q^T\gamma\ F^1 \mid Q^T\gamma\ F^2 \mid \ldots \mid Q^T\gamma\ F^m]^T. \tag{4.13}$$

The submatrices in the above are given by

$$\hat{\Phi}_{F,j} = -F^{j^T}\ \gamma^T\ D^n,$$

$$\hat{\Phi}_{R_l,j} = R_l^{j^T}\ \gamma^T\ D^n,$$

$$\hat{\Phi}_{P,j} = P^{j^T}\ \gamma^T\ D^n.$$

The vectors F^j, R_l^j and P^j are as follows:

$$F^j = [f_o^j,\quad f_1^j,\quad \ldots,\ f_{q-1}^j]^T,$$

$$R_l^j = [f_{l,o}^j,\ r_{l,1}^j\ \ldots,\ r_{l,q-1}^j]^T,$$

$$P^j = [p_o^j,\quad p_1^j,\quad \ldots,\ p_{q-1}^j]^T.$$

In the above, $j = 1,2,\ldots,m$ and $l = 1,2,\ldots,M$.

<u>Example 4.2:</u> Consider for illustration the same model given by equation (4.8). In this case we consider $q = (2+1) = 3$. Taking PMF's about t_j: $j = 1,2,\ldots,8$, we obtain

$$F^j = [f_o^j,\quad f_1^j,\quad f_2^j]^T,$$

$$R_1^j = [r_{1,o}^j,\ r_{1,1}^j,\ r_{1,2}^j]^T,$$

$$R_2^j = [r_{2,o}^j,\ r_{2,1}^j,\ r_{2,2}^j]^T,$$

$$P^j = [p_o^j,\quad p_1^j,\quad p_2^j]^T.$$

Here,

$$\gamma = \begin{bmatrix} 1 & -2\lambda & \lambda^2 \\ 0 & 1 & -\lambda \\ 0 & 0 & 1 \end{bmatrix}.$$

Therefore,

$$\hat{\Phi}_{F,1} = [-(f_1^1-\lambda f_2^1),\ -f_2^1],\ \ldots,\ \hat{\Phi}_{F,8} = [-(f_1^8-\lambda f_2^8),\ -f_2^8],$$

$$\hat{\Phi}_{R_1,1} = [(r_{1,1}^1-\lambda r_{1,2}^1),\ r_{1,2}^1],\ \ldots,\ \hat{\Phi}_{R_1,8} = [(r_{1,1}^8-\lambda r_{1,2}^8),\ r_{1,2}^8],$$

$$\hat{\Phi}_{R_2,1} = [(r_{2,1}^1-\lambda r_{2,2}^1),\ r_{2,2}^1],\ \ldots,\ \hat{\Phi}_{R_2,8} = [(f_{2,1}^8-\lambda r_{2,2}^8),\ r_{2,2}^8],$$

$$\hat{\Phi}_{P,1} = [(p_1^1-\lambda p_2^1),\ p_2^1],\ \ldots,\ \hat{\Phi}_{P,8} = [(p_1^8-\lambda p_2^8),\ p_2^8].$$

Substituting these submatrices in equation (4.12), we get $\hat{\Phi}$. The vector $\hat{C}$ is obtained as

$$\hat{C} = [(f_o^1-2\lambda f_1^1+\lambda^2 f_2^1),\ (f_o^2-2\lambda f_1^2+\lambda^2 f_2^2),\ (f_o^3-2\lambda f_1^3+\lambda^2 f_2^3),\ (f_o^4-2\lambda f_1^4+\lambda^2 f_2^4),$$
$$(f_o^5-2\lambda f_1^5+\lambda^2 f_2^5),\ (f_o^6-2\lambda f_1^6+\lambda^2 f_2^6),\ (f_o^7-2\lambda f_1^7+\lambda^2 f_2^7),\ (f_o^8-2\lambda f_1^8+\lambda^2 f_2^8)]^T.$$

The vector of unknowns may now be obtained as

$$U = \hat{\Phi}^{-1}\ \hat{C}. \tag{4.14}$$

In the process modelled by equation (4.8) (Example 4.1), the PMF's of $f(t)$, $r_1(t)$ and $r_2(t)$ about 0.2, 0.4, 0.6, 0.8, 1.0, 1.2, 1.4 and 1.6 secs with $\lambda = 1$ are obtained. The vector P^j with elements corresponding to different time instants is also obtained to form the following:

$$\hat{\Phi} = \begin{bmatrix} -0.23755225D-05 & -0.80501828D-07 & 0.24146238D-05 & 0.81637097D-07 \\ 0.11484812D-02 & 0.59175527D-04 & 0.14737154D\ 00 & 0.16374615D-01^{*} \\ -0.67861071D-04 & -0.46743235D-05 & 0.70064861D-04 & 0.48043629D-05 \\ 0.79263319D-02 & 0.84177862D-03 & 0.21450241D\ 00 & 0.53625604D-01 \\ -0.46101571D-03 & -0.48391857D-04 & 0.48314397D-03 & 0.50382063D-04 \\ 0.23115288D-01 & 0.37949661D-02 & 0.23050089D\ 00 & 0.98786094D-01 \\ -0.17417234D-02 & -0.24756000D-03 & 0.18514329D-02 & 0.26092820D-03 \\ 0.47422596D-01 & 0.10698503D-01 & 0.21567790D\ 00 & 0.14378527D\ 00 \\ -0.47756439D-02 & -0.86135419D-03 & 0.51453089D-02 & 0191856365D-03 \\ 0.80301397D-01 & 0.23336926D-01 & 0.18393972D\ 00 & 0.18393972D\ 00 \\ -0.10699748D-01 & -0.23500140D-02 & 0.11675733D-01 & 0.25341689D-02 \\ 0.12051290D\ 00 & 0.43308577D-01 & 0.14457322D\ 00 & 0.21685983D\ 00 \\ -0.20867639D-01 & -0.54238255D-02 & 0.23045943D-01 & 0.59109955D-02 \\ 0.16650226D\ 00 & 0.71927416D-01 & 0.10357072D\ 00 & 0.24166502D\ 00 \\ -0.36789591D-01 & -0.11080454D-01 & 0.41090063D-01 & 0.12197105D-01 \\ 0.21664151D\ 00 & 0.11018595D\ 00 & 0.64606886D-01 & 0.25842754D\ 00 \end{bmatrix}$$

* The second line in each row corresponds to 5,6,7 and 8th columns of the matrix.

$$\hat{C} = [0.58027434D-04,\ 0.81011689D-03,\ 0.35875816D-02,\ 099440353D-02\ 0.21347374D-01,\ 0.39026765D-01,\ 0.63915485D-01,\ 0.96649957D-01]^T.$$

Again, solving equation (4.14), we obtain the TFM as

$$H(s) = \left[\frac{1.00000001s + 0.50000001}{s^2 + 1.50000001s + 0.50000002}, \frac{0.00000000s + 1.00000000}{s^2 + 1.50000001s + 0.50000002}\right].$$

The above example is considered with data over an interval (0.2, 1.8 sec). The PMF's of $f(t)$ and $r_1(t)$ and $r_2(t)$ about 0.4, 0.6, 0.8, 1.0, 1.2, 1.4, 1.6 and 1.8 secs with $\lambda = 1$ are obtained. The vector P^j with elements corresponding to different time instants is also obtained to form $\hat{\Phi}$ and $\hat{C}$. The results are found to be

$$H(s) = \left[\frac{0.99999999s + 0.49999998}{s^2 + 1.49999999s + 0.49999997} \frac{0.00000000s + 1.00000000}{s^2 + 1.49999999 + 0.49999997}\right].$$

The θ's are as follows:

$$[0.00130192,\ 0.02000063].$$

<u>Example 4.3:</u> Consider for illustration the 2-input 2-output system whose TFM is modelled as

$$H(s) = \begin{bmatrix} \dfrac{b^1_{1,1}s^2 + b^1_{1,2}s + b^1_{1,3}}{s^3 + a^1_1 s^2 + a^1_2 s + a^1_3} & \dfrac{b^1_{2,1}s^2 + b^1_{2,2}s + b^1_{2,3}}{s^3 + a^1_1 s^2 + a^1_2 s + a^1_3} \\ \\ \dfrac{b^2_{1,1}s + b^2_{1,2}}{s^2 + a^2_1 s + a^2_2} & \dfrac{b^2_{2,1}s + b^2_{2,2}}{s^2 + a^2_1 s + a^2_2} \end{bmatrix}.$$

Here the superscripts 1 and 2 denote the respective rows. In this model, the vectors of the unknowns to be identified are

$$U^1 = [a^1_1,\ a^1_2,\ a^1_3,\ b^1_{1,1},\ b^1_{1,2},\ b^1_{1,3},\ b^1_{2,1},\ b^1_{2,2},\ b^1_{2,3},\ \theta^1_1,\ \theta^2_2,\ \theta^3_3]^T,$$

and

$$U^2 = [a^2_1,\ a^2_2,\ a^2_3,\ b^2_{1,1},\ b^2_{1,2},\ b^2_{2,1},\ b^2_{2,2},\ \theta^2_1,\ \theta^2_2]^T,$$

where θ^1_1, θ^1_2, θ^1_3, θ^2_1, θ^2_2 are the additional unknowns due to initial conditions.

The unknown parameters including those due to initial conditions are identified by the second algorithm and are given as follows

$$\begin{aligned} U^1 = [&8.00323963,\ 21.01938152,\ 18.02898121,\ 1.00033934,\\ &6.00249738,\ 9.01445228,\ 4.00000050,\ 12.01294726,\\ &8.01271373,\ 0.00000003,\ 0.00000023,\ 0.00000060]^T, \end{aligned}$$

$$\begin{aligned} U^2 = [&4.99996168,\ 5.99988727,\ 1.00000384,\ 2.99994674,\\ &1.99999985,\ 3.99992429,\ 0.00000000,\ 0.0000000]^T. \end{aligned}$$

In fact, the actual TFM from which output signal is generated is taken as

$$H(s) = \begin{bmatrix} \dfrac{s^2 + 6s + 9}{s^3 + 8s^2 + 21s + 18} & \dfrac{4s^2 + 12s + 8}{s^3 + 8s^2 + 21s + 18} \\ \\ \dfrac{s + 3}{s^2 + 5s + 6} & \dfrac{2(s+2)}{s^2 + 5s + 6} \end{bmatrix}.$$

Here θ's correspond to the initial conditions which happen to be all zero in the simulated model. In the simulation of the above process, the inputs are as follows:

$$r_1(t) = t^5/120 \text{ and } r_2(t) = t^2/2.$$

The error appearing in the last few decimal places is due to round off error in the computer.

4.4. Discussion

The two PMF algorithms presented here for the identification of MIMO systems may be considered as a culmination of the process of generalisation of the PMF method introduced in the earlier chapters. The size of the matrices Φ and $\hat{\Phi}$ is naturally large for systems of high order. Their size further increases with number of inputs. The number of outputs does not effect their size since the method involves identification of each row of TFM separately. In the first method in which PMF's at a single instant of time alone are considered, the higher order PMF's would be considerably large. Physically, the higher order PMF's are increasingly weak. Consequently, the matrix Φ has greater tendency to become singular. This situation in practice in higher order systems with large number of inputs is not well posed. On the other hand, in the second method that employs minimal order PMF's sampled at several instants, the matrix $\hat{\Phi}$ is better posed.

CHAPTER V

CONDITIONS OF IDENTIFIABILTY

5.1. Introduction

Identifiability in the context of an identification algorithm is practically very important and should be discussed thoroughly. Certain conditions of identifiability in the context of PMF approach provide useful guidelines towards proper choice of test signals, model structure and reduction of problem size. This chapter is concerned with the discussions on identifiability conditions in the context of PMF approach both for SISO and MIMO systems. In MIMO systems, since the number of inputs is more, the complexity of the problem increases. It needs some more additional conditions of identifiability over and above those required for SISO systems. Section 5.2 discusses the conditions of identifiability for SISO systems and section 5.3 extends the results of Section 5.2 for MIMO systems.

5.2. Some important aspects of identifiability for SISO systems

The determination of the vector of unknowns U, depends on the invertibility of Φ and $\hat{\Phi}$. The conditions which make Φ and $\hat{\Phi}$ singular should be avoided. These can be foreseen in the context of PMF approach. In view of the generality of the model and arbitrariness of the input-output data record, the vector of unknowns is considerably lengthened. The vector of unknowns U may, in fact, be partitioned as

$$U = [U_F^T \mid U_R^T \mid U_\Theta^T]^T \tag{5.1}$$

where U_F, U_R and U_Θ contain parameters of the system, input process and initial conditions respectively arranged in the order of their importance in practice.

An analysis of various conditions under which Φ and $\hat{\Phi}$ become singular with reference to the model (3.1) leads to the understanding of the following.

5.2.(a) Input signals due to which the matrices Φ and $\hat{\Phi}$ become singular

When the initial conditions are treated as unknown in the problem (with data on an arbitrary but active period), the columns of Φ_R and Φ_P (or $\hat{\Phi}_R$ and $\hat{\Phi}_P$) become linearly dependent due to certain input signals. Such signals are termed here as singularising inputs. The signals which do not lead to singular Φ or $\hat{\Phi}$ in the context of the PMF approach are termed here as Poisson suitable signals.

The columns of Φ_R and Φ_P (or $\hat{\Phi}_R$ and $\hat{\Phi}_P$) become linearly dependent irrespective of the instant about which respective PMF's are employed, when all rows of these matrices are such that

$$[R^T E^{(i-1)} \mathcal{J}_{n-i+1,1} D \;\vdots\; R^T E^{(i-1)} \mathcal{J}_{n-i+1,2} D \;\vdots \ldots\; R^T E^{(i-1)} \mathcal{J}_{n-i+1,m+1} D]\alpha$$

$$= [P^T E^{(i-1)} \mathcal{J}_{n-i+1,1} D]\beta \tag{5.2}$$

for any arbitrary α and β and for all i (i-th row of Φ or $\hat{\Phi}$).

The vectors R and P and the matrix $\mathcal{J}$ will contain functions of time, instead of constant quantities corresponding to fixed t_i, in view of our search for the condition of dependence for all t in the given record. We now take the Laplace transform of (5.2) to get

$$R(s)[\ldots \vdots P^T(s) E^{(i-1)} \mathcal{J}(s)_{n-i+1,j} D \ldots]\alpha = [P^T(s) E^{(i-1)} \mathcal{J}(s)_{n-i+1,1} D]\beta \tag{5.3}$$

$$j = 1, 2, \ldots, (m+1),$$

where R(s) is the Laplace transform of r(t),

$$P(s) = \left[\frac{1}{s+\lambda}, \frac{1}{(s+\lambda)^2}, \ldots, \frac{1}{(s+\lambda)^q}\right]^T,$$

$$\mathcal{J}_{k,j}(s) = (\text{j-th row of } T_k(s))^T \otimes I_{(n+1)x(n-1)},$$

$$D = \left[\begin{array}{c} 0 \quad 0 \quad \ldots \quad 0 \\ \hline I_{(nxn)} \end{array}\right],$$

and $T_k(s)$ is the Laplace transform of T_k with t in place of t_i.

$$R(s) = \frac{\left[P^T(s) E^{(i-1)} \mathcal{J}(s)_{n-i+1,1} D\right]\beta}{\left[\ldots \vdots P^T(s) E^{(i-1)} (s)_{n-i+1,j} D \vdots \ldots\right]\alpha} \tag{5.4}$$

$$j = 1, 2, \ldots, (m+1).$$

To illustrate the possibility of a singularizing input, let us consider the case of parameter identification in a second order time-invariant system model as shown in Example 3.1 (Chapter III). We set i=1, and the related quantities in (5.4) to get

$$\left[\frac{1}{(s+\lambda)}, \frac{1}{(s+\lambda)^2}, \ldots, \frac{1}{(s+\lambda)^8}\right]\begin{bmatrix}1 & 0 & 0\\ -2\lambda & 1 & 0\\ \lambda^2 & -\lambda & 1\\ 0 & 0 & 0\\ 0 & 0 & 0\\ 0 & 0 & 0\\ 0 & 0 & 0\end{bmatrix}\cdot\begin{bmatrix}\frac{1}{s} & 0 & 0\\ 0 & \frac{1}{s} & 0\\ 0 & 0 & \frac{1}{s}\end{bmatrix}$$

$$R(s) = \frac{\begin{bmatrix}0 & 0\\ 1 & 0\\ 0 & 1\end{bmatrix}\begin{bmatrix}\beta_1\\ \beta_2\end{bmatrix}}{\left[\frac{1}{(s+\lambda)}, \frac{1}{(s+\lambda)^2}, \ldots, \frac{1}{(s+\lambda)^8}\right]\begin{bmatrix}1 & 0 & 0\\ -2\lambda & 1 & 0\\ \lambda^2 & -\lambda & 1\\ 0 & 0 & 0\\ 0 & 0 & 0\\ 0 & 0 & 0\\ 0 & 0 & 0\\ 0 & 0 & 0\end{bmatrix}\begin{bmatrix}\frac{1}{s} & 0 & 0\\ 0 & \frac{1}{s} & 0\\ 0 & 0 & \frac{1}{s}\end{bmatrix}\begin{bmatrix}0 & 0\\ 1 & 0\\ 0 & 1\end{bmatrix}\begin{bmatrix}\alpha_1\\ \alpha_2\end{bmatrix}}$$

$$= \frac{\beta_1 s+\beta_2}{\alpha_1 s+\alpha_2} .$$

An input of this form makes columns 3, 4, 5, 6 of Φ linearly dependent. A similar result follows for $\hat{\Phi}$ also. Consequently, inputs such as step functions and exponential functions should be avoided if Φ and $\hat{\Phi}$ with all their 6 columns are to be invertible. The authors have verified this fact by numerical experiment. On the other hand, Φ and $\hat{\Phi}$ with all their 6 columns have been inverted with a ramp input which does not fall into this category.

An input signal r(t) in (O,T) is Poisson suitable for identification of parameters and initial condition terms in the general model (Equation 3.1) if the Wronskians defined as

$$W_S = \begin{vmatrix} r_o^o & r_1^o \dots r_{n-1}^o & p_o^o & p_1^o & \dots p_{n-1}^o \\ r_1^o & r_2^o \dots r_n^o & p_1^o & p_2^o & \dots p_n^o \\ \vdots & \vdots \quad\quad \vdots & \vdots & \vdots & \vdots \\ r_{2n-1}^o & r_{2n}^o \dots r_{3n-2}^o & p_{2n-1}^o & p_{2n}^o & \dots p_{3n-2}^o \end{vmatrix} \neq 0,$$

or alternatively,

$$\hat{W}_S = \begin{vmatrix} r_o^1 & r_1^1 \dots r_{n-1}^1 & p_o^1 & p_1^1 & \dots p_{n-1}^1 \\ r_o^2 & r_1^2 \dots r_{n-1}^2 & p_o^2 & p_1^2 & \dots p_{n-1}^2 \\ \vdots & \vdots \quad\quad \vdots & \vdots & \vdots & \\ r_o^{2n} & r_1^{2n} \quad r_{n-1}^{2n} & p_o^{2n} & p_1^{2n} & \dots p_{n-1}^{2n} \end{vmatrix} \neq 0.$$

It is to be noted that these Wronskians which are expressed entirely in terms of the PMF's of the input r(t) and various ordered Poisson pulse functions, are derived by PMF transforming the conventional Wronskian which is normally in terms of functions and their derivatives.

In the case of parameter identification in the general n-th order model an input given by (5.4) which happens to be of the form

$$R(s) = \frac{\sum_{i=o}^{n-1} \beta_i s^i}{\sum_{n=o}^{n-1} \alpha_i s^i}$$

is Poisson unsuitable. The case of n=2 has been verified both in theory and numerical experiments.

This interesting phenomenon of singularizing inputs, which is characteristic of the PMF approach, may well be used advantageously towards reducing the size of the existing large scale system parameter identification problem. To do this, we would first obtain the form of the singularizing input function and deliberately employ the same simultaneously replacing all the linearly dependent columns by a single effective column. The section of the U vector i.e. $[U_R \,|\, U_\theta]$ will then be linearly combined (according to the chosen input form) into a single element to be obtained along with the essential section U_F. Having obtained U_F, we may return to the general model. Inserting the values of the parameters thus obtained, the model may be reduced and the identification of the remaining parameters may be carried out, of course, now by avoiding the singularizing input. This procedure will be practically very useful particularly in situations that compel modelling with a large number of parameters in the general model.

Even after the aspects of singularizing inputs are considered, the reduced matrices Φ and $\hat{\Phi}$ may still be singular due to certain columns in Φ_F and $\hat{\Phi}_F$ becoming linearly dependent. Such situations when analysed, automatically lead to guidelines towards proper choice of model structure. This aspect will be taken up in the next chapter.

5.3. Identifiability conditions in the case of MIMO systems

There are two essential requirements for successful identification of TF matrices in MIMO systems:

(i) Input-output pair suitability: Although the output signals are always uniquely determined from the input signals and the TFM of the system, however, for a given set of input-output signals the input-output relation may be satisfied by more than one TFM. Consider for instance, the example discussed by Mathew and Fairman [P7], of a system which is initially at rest having a TFM

$$H(s) = \left[\frac{1}{s+2}, \frac{-1}{s+1}\right],$$

with input vector

$$R(s) = \left[\frac{1}{s(s+1)}, \frac{1}{(s+2)(s+3)}\right]^T.$$

Then, the output

$$F(s) = \frac{3}{s(s+1)(s+2)(s+3)}.$$

The same input-output pair is also satisfied by the TFM

$$H(s) = \left[\frac{3}{s+3}, \frac{-3}{s}\right].$$

Mathew and Fairman [P7] have rightly raised this important prcblem but wrongly attributed this non-uniqueness to the so called L-suitability which pertains to input signals alone.

If we carefully observe the pair of input signals in question and the corresponding output signal, viz. $r_1(t) = 1-e^{-t}$; $r_2(t) = e^{-2t}-e^{-3t}$; and $f(t) = \frac{1}{2} - \frac{3}{2}e^{-t} + \frac{3}{2}e^{-2t} - \frac{1}{2}e^{-3t}$, we find that the output signal f(t) happens to contain a linear combination of the various modes of the input signals. This situation raises doubts even about the possibility of any dynamic relation between (r_1,r_2) and f. No clues regarding pole canellation and the like to clarify the matter are available a priori in the identification problem. We should therefore diagonise the trouble by performing suitable tests on the input-output data alone prior to applying any parameter identification algorithm. It is thus reasonable to suggest tests involving output signals also to detect such situations. A condition termed as 'Pair suitablity' discussed here will be useful in this context.

Definition 1: A given pair of sets of input and output signals $[\{r_j(t),\ j=1,2,\ldots,M\},\ \{f_i(t),\ i=1,2,\ldots,N\}]$ is pair suitable in (O,T) provided for every i the elements in $\mathcal{D}_i$ are linearly independent on (O,T), where

$$\mathcal{D}_i = f_i(t) \cup \{r_j(t),\ j=1,2,\ldots,M\}.$$

The term linear independence here is in the field of real numbers and relates to all the individual modes of the signals. The symbol $\cup$ represents union.

The pair suitablility of an output signal with all input signals may be expressed in terms of PMF transformed Wronskians. The input-output data is pair suitable if and only if for each k

$$W_{k_p} = \begin{vmatrix} r^o_{1,o} & r^o_{2,o} & \cdots & r^o_{M,o} & f^o_{k,o} \\ r^o_{1,1} & r^o_{2,1} & \cdots & r^o_{M,1} & f^o_{k,1} \\ \vdots & \vdots & & \vdots & \vdots \\ r^o_{1,M} & r^o_{2,M} & \cdots & r^o_{M,M} & f^o_{k,M} \end{vmatrix} \neq 0,$$

or alternatively,

$$\hat{W}_{k_p} = \begin{vmatrix} r^1_{1,o} & r^1_{2,o} & \cdots & r^1_{M,o} & f^1_{k,o} \\ r^2_{1,o} & r^2_{2,o} & \cdots & r^2_{M,o} & f^2_{k,1} \\ \vdots & \vdots & & \vdots & \vdots \\ r^{M+1}_{1,o} & r^{M+1}_{2,o} & \cdots & r^{M+1}_{M,o} & f^{M+1}_{k,o} \end{vmatrix} \neq 0.$$

(ii) Poisson suitablility of input signals: An important additional requirement for successful identification of TFM by this approach is a necessary condition of 'Poisson-suitability' of input signals defined below.

Definition 2. A given set of signals $\{r_j(t),\ j=1,2,\ldots,M\}$ is Poisson suitable in (O,T) provided the individual elements in ε are linearly independent on (O,T) where

$$\varepsilon = \mu \cup \Omega,$$
$$\mu = \{r^i_{j,k},\ j=1,2,\ldots,M;\ k=0,1,\ldots,(q-1)\},$$
$$\Omega = \{p^i_k,\ k=0,1,\ldots,(q-1)\}.$$

It may be seen that L-suitability of Mathew and Fairman [P7] is a special case of Poisson-suitability (λ=O), with the test set twice as large as above.

The test for Poisson suitability of input signals in a MIMO system may be performed on the following PMF transformed Wronskians.

$$W_p = \begin{vmatrix} r^o_{1,o} & \cdots & r^o_{1,n'} & r^o_{2,o} & \cdots & r^o_{2,n'} & \cdots & r^o_{M,o} & \cdots & r^o_{M,n'} & p^o_o & \cdots & p^o_{n'} \\ r^o_{1,1} & \cdots & r^o_{1,n_{max}} & r^o_{2,1} & \cdots & r^o_{2,n_{max}} & & r^o_{M,1} & \cdots & r^o_{M,n_{max}} & p^o_1 & & p^o_{n_{max}} \\ \vdots & & \vdots & \vdots & & \vdots & & \vdots & & \vdots & \vdots & & \vdots \\ r^o_{1,M} & & r^o_{1,M''} & r^o_{2,M'} & \cdots & r^o_{2,M''} & & r^o_{M,M} & \cdots & r^o_{M,M''} & p^o_M & & p^o_{M''} \end{vmatrix},$$

or

$$\hat{W}_p = \begin{vmatrix} r^1_{1,o} & \cdots & r^1_{1,n'} & r^1_{2,o} & \cdots & r^1_{2,n'} & r^1_{M,o} & \cdots & r^1_{M,n'} & p^1_o & \cdots & p^1_{n'} \\ r^2_{1,o} & \cdots & r^2_{1,n'} & r^2_{2,o} & \cdots & r^2_{2,n'} & r^2_{M,o} & \cdots & r^2_{M,n'} & p^2_o & \cdots & p^2_{n'} \\ \vdots & & \vdots & \vdots & & \vdots & \vdots & & \vdots & \vdots & & \vdots \\ r^{M'+1}_{1,o} & \cdots & r^{M'+1}_{1,n'} & r^{M'+1}_{2,o} & \cdots & r^{M'+1}_{2,n'} & r^{M'+1}_{M,o} & \cdots & r^{M'+1}_{M,n'} & p^{M'+1}_o & \cdots & p^{M'+1}_{n'} \end{vmatrix},$$

where $n' = (n_{max}-1)$, $M' = \{(M+1)n_{max}-1\}$, and $M'' = \{(M+2)n_{max}-2\}$.

In this case, if the initial conditions are all known a priori to be zero, W_p and $\hat{W}_p$ should still be tested for Poisson suitability without the columns containing the p's. The remaining columns with r's should all be linearly independent. Notice that this is not so in the SISO case in which for the single input with all zero initial conditions, the question of Poisson suitability does not arise.

The above results lead to the following important theorem, which can be proved along the lines applicable to the uniqueness problem of linear equations.

Theorem 1. The TFM of a MIMO system is uniquely identifiable if and only if the given data is pair suitable and Poisson suitable.

CHAPTER VI

A MICROPROCESSOR BASED SYSTEM FOR ON LINE PARAMETER IDENTIFICATION IN CONTINUOUS DYNAMICAL SYSTEMS [P11]

6.1. Introduction

This chapter proposes a microprocessor based unit for on line identification of the parameters in linear continuous lumped dynamical systems. The unit implements the algorithm which is based on Poisson moment functionals of input-output data, as already established in the previous chapters, from the actual process under identification. The development and performance of the unit are discussed in detail in the chapter. Section 6.2 presents the development of an interface between the main process and the microprocessor. A pair of Poisson filter chains (PFC) transforms the input output data from the main process into respective PMF's. The microprocessor receives the digital version of the respective PMF's and is programmed to execute the parameter identification algorithm. The results may be either displayed or used further in appropriate control/optimization algorithms. Sections 6.3 and 6.4 respectively discuss the performance of the unit and practical aspects of application.

The PMF method, for parameter identification in a first order time varying system with all initial conditions known a priori to be zero, is schematically shown in Fig. 6.1.

6.2. Development of interface between the process and microprocessor

A microprocessor unit dedicated to the task of estimating the parameters of a continuous dynamic process through the PMF method requires an interface for on line operation with the process under identification. In this section we discuss some details of development of such an interface. The interfacing unit consists of three subsystems:

i) A pair of Poisson filter chains (PFC), one each to generate the PMF's of the process input and the process output.

ii) A multiplexer (to essentially economize hardware) enabling a single A/D converter to handle a number of signals arising out of the PFC.

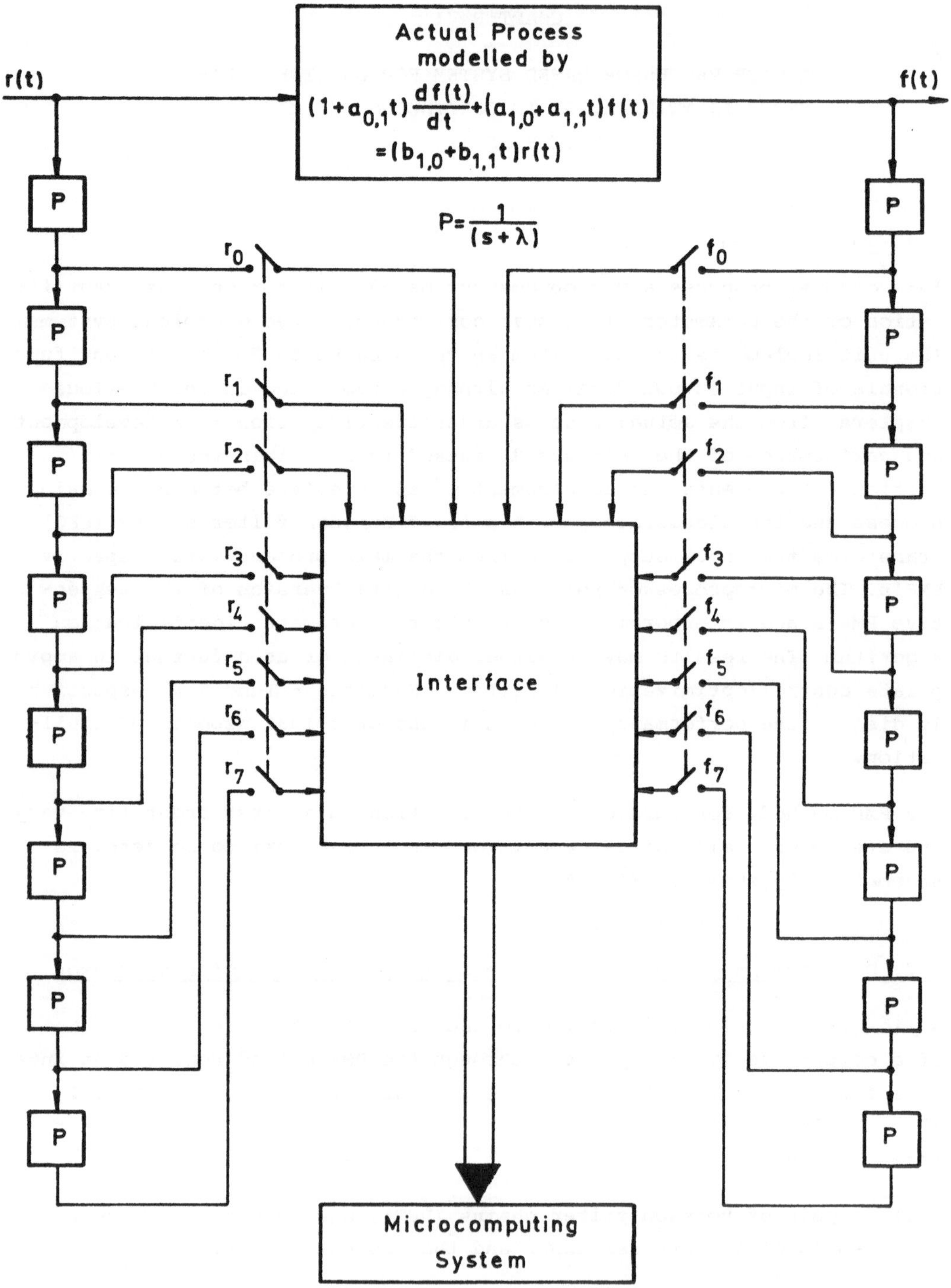

Fig. 6.1. PMF method of parameter identification in a first order time-varying model

iii) An A/D converter to convert the analog PMF signals into digital form.

a) Poisson filter chains: Two identical filter chains with a number of stages, each stage having transfer function of the form $-\lambda/(s+\lambda)$, have been incorporated. Poisson filter element of this type is easily realized by means of an OP Amp (IC 741) in the inverting mode with RC feedback as shown in Fig. 6.2 that can be set to any desired value. The effect of the gain term '$-\lambda$' in the PFC element can be easily included in the original PMF formulation. This additional gain term will helpfully strengthen the higher order PMF's (outputs of long PFC at the far end). These are usually quite weak due to multistage filtering in actual practice.

Since the Poisson filter element is designed for inversion, the PMF's of order 0,1,2,3,... will have signs -,+,-,+,... respectively. This alternation of the signs of the PMF's must be taken into consideration in A/D conversion. It is economical to use an A/D converter unit with facility for bipolar operation, as in Fig. 6.3, instead of using unipolar converter with additional compensatory inverters at the required stages of output of the PFC. In the system, developed by the authors, each PFC has 3 stages.

b) The Multiplexer: An 8 channel analog multiplexer (MP 7501) has been used to multiplex the PMF's. f_o, f_1, f_2, r_o, r_1, r_2 are handled through the input lines s_1 to s_6 in 6 channels and the unused channels have been grounded.

The analog inputs are selected by 3 address logic lines (A_2, A_1,A_o). These address and enable lines are connected to port A (in the output mode) of a standard microprocessor kit (SDK 85). The multiplexer address is sequentially incremented so as to access all the PMF's. Connections between PFC and multiplexer, and between the multiplexer and the output port are shown functionally in Fig. 6.4.

The analog output line of the multiplexer is connected to the analog input of the A/D converter. Since the enable line of the multiplexer is tied to the START line of the 74121 chip which triggers the A/D converter, addressing any input line will automatically initiate the conversion process without any further control signals from the microprocessor.

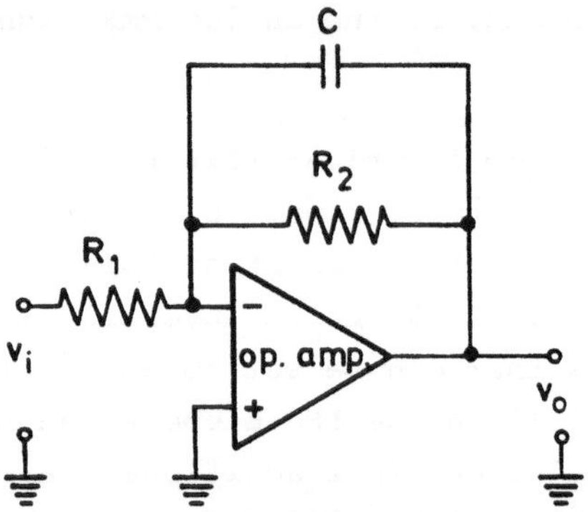

Fig. 6.2. Poisson filter element ($P(s) = \frac{-\lambda}{s+\lambda}$)

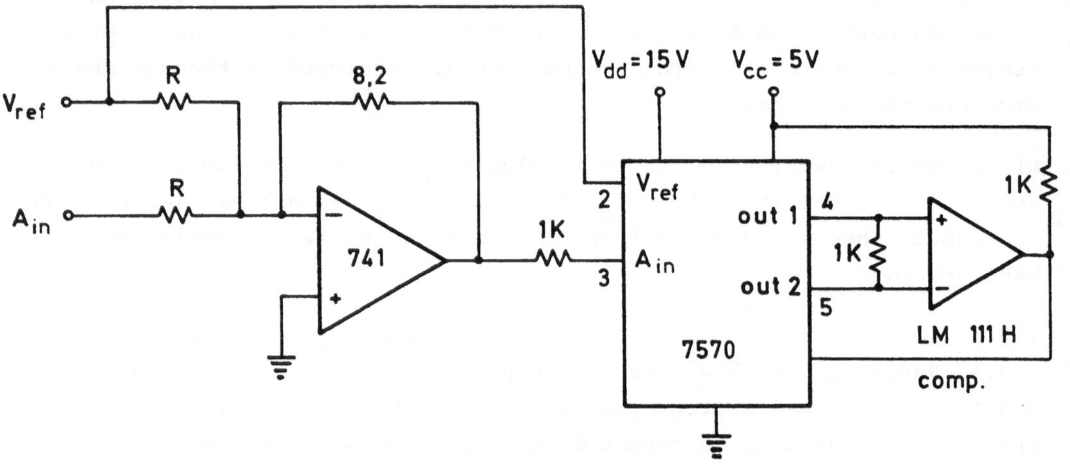

Fig. 6.3. Bipolar operation

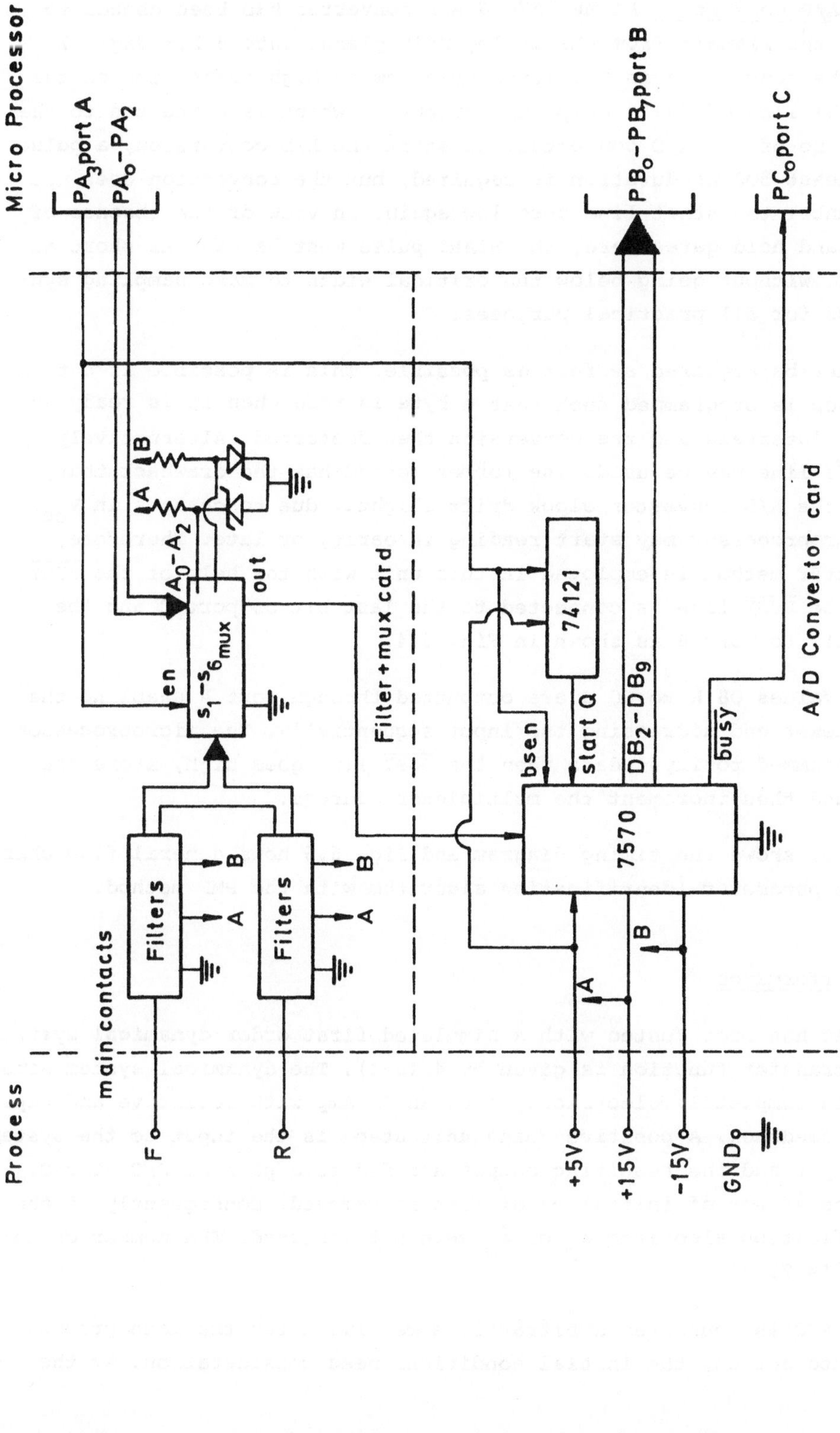

Fig. 6.4. The interface

<u>c) The A/D Converter:</u> An MP 7570 J A/D converter has been chosen to convert the signals from the analog multiplexer into 8 bit digital form. The conversion is initiated by a low to high transition on the START (B) line of 74121 chip, the output of which is connected to the START line of the A/D converter. To start the A/D conversion, a pulse of at least 500 ns duration is required, but the conversion does not start until the start line goes low again. In view of the absence of sample and hold gates here, the START pulse must be made as short as possible without going below the critical width to make sampling synchronous for all practical purposes.

Data must be acquired as fast as possible. This is possible if a tight wait loop is programmed such that a byte is read when it is ready at regular intervals and the conversion then restarted. Alternatively, the $\overline{\text{BUSY}}$ line may be used. The former method has the drawback that, should the A/D converter clock drift slightly due to changes in V_{CC}, the microprocessor may start reading in early, or late. Therefore, the latter method is employed in this unit with the help of the $\overline{\text{BUSY}}$ line. The $\overline{\text{BUSY}}$ line is connected to the last bit of port C and the data bits to port B as shown in Fig. 6.4.

Binary values 08 H to OC H are outputted through port A enabling the multiplexer and addressing the input sequentially. The microprocessor is programmed to input data when the $\overline{\text{BUSY}}$ line goes high, store the value and then increment the multiplexer address.

Fig. 6.5. shows the timing diagram and Fig. 6.6 hows general flow chart for the parameter identification algorithm with the PMF method.

6.3. Performance

The unit has been tested with a simulated first order dynamical system whose transfer function is given by 4/(s+4). The dynamical system simulated is completely electrical, i.e. an OP Amp with resistive and capacitive feedback. A positive going unit step is the input to the system. This input and the resulting output are fed to a pair of PFC at t=O. Thus the effect of initial conditions is removed. Consequently in the identification algorithm Φ_p or $\hat{\Phi}_p$ were not inserted. The number of unknowns is 2.

If the PFC is connected arbitrarily some time after the main process went into action, the initial conditions need consideration. At the

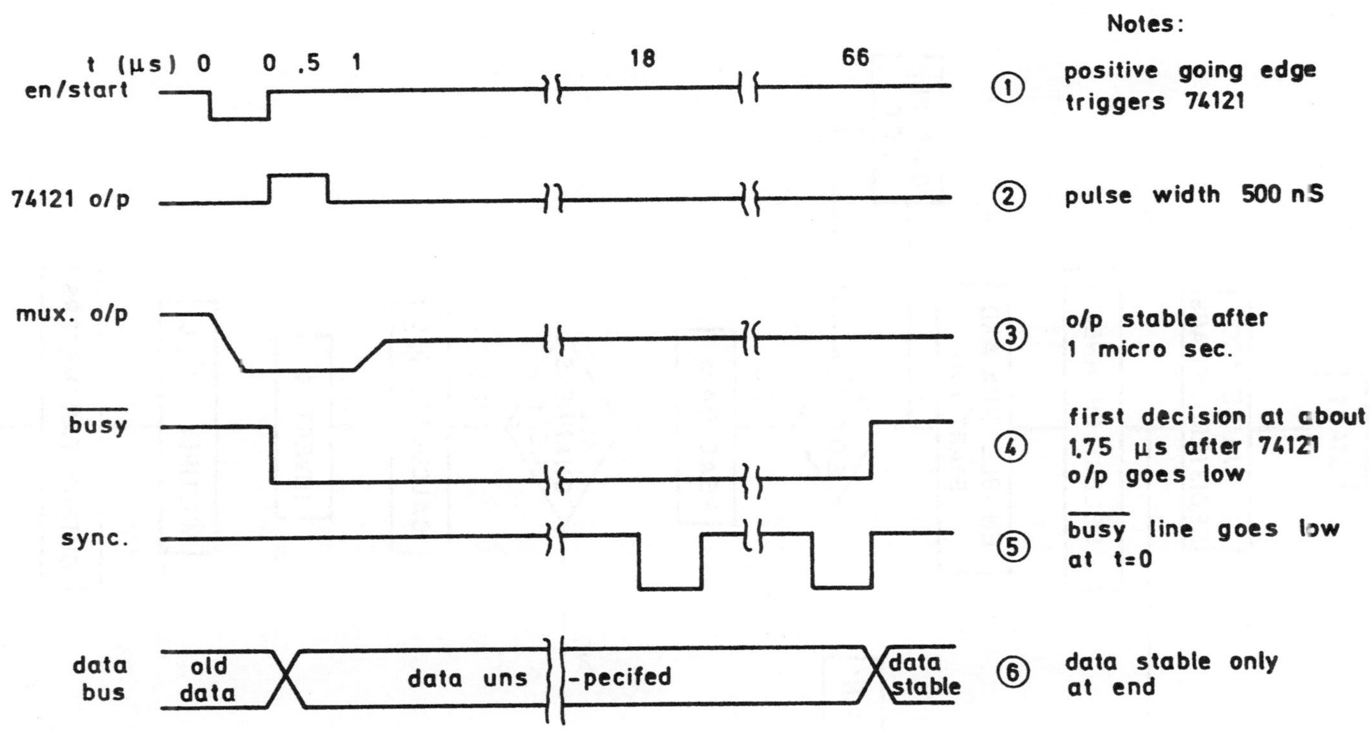

Notes:
t (µs) 0
0 .5 1
18
66
en/start
74121 o/p
mux. o/p
busy
sync.
data
bus
old
data
data uns
-pecifed
data
stable
① positive going edge triggers 74121
② pulse width 500 nS
③ o/p stable after 1 micro sec.
④ first decision at about 1,75 µs after 74121 o/p goes low
⑤ busy line goes low at t=0
⑥ data stable only at end

Fig. 6.5. Timing diagram

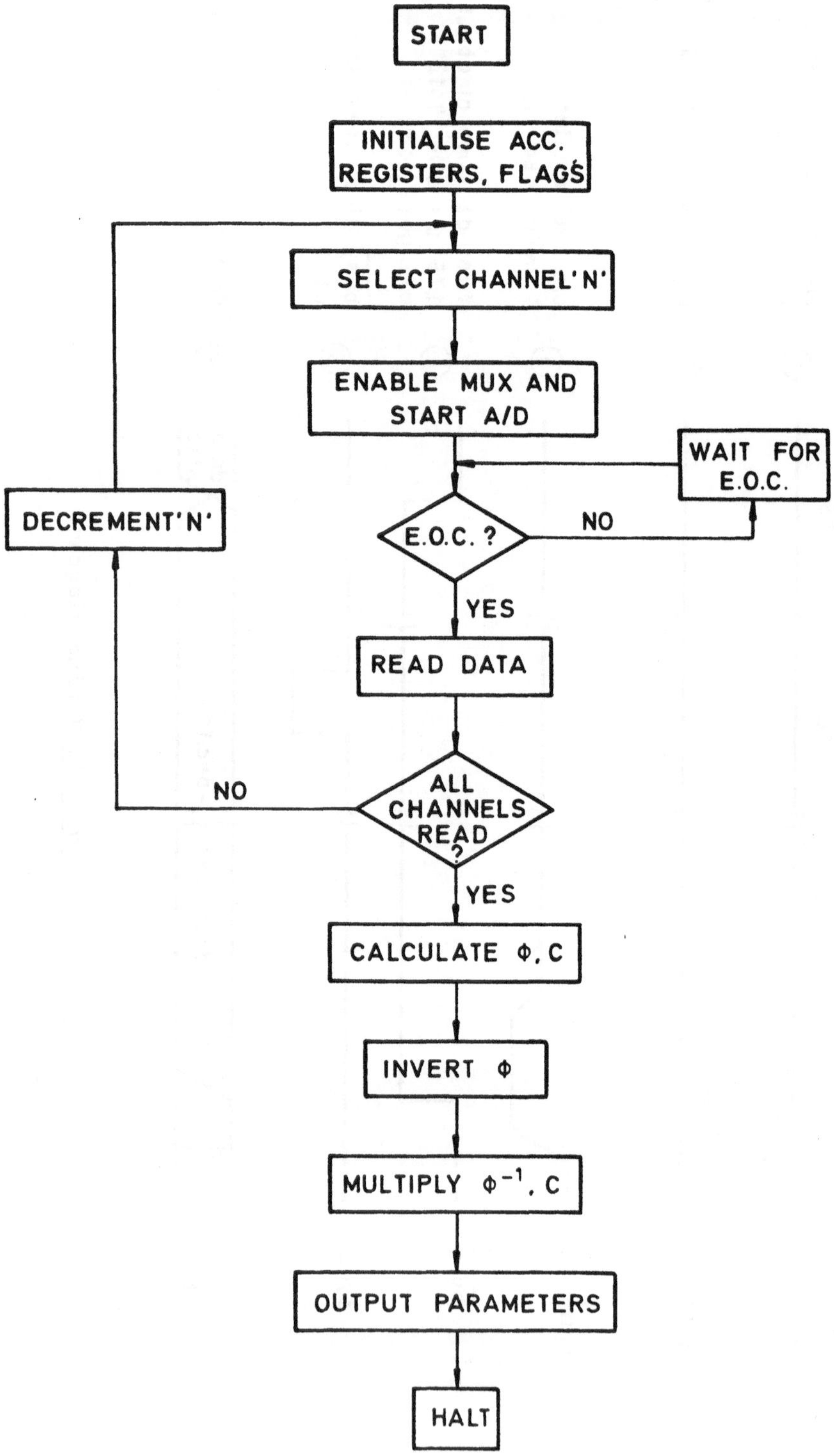

Fig. 6.6. Flow chart

same time if λ is chosen sufficiently large, and if t_o is also long, the effect of initial conditions will decay very fast in the PMF's measured about that time. Our algorithms therefore, may be written ignoring the initial conditions for all purposes. In the general algorithm, however, the choice of λ is completely free.

Returning to the discussions of our simulation , we choose $\lambda = 3.33$ (R = 150 kilo ohm and C = 2 microfarad). The parameters of the main process are found to be 4.34 and 4.32 in Method 1 and 3.23 and 2.91 in Method 2. The errors are due to the following:

i) Limited A/D converter resolution: The 8 bit A/D converter finds it difficult to resolve accurately the higher order PFM's. Higher order PFM's are generally weaker than the lower order ones. This generally weakens the determinant of Φ or $\hat{\Phi}$. Consequently, the results become very sensitive to errors in Φ (or $\hat{\Phi}$) and C (or $\hat{C}$).

ii) Lack of truely synchronized samples: The PMF's corresponding to an instant of time are not truely synchronous in the present unit which emplys only one A/D converter for reasons of economy of hardware. The various PMF's corresponding to an instant of time are actually "queued" for a short time which includes the conversion time. The slight delay is considered negligible in view of large time constant of the main process and the consequent slow modes of the signals. When λ is large, this however, cannot be considered negligible. Moreover, when a large number of PMF's are queued, the largest delay experienced by the last PMF for conversion may not be negligible.

Additional hardware may be used to elemininate this error by admitting truely synchronous samples.

6.4. Conclusion and discussion

An implementation of the PMF method of parameter identification in linear continuous systems is presented. The PMF algorithm may be modified to handle models with unknown time lags [P10, P16]. In fact, all models which are linear in the parameters may be directly handled with suitable modification of the basic algorithm. It is interesting to note that the interface in all such cases remains the same in form. It will have to be expanded only in size to handle larger data in more complicated models.

This universality of the PMF technique makes it practically attractive.

The PMF's of the process signals are found to be considerably immune to zero mean additive noise, if λ is fairly small. In spite of the freedom available to us in the choice of λ, we will be guided by the actual situation in the particular application to choose a suitable value for λ. Large λ will practically eliminate the effects of the initial conditions, but owing to its large band-width in this condition, the PFC will admit more noise than when λ is small. It is possible to use Kalman filtered PMF's [P23] if we wish to have optimal filtering.

The PMF's of higher order are generally weak. Consequently,when higher order PMF's are to be used,(inevitably in Method 1 and particularly when the model order is high) the matrices Φ and $\hat{\Phi}$ have weakened determinants, making the results more sensitive to errors. In order to overcome this problem, we suggest the use of multiple PFC with various values of λ to generate data for the required number of independent equations, inspite of its increased cost.

CHAPTER VII

SYSTEM STRUCTURE IDENTIFICATION [P19, G9, G29]

7.1. Introduction

The general algorithm, which considers the model in the form of equation (3.1) presented in Chapter III, suffers from the limitation that the structure of the system in terms the structure indices 'm' and 'n' have to be assumed to be known a priori. This chapter deals with the problem of determining the structure indices of the system, from a knowledge of the input-output data. At the outset, the conventional approach based on "matrix rank method" (MRM) [G9], is outlined and its limitations are discussed in Section 7.2 of this chapter. Then an effective method termed here as "parameter error function method" (PEFM), is described for system structure identification in Section 7.3. This method is shown to be superior to rank evaluation method through illustrative examples both with deterministic and noisy data. It is based on minimisation of a parameter error function reflecting a measure of the total variation of the parameters. The results of the above methods are discussed in Section 7.4.

7.2. Matrix Rank Method (MRM) for determination of system order 'n'

The order of the system is directly related to the rank of matrices Φ or $\hat{\Phi}$. An attempt to fit oversized models in the case of process data actually from a lower order system will singularize Φ and $\hat{\Phi}$. The MRM is based on this phenomenon. To simplify our discussion without loss of generality, consider the case when m=0 and n alone is to be determined. It can be shown that n is equal to half the size of the largest nonsingular matrix V_{2k} (or $\hat{V}_{2k}$) considered in the Hurwitzian way, here

$$V_{2k} = \begin{bmatrix} f_o^o & r_o^o & f_1^o & r_1^o & \cdots & f_{k-1}^o & r_{k-1}^o \\ f_1^o & r_1^o & f_2^o & r_2^o & \cdots & f_k^o & r_k^o \\ \vdots & \vdots & \vdots & \vdots & & \vdots & \vdots \\ f_{2k-1}^o & r_{2k-1}^o & f_{2k}^o & r_{2k}^o & \cdots & f_{3k-2}^o & r_{3k-2}^o \end{bmatrix}, \tag{7.1}$$

and

$$\hat{V}_{2k} = \begin{bmatrix} f_o^1 & r_o^1 & f_1^1 & r_1^1 & \cdots & f_{k-1}^1 & r_{k-1}^1 \\ f_o^2 & r_o^2 & f_1^2 & r_1^2 & \cdots & f_{k-1}^2 & r_{k-1}^2 \\ \vdots & \vdots & \vdots & \vdots & & \vdots & \vdots \\ f_o^{2k} & r_o^{2k} & f_1^{2k} & r_1^{2k} & & f_{k-1}^{2k} & r_{k-1}^{2k} \end{bmatrix}. \tag{7.2}$$

For example, if we find that the data in a certain case is such that

$$\begin{bmatrix} f_o^o & r_o^o \\ f_1^o & r_1^o \end{bmatrix} \quad \text{or} \quad \begin{bmatrix} f_o^1 & r_o^1 \\ f_o^2 & r_o^2 \end{bmatrix}$$

is the largest nonsingular submatrix of V_{2k} (or $\hat{V}_{2k}$) considered in the Hurwitzian way, the data belongs to a <u>first order system</u> (i.e. n=1). The above result is derived by using the concept of linear dependence of process signals and their derivatives in terms of Wronskians. The matrices V_{2k} and $\hat{V}_{2k}$ are, in fact, Wronskians in the PMF domain. Accommodating excessive PMF information in additional rows of V_{2k} or $\hat{V}_{2k}$ in a least squares sense, we may form matrices

$$\overset{*}{V}_{2k} = V_{2k}^T\, V_{2k} \quad \text{and} \quad \hat{V}_{2k}^* = \hat{V}_{2k}^T\, \hat{V}_{2k}$$

and compute

$$\Lambda_k = \det\, [V_{2k}^*]$$

and

$$\hat{\Lambda}_k = \det\, [\hat{V}_{2k}^*] .$$

To examine the rank we study either the magnitude of Λ_k (or $\hat{\Lambda}_k$) or the ratio Λ_k/Λ_{k+1} (or $\hat{\Lambda}_k/\ \hat{\Lambda}_{k+1}$). Notice that the PMF matrix V_{2k} (or $\hat{V}_{2k}^*$) is close in spirit to the so called product moment matrix [G27]. In the process of applying the general algorithm, we may conduct the rank tests on the readily available matrices Φ and $\hat{\Phi}$. Thus the order of the system may be seen to be the size of the largest non-singular matrix Φ (or $\hat{\Phi}$). In all our further discussions we will follow this approach.

<u>Example 7.1.</u> Consider the input-output data from a system which is actually time-invariant and one of second order

$$\ddot{f}(t) + 5\,\dot{f}(t) + 6\,f(t) = r(t)\ ,$$

with r(t) as unit step and zero initial conditions. The data is fitted to models with different values of n and the determinats of Φ at t_o=1 sec. denoted as $|\Phi(0,n)|$, are shown in Table 7.1.

Table 7.1. Determinant of Φ as a function of n in time-invariant system structure determination from the data of Example 7.1.

n	$\|\Phi(0,n)\|$			
	0./.Noise	5./.Noise	10./.Noise	50./.Noise
1	0.2806×10^{-3}	0.2610×10^{-3}	0.2750×10^{-3}	0.3221×10^{-3}
2	0.5555×10^{-14}	0.1128×10^{-13}	0.9403×10^{-14}	0.2339×10^{-13}
3	-0.2138×10^{-37}	0.7491×10^{-32}	-0.7222×10^{-35}	0.7507×10^{-31}
4	0.1007×10^{-68}	0.6899×10^{-59}	0.1069×10^{-58}	-0.4489×10^{-57}

In the MRM the decision is based on a search for n at which $|\Phi(0,n)|$ vanishes. This search is made difficult in practice due to uncertainty resulting from computational errors. The presence of noise in the data further complicates the matter. Under these conditions, as has been the existing practice, abrupt decrease in the value of the determinant may be taken as an indicator. A study of the values of $|\Phi(0,n)|$ in Table 7.1 would reveal the difficulties even in this decision. For instance, even with 0./. noise in the results in Table 7.1, which have been computed with double precision arithmetic, the point at which the determinant "abruptly decreased" is not clear. The determinant ratios $|\Phi(0,n)|/|\Phi(0,n+1)|$, n=1,2,3 are respectively of orders 10^{11}, 10^{23}, 10^{31}. Noise in the data modified these ratios only slightly in view of inherent noise rejection property of PMF's. The determinant values are usually improved, the ratios still maintaining similar orders of magnitude. Decision making on the basis of these, is therefore not reliable.

Another important feature of the PMF technique is the possibility of certain inputs singularizing the matrices Φ and $\hat{\Phi}$ even if the order of the model is chosen correctly. Such singularizing inputs have been termed as Poisson unsuitable signals and these may occur accidentally when we try to include the effect of unknown initial conditions while using data from an arbitrary period of time. Poisson unsuitable signals lead to a situation wherein the columns of matrix block Φ_R and Φ_P (or $\hat{\Phi}_R$ and $\hat{\Phi}_P$) become linearly dependent. It had been shown in chapter V that an input of the form

$$R(s) = \frac{\sum_{i=0}^{n-1} \beta_i s^i}{\sum_{i=0}^{n-1} \alpha_i s^i}$$

is Poisson unsuitable. While Poisson suitability will not matter if the initial conditions are not treated, since Φ_p (or $\hat{\Phi}_p$) is dropped from Φ (or $\hat{\Phi}$) in our algorithm in such a case, however, in the general case, singularization due to unsuitable input signals is bound to cause difficulties in order determination through MRM. In view of such practical difficulties in MRM, we follow an alternative approach discussed in the next section.

7.3. Parameter error function method (PEFM)

The general model, (equation 3.1), has parameters $a_{i,j}$ and $b_{i,j}$ which are constant even if the dynamical system is time-varying. If the structure is correctly identified, the corresponding parameters $a_{i,j}$ and $b_{i,j}$ should maintain invariance with tespect to $t_o, t_o \in (0,T)$, where t_o is the instant about which PMF's are evaluated, the input-output data being available on (0,T). We will base our decision mainly on this invariance property. To do this we define a parameter error function based on L instants of time in (0,T), i.e., with PMF's about t_i: i=1,2,...,L.

$$P_e(m,n) = \frac{\sum_{i=1}^{L} (U_i-\bar{U})^T (U_i-\bar{U})}{M} , \tag{7.3}$$

where

$$\bar{U} = \frac{\sum_{i=1}^{L} U_i}{L} . \tag{7.4}$$

Notice that division by M in P_e is to normalise the total measure of this parametric error with respect to the number of parameters. This scalar measure is conceptually similar to the EVN norm of the covariance matrix, P* of parametric error [G33]. The consistency measure employed by Desai and Fairman [G9], and the several other variants of the scalar measure of parametric errors such as EEVN, GEVN [G33] are all heuristically expected to provide the indication regarding model structure. Statistical interpretations are valid only when large values of L are involved. Equation (7.3) inplies that $P_e \geq 0$. $P_e = 0$ only in the noise free case correspnding to the exact structure indices m and n. In the presence of noise $P_e > 0$, attaining a minimum for true values of m and n.

Example 7.2. Let us consider a system actually described by (3.1) with m=0, and n=2, i.e., in particular

$$\ddot{f}(t) + 5\,\dot{f}(t) + 6\,f(t) = r(t).$$

With r(t) as a unit step, input-output data is simulated without noise. This data has been employed to evaluate $P_e(m,n)$. For various indices of model structure the function is shown in Table 7.2.

Table 7.2. Parameter error function $P_e(m,n)$ with data from Example 7.2

Case	(m,n)	$P_e(m,n)$	Remark
1	(0,1)	7.18×10^{-2}	
2	(1,1)	2.70×10^{-3}	
3*	(0,2)	1.20×10^{-11}	*Actual Structure
4	(2,1)	8.65×10^{-1}	
5	(0,3)	2.37×10^{-1}	

The parameters obtained in case 3, with m=0, n=2 are

5.0000330, 6.0000158, 0.7747407×10^{-5} and 1.0000051

while the actual values are 5, 6, 0 and 1 respectively.

Example 7.3. Let us consider a system whose structural indices are actually m=1, n=1; the system equation being in particular

$$\dot{f}(t) + 2\,f(t) = 4t\,r(t).$$

With r(t) as a unit step, the input-output data so simulated is used to compute $P_e(m,n)$ which is shown in Table 7.3.

Table 7.3. Parameter error function $P_e(m,n)$ with data from Example 7.3

Case	(m,n)	$P_e(m,n)$	Remarks
1	(0,1)	1.36	
2*	(1,1)	9.28×10^{-6}	*Actual Structure
3	(0,2)	0.14	
4	(2,1)	0.09	
5	(0,3)	4.89	

The parameters obtained in case 2 (m=1, n=1) are:

0.4354462×10^{-2}, $-0.11495777 \times 10^{-1}$, 2.0056571, $0.36543012 \times 10^{-4}$ and 3.9990392

while the actual parameters are 0, 0, 2, 0 and 4 respectively.

Example 7.4. Let us consider a system known to be time-invariant (i.e. m=0). We have to determine the appropriate order n with the available noisy input-output data.

$$r(t) = \text{unit step} + \text{noise}$$
$$f(t) = 1 - \exp(-t) + \text{noise}$$

The parameter error function is computed for various values of n and shown in Table 7.4.

Table 7.4. Parameter error function $P_e(0,n)$ with noisy data of Example 7.4

Order	$P_e(0,n)$				Remarks
n	0./.Noise	5./.Noise	10./.Noise	50./.Noise	
1*	0	0.0165	0.0183	0.0040	*P_e is minimum. Appropriate model
2	3.1907	5.9962	19.1170	42.4000	
3	1064.22	12925.63	4904.1445	564.75	
4	84821803.00	21422250.00	12579625.00	9731157.50	

One may also normalise the variation in each parameter by expressing it as a fraction of the mean value of the parameter itself. We may denote the normalised version of P_e as P_e^*, i.e.,

$$\bar{u}_j = \left(\sum_{i=1}^{L} u_{ij}\right)/L$$

and

$$P_e^* = \frac{1}{M} \sum_{i=1}^{L} \left[\frac{u_{ij}-\bar{u}_j}{\bar{u}_j}\right]^2 ,$$

where $\bar{u}_j$ is the j-th element of $\bar{U}$
and u_{ij} is the j-th element of U_i.

Table 7.5, which shows P_e^* in the case of Example 7.4, maintains the decision arrived through P_e.

Table 7.5. Normalised parameter error function $P_e^*(0,n)$ with noisy data of Example 7.4

Order n	$P_e^*(0,n)$				Remarks
	0./.Noise	5./.Noise	10./.Noise	50./.Noise	
1+	0	0.0152	0.0150	0.0026	+P_e^* is minimum.
2	0.0693	0.7280	5.2231	0.7210	Appropriate
3	0.2266	0.5128	0.6647	0.7189	model
4	0.3586	1.0762	261.1035	15.4821	

Notice that case 1 shows P_e or P_e^* under all conditions of noise strength. Therefore, a first order model (n=1) is the most appropriate to represent the system. The corresponding parameters evaluated at t_o=3 sec. are shown in Table 7.6.

Table 7.6. Identified parameters in Example 7.4.

Noise	Parameters
0./.	1.0000, 1.0000
5./.	1.0237, 1.0653
10./.	1.0544, 0.9844
50./.	1.0179, 0.9378

The process data actually belongs to a system described by $\dot{f}(t) + f(t) = r(t)$.

7.4. Conclusion

The problem of structure identification in continuous linear lumped systems has been examined in two approaches using the PMF method. The first, based on rank evaluation, is usually corrupted by singularizing features of Poisson unsuitable input signals when the identification algorithm is employed with an arbitrary record of data necessitating determination of unknown initial conditions. However, in our present discussion, this situation is averted by considering models with initial conditions known to be zero, and the influence of model structure alone on the rank of Φ matrix is examined. Practical difficulties in decision making in this approach have been pointed out. The second approach uses the concept of a parameter error function. Decision making is based on the minimum of this function and is found to be clearer than in the former approach. In the second approach the parameters of the system are those corresponding to the minimum value of the parameter error function. According to the authors' experience, P_e or P_e^* can be computed with few instants of time (even just two). A recursive evaluation allowing for all instants of time may also be performed, in which case (7.3) and (7.4) will be used recursively.

CHAPTER VIII

IDENTIFICATION OF TIME-LAG AND NONLINEAR SYSTEMS

8.1. Introduction

This chapter deals with parameter identification in some special types of systems such as time-lag, nonlinear and piecewise linear systems. Mathematical models encountered in the control of processes such as thermal systems, rocket motor combustion, travelling wave systems, systems with human links, high speed aerodynamic systems, economic systems, etc. involve differential equations with delays. The problem of parameter identification is, therefore, of practical importance.

Many control systems are actually nonlinear. When the process signals are wide ranging in magnitude, nonlinear effects cannot be ignored. The presence of nonlinear dynamics may be described in various ways. It is not possible to have a general model for nonlinear systems. Volterra series representations are no doubt quite general, but accuracy of the description depends on the level of truncation. The description is analytic. There may be other models as well in the differential equation form. We will consider the problem of parameter identification in differential equation models and those in the form of blocks with nonlinear elements separable from linear elements.

Inspite of their undoubted generality, analytic models have the limitation of being less accurate for systems which are highly nonlinear, such as those exhibiting switching phenomena. For instance, characteristics exhibiting abrupt saturation and dead zone are better modelled by piecewise linear characteristics. Piecewise linear models in such cases have less number of parameters than the corresponding analytical models. Consequently, in algorithms for parameter identification, piecewise linear models are lighter to handle. In view of this situation, we will discuss a method of parameter identification in nonlinear systems using piecewise linear models.

Section 8.2 presents a parameter identification technique for time-lag systems. Section 8.2(a) discusses an iterative shift algorithm for time-lag system identification in general and 8.2(b) proposes a direct identification algorithm for small delays. An algorithm for nonlinear system identification is discussed in Section 8.3. Section 8.4 presents an algorithm for piecewise linear system identification.

8.2. Parameter identification in time-delay systems

Consider for the sake of an illustrative development, a process modelled by an n-th order differential equation, known a priori to have a single delay in the input side, as

$$\frac{d^n f(t)}{dt^n} + \sum_{i=1}^{n} a_i \frac{d^{n-i} f(t)}{dt^{n-i}} = br(t-\tau), \tag{8.1}$$

with f(t) and r(t) over an arbitrary but active period of operating record. In such a case the initial conditions $f^{(o)}(0)$, $f^{(1)}(0)$, ..., $f^{(n-1)}(0)$, the parameters a_1, a_2, ..., a_n, b and τ are unknowns to be determined from the given data. The total number of unknowns is $N = 2(n+1)$. Taking the k-th PMF transformation about t_i, $i = 1, 2, \ldots, (N+1)$, with $k = n$, we get N simultaneous linear algebraic equations in the form

$$\Phi U = C,$$

or

$$\hat{\Phi} U = \hat{C}, \tag{8.2}$$

if τ were known, with our usual notation. We are now in a position to determine the unknowns. Usually the value of τ is not known exactly, but the neighbourhood of τ may often be known a priori. If τ is completely unknown we can make some guess work and determine iteratively. If it is known that τ is very small we can approximate the PMF's of the delayed function. Based on these, two methods are developed, namely i) iterative shift algorithm for a general unknown delay and ii) a direct algorithm evaluating the PMF's of the delayed function by a simple interpolation technique.

8.2(a). The Iterative Shift Algorithm (ISA) [P 10]

In this technique we can use some guess or trial value of τ to obtain the identification equation (8.2). The vector of unknowns U so obtained will be true if the guessed τ is correct. Otherwise, U will be in error. That the unknowns U are in error may be detected by computing U with data on some subintervals $(0,T_1)$, $(0,T_2)$ and then comparing the resultant vectors U. If τ is correctly guessed, the vector U will be invariant with data on various subintervals. With this in mind we propose an iterative shift algorithm (ISA) as follows:

a) Guess a value of τ and determine the PMF expansions of the delayed signals corresponding to the chosen model.

b) Consider subintervals I_i, $(0,T_i)$; $T_i \in (0,T)$, $i = 1,2,\ldots,L$.

c) With the data on each subinterval, determine separately the unknown vector U_i with appropriate model following the general algorithm.

d) Compute the error function

$$H(\tau) = \sum_{i=1}^{L-1} ||U_{i+1} - U_i|| . \tag{8.3}$$

Notice here that the error function may be taken also in the normalised form.

e) Minimise $H(\tau)$ with respect to τ.

This value of $\tau = \tau^o$ say, along with the corresponding vector U, completely identifies the system under consideration. The true value of lag in the system satisfies $H(\tau) = 0$. These roots are simultaneously accompanied by the true values of the plant parameters and also of the unknown terms due to initial conditions. Solution of $H(\tau) = 0$ has been via Newton-Raphson iteration in the illustrative examples. An a priori knowledge (if available) of the neighbourhood of τ^o will help in making good initial start of iteration.

<u>Illustrative examples:</u>

Example 8.1: Linear time invariant systems with a lag.

Consider a system described by

$$\frac{d^2c(t)}{dt^2} + a_1 \frac{dc(t)}{dt} + a_2c(t) = r(t-\tau), \tag{8.4}$$

where c(t) is the output, r(t) is the input, a_1 and a_2 are the unknown system parameters and τ is an unknown lag. With $a_1 = 3.0$, $a_2 = 1.25$, $\tau = 0.6$, and zero initial conditions, the input-output data along with the respective moment functionals are generated. Fig. 8.1 shows the function $H(\tau)$. The converged results are given in Table 8.1.

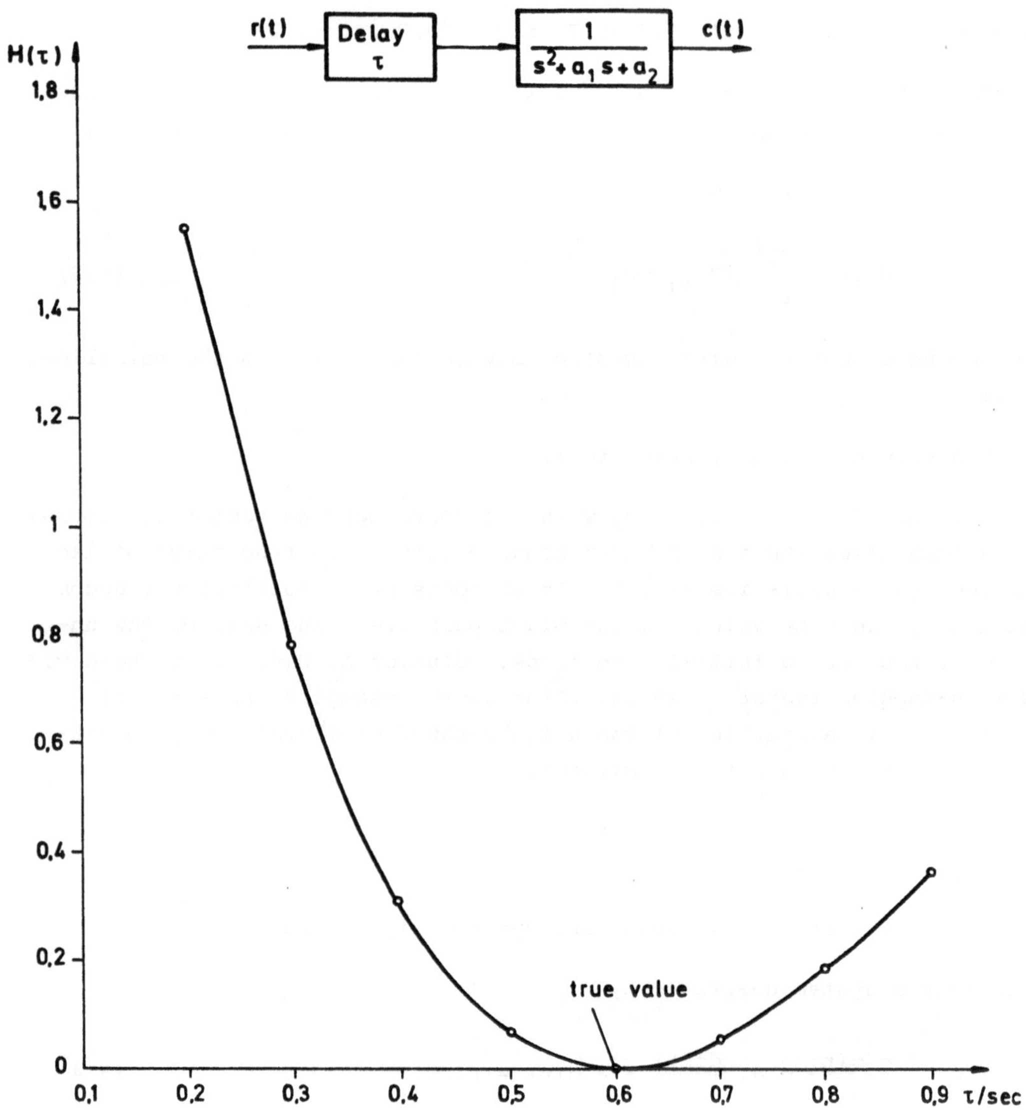

Fig. 8.1. $H(\tau)$ in Example 8.1.

Example 8.2: Linear TVP system with a lag.

For the case of a simple TVP system

$$\frac{dc(t)}{dt} + a_1 c(t) = a_2 r(t-\tau), \tag{8.5}$$

with $a_1 = 1.5$, $a_2 = 0.5$, $\tau = 0.6$ and zero initial conditions the input-output data along with the respective moment functionals are generated. Fig. 8.2 shows $H(\tau)$ and the results are given in Table 8.1.

Example 8.3: Nonlinear system with a lag.

For the case of a nonlinear system

$$\frac{dc(t)}{dt} + a_1 c(t) = a_2 r^3(t-\tau), \tag{8.6}$$

with $a_1 = 1.0$, $a_2 = 1.0$, $\tau = 0.6$, and zero initial conditions, the input-output data and their moment functionals are generated. Fig. 8.3 shows the function $H(\tau)$. The results through Newton-Raphson iteration are given in Table 8.1.

Table 8.1. Results of the Iterative Shift Algorithm (ISA)

System	True values			Initial value of	Converged results			Number of iterations
	a_1	a_2	τ		a_1	a_2	τ	
Example 8.1	3.0	1.25	0.6	0.00	3.008	1.2470	0.5993	9
Example 8.2	1.5	0.50	0.6	0.75	1.505	0.5016	0.6009	11
Example 8.3	1.0	1.00	0.6	0.75	1.005	1.0030	0.6005	13

In all these illustrative examples, choosing a unit ramp function as the input signal, the output and the required input and output moment functionals have been generated at $t_o = 0.0, 0.1, \ldots, 6.0$. The filter constant λ has been set equal to 1.5 for the linear time invariant problem and 1.0 for all other cases. Ten parameter sets have been computed using the attributes of signals at ten pairs of time instants (2.5, 4.0) (2.6, 4.1) ..., (3.4, 4.9) s to evaluate the loss function at any value of the lag. $\Delta\tau_g$ is set equal to 0.1 initially and for the k-th iteration it is chosen as $\Delta\tau_g/2^{k-1}$.

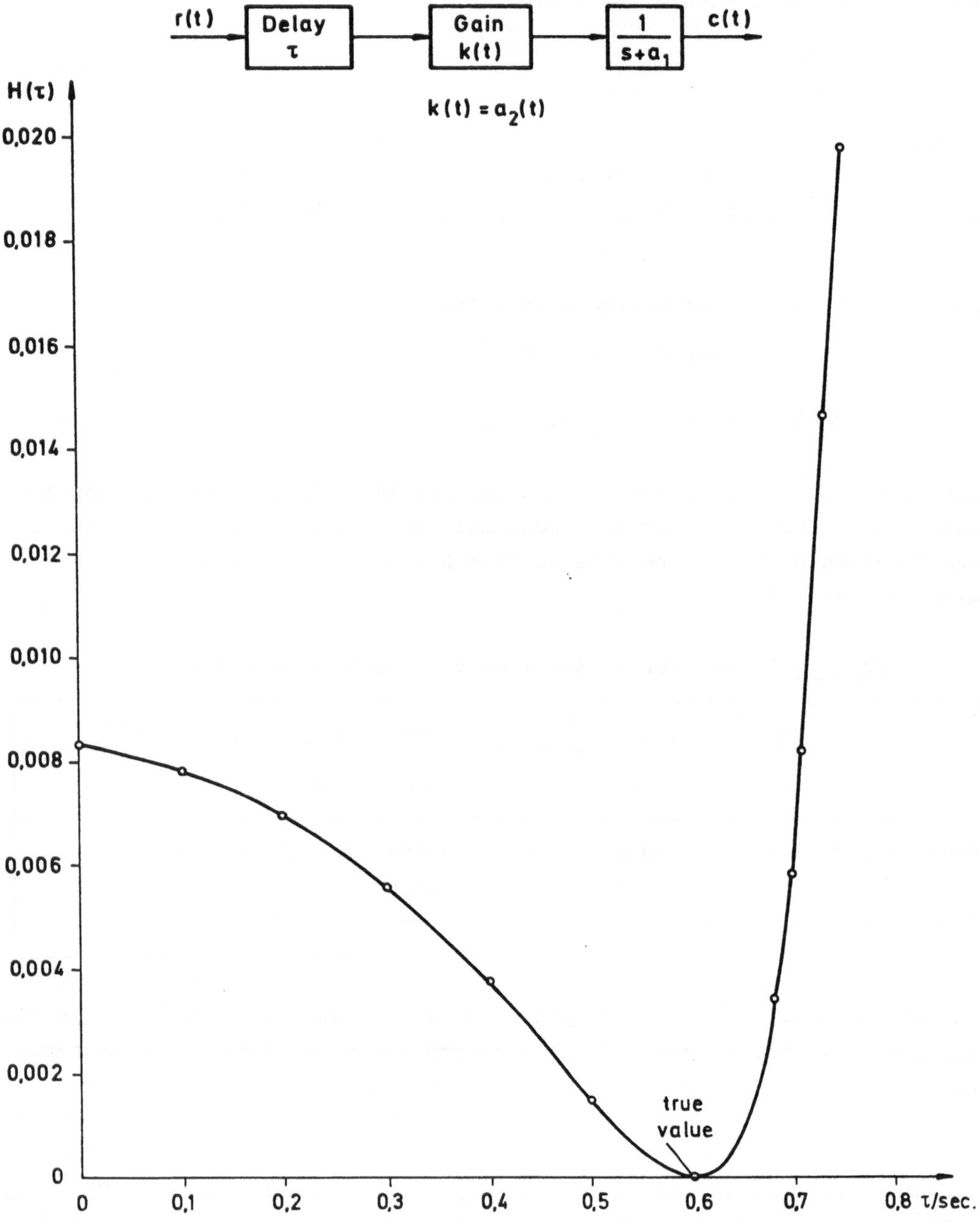

Fig. 8.2. $H(\tau)$ in Example 8.2.

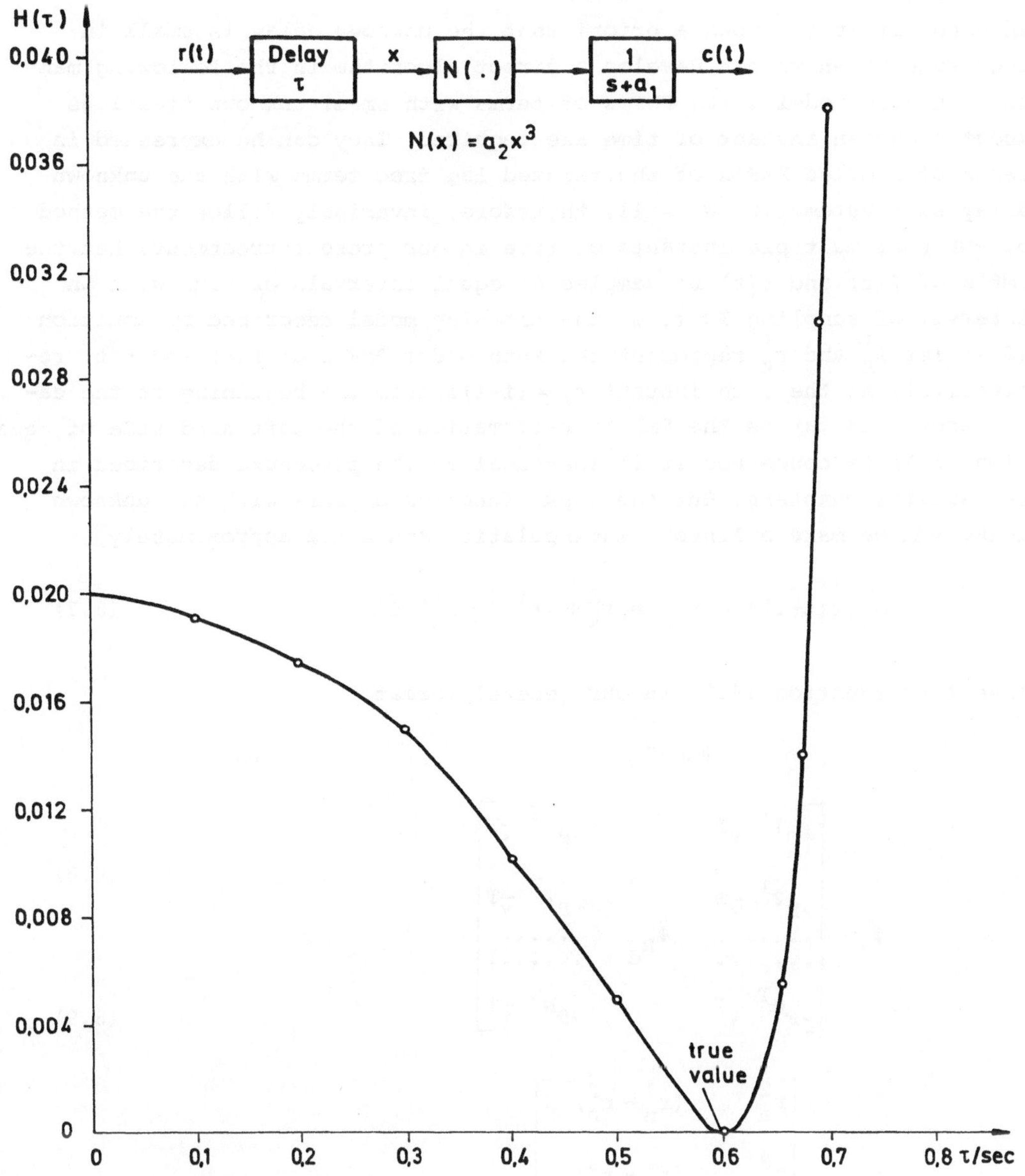

<u>Fig. 8.3.</u> $H(\tau)$ in Example 8.3.

8.2(b). Direct identification algorithm in the case of small delays

In case if it is known a priori that the unknown delay is small in magnitude, then we can develop a direct algorithm in the following manner. In such models, the PMF's of terms with small unknown time-lags about a chosen instant of time are required. They can be expressed in terms of sampled PMF's of the related lag free terms with the unknown delay as a parameter. We will, therefore, invariably follow the method of PMF's at multiple instants of time in our present treatment. Let the PMF's of f(t) and r(t) be sampled at equal intervals of time with an interval of sampling $T > \tau$. In the time-lag model described by equation (8.1) let f_k^i and r_k^i represent the k-th order PMF's of f(t) and r(t) respectively at the i-th instant $t_i = (i-1)T$ from the beginning of the data record. As far as the PMF transformation of the left hand side of equation (8.1) is concerned it is identical to the procedure described in the earlier chapters. But the input function appears with an unknown delay $< T$. We make a linear interpolation and write approximately

$$M_k\{r(t-\tau)\} \triangleq r_{d_k} = r_k^i + (r_k^{i-1} - r_k^i)\,\frac{\tau}{T}\,. \tag{8.7}$$

Inserting equation (8.7) in our general format

$$\hat{\Phi}\,U = \hat{C}\,,$$

$$\hat{\Phi} = \begin{bmatrix} -F^{1^T} & \bar{\gamma}^T & & -P^{1^T} & \bar{\gamma}^T \\ -F^{2^T} & \bar{\gamma}^T & & -P^{2^T} & \bar{\gamma}^T \\ \cdots & \cdots & \hat{\Phi}_{R_d} & \cdots & \cdots \\ \cdots & \cdots & & \cdots & \cdots \\ -F^{N^T} & \bar{\gamma}^T & & -P^{N^T} & \bar{\gamma}^T \end{bmatrix}, \tag{8.8}$$

(8.9)

$$\hat{\Phi}_{R_d} = \begin{bmatrix} r_n^2 & (r_n^1 - r_n^2) \\ r_n^3 & (r_n^2 - r_n^3) \\ \vdots & \vdots \\ r_n^{N+1} & (r_n^N - r_n^{N+1}) \end{bmatrix}, \tag{8.10}$$

$$\hat{C} = [Q^T \gamma F^1 \mid Q^T \gamma F^2 \mid \ldots \mid Q^T \gamma F^N]^T, \tag{8.11}$$

$$U = [a_1, a_2, \ldots, a_n, b, b(\tau/T), \theta_1, \theta_2, \ldots, \theta_n]^T, \quad (8.12)$$

$$\theta_j = -[1, a_1, a_2, \ldots, a_n] S_f . \quad (8.13)$$

The section $\hat{\Phi}_{Rd}$ of $\hat{\Phi}$ will depend upon the way in which delay terms appear in the input side. The present form of course, is the result of a particular single delay term in the model equation. In case there are delay terms in the left hand side involving the output f(t) also, an additional section $\hat{\Phi}_{Fd}$ has to be suitably inserted in $\hat{\Phi}$ after due interpolation for PMF's of terms with small delay. The vector of unknowns is obtained as

$$U = \hat{\Phi}^{-1} \hat{C} . \quad (8.14)$$

The results of this direct step given by (8.14) may sometimes be considerably in error. This error is mainly due to interpolation of PMF's of delayed terms. To keep this error low, we use samples at sufficiently close intervals of time from recorded data. The interpolation error and hence the error of identification will approach zero as τ/T tends to zero or unity. Now, let τ_k be the value of delay obtained approximately with sampling interval of T_k at any stage. We now set the new sampling interval at $T_{k+1} = \tau_k$ and repeat the process of identification until the parameters obtained change little in the next step. In practice a suitable error bound may be specified for the parameters and the delay to terminate this iteration. For instance, one may specify an upper bound for the error in parameters, defined by

$$\varepsilon = \frac{\|U_k - U_{k-1}\|}{\|U_k\|}$$

where k represents the iteration number. The scheme is shown in the Figure 8.4.

Illustrative examples:

Example 8.4.

Consider a process modelled by

$$\frac{df(t)}{dt} + af(t) = br(t-\tau), \quad (8.15)$$

excited by a unit step input delayed by a small unknown time-lag with initial conditions known a priori to be all zero. In order to test the present algorithm, the input-output data generated for various values of τ with $a = 0.1$ and $b = 1$ over $t \in (0, 2.0\,s)$ has been used. The PMF's are initially sampled at intervals of $T = 0.5$ s. In this case the identification equation may be shown to be in the form

$$\begin{bmatrix} -f_1^2 & r_1^2 & (r_1^1 - r_1^2) \\ -f_1^3 & r_1^3 & (r_1^2 - r_1^3) \\ -f_1^4 & r_1^4 & (r_1^3 - r_1^4) \end{bmatrix} \begin{bmatrix} a \\ b \\ b(\tau/T) \end{bmatrix} = \begin{bmatrix} f_o^2 - f_1^2 \\ f_o^3 - f_1^3 \\ f_o^4 - f_1^4 \end{bmatrix}. \tag{8.16}$$

Table 8.2 gives numerical results with the present algorithm for various τ with the sampling interval fixed at 0.5 s.

Table 8.2. Parameter estimation in eq. (8.15)

Actual time-lag	Parameters and time-lag determined		
	a	b	τ
0.05	0.1242	1.0334	0.0697
0.10	0.1441	1.0591	0.1327
0.15	0.1593	1.0770	0.1903
0.20	0.1695	1.0872	0.2434
0.25	0.1742	1.0898	0.2927
0.30	0.1730	1.0852	0.3389
0.35	0.1655	1.0735	0.3824
0.40	0.1512	1.0552	0.4236
0.45	0.1296	1.0306	0.4627

Example 8.5.

Consider a second order system modelled as

$$\frac{d^2f(t)}{dt^2} + a_1 \frac{df(t)}{dt} + a_2 f(t) = br(t-\tau), \tag{8.17}$$

excited by a unit step input delayed by a small unknown time lag. The PMF's are sampled at intervals of 0.4 s and are used to determine the parameters a_1, a_2 and b. All initial conditions are assumed to be zero. Table 8.3 shows the numerical results for various values of τ while T is fixed at 0.4 s.

Table 8.3. Parameter estimation in eq.(8.17)

Actual time-lag	Parameters and time-lag determined			
	a_1	a_2	b	τ
0.04	3.0115	2.0228	1.0086	0.0389
0.08	3.0085	2.0295	1.0097	0.0753
0.12	2.9941	2.0231	1.0050	0.1100
0.16	2.9713	2.0066	0.9960	0.1435
0.20	2.9429	1.9827	0.9840	0.1765
0.24	2.9124	1.9547	0.9707	0.2099
0.28	2.8843	1.9266	0.9582	0.2447
0.32	2.8670	1.9057	0.9499	0.2831
0.36	2.8807	1.9093	0.9540	0.3298

The true values of the parameters are: $a_1 = 3$, $a_2 = 2$, and $b = 1$.

Notice that the interpolation error and the consequent error in parameter identification reduce as τ/T approaches zero or unity. The results are, of course, considerably in error when $\tau/T \approx 0.5$. This is mainly due to the error in linear interpolation employed to approximate PMF's of delayed terms in terms of successive samples. This error may be efficiently reduced, if necessary, by the technique described in the Figure 8.4. We consider, for illustration, the particular case when the actual model is described by eq.(8.15) with $a = 0.1$, $b = 1.0$ and $\tau = 0.3$. Initially by setting $T = 0.5$ s, the direct step gives

$$a = 0.1730, \quad b = 1.0851 \text{ and } \tau = 0.3389.$$

This step is repeated with modified sampling such that $T = 0.3389$. The process of convergence is displayed in Table 8.4.

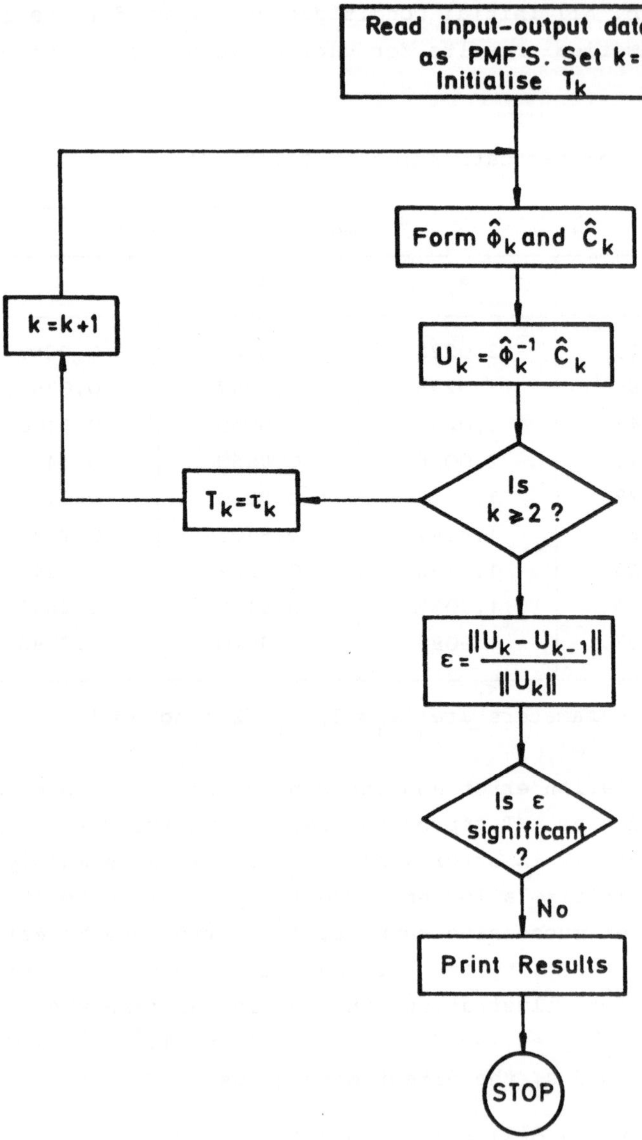

Fig. 8.4. Iterative sampling scheme

Table 8.4. Results of iterative sampling scheme for parameter estimation in eq.(8.15)

Iteration number k	Parameters and time-lag determined		
	a_k	b_k	τ_k
1	0.1730	1.0851	0.3389
2	0.1574	1.0410	0.3125
3	0.1244	1.0154	0.3043
4	0.1093	1.0056	0.3015
5	0.1034	1.0020	0.3005
6	0.1012	1.0007	0.3001
7	0.1005	1.0003	0.3001
8	0.1002	1.0001	0.3000
9	0.1001	1.0000	0.3000
10	0.1000	1.0000	0.3000

8.3. Parameter identification in dynamical systems containing analytic non-linear characteristics

In this section we will consider the problem of parameter identification in differential equation models and those in the form of blocks with non-linear elements separable from linear elements.

First, consider for the sake of illustrative development, a class of nonlinear models of the form:

$$\frac{d^n f(t)}{dt^n} + \sum_{i=1}^{n-1} a_i \frac{d^{n-i} f(t)}{dt^{n-i}} + \sum_{j=1}^{m_f} a_{n_j} [f(t)]^j$$

$$= \sum_{i=1}^{n-1} b_i \frac{d^{n-i} r(t)}{dt^{n-i}} + \sum_{j=1}^{m_r} b_{n_j} [r(t)]^j. \tag{8.18}$$

Let us denote $a_{n_1} = a_n$ and $b_{n_1} = b_n$. The coefficients $a_1, a_2, \ldots, a_n$; $b_1, b_2, \ldots, b_n$ characterize the linear part of the model and a_{n_j}, b_{n_j} $(j = 2, \ldots)$ are coefficients in a polynomial representation of the non-linear system. Notice that $[f(t)]^j$ and $[r(t)]^j$ can be generated either numerically or by analog means.

It is possible to show that PMF transformation of (8.18) leads to an equation of the form

$$\Phi U = C \ ,$$

where

$$C = [c_o \;\; c_1 \; \dots \; c_{k_f}]^T ,$$

$$U = [a \,\vdots\, a_n \,\vdots\, b \,\vdots\, b_n \,\vdots\, \theta]^T ,$$

$$\Phi = \left[\begin{array}{c|c|c|c|c} -F^{o^T}\,\bar{\Gamma}(o)^T & & R^{o^T}\,\bar{\Gamma}(o)^T & & -P^{o^T}\,\bar{\Gamma}(o)^T \\ -F^{o^T}\,\bar{\Gamma}(1)^T & \Phi_{FN} & R^{o^T}\,\bar{\Gamma}(1)^T & \Phi_{RN} & -P^{o^T}\,\bar{\Gamma}(1)^T \\ \vdots & & \vdots & & \vdots \\ -F^{o^T}\,\bar{\Gamma}(k_f)^T & & R^{o^T}\,\bar{\Gamma}(k_f)^T & & -P^{o^T}\,\bar{\Gamma}(k_f)^T \end{array}\right] ,$$

and $k_f = m_f + m_r + 3(n-1)$.

Alternatively, if PMF's are considered at several instants of time, equation (8.18) takes the form

$$\hat{\Phi} U = \hat{C} \ ,$$

where

$$\hat{\Phi} = \left[\begin{array}{c|c|c|c|c} -F^{o^T}\,\bar{\gamma}^T & & R^{o^T}\,\bar{\gamma}^T & & -P^{o^T}\,\bar{\gamma}^T \\ -F^{1^T}\,\bar{\gamma}^T & \hat{\Phi}_{FN} & R^{1^T}\,\bar{\gamma}^T & \hat{\Phi}_{RN} & -P^{1^T}\,\bar{\gamma}^T \\ \vdots & & \vdots & & \vdots \\ -F^{k_f^T}\,\bar{\gamma}^T & & R^{k_f^T}\,\bar{\gamma}^T & & -P^{k_f^T}\,\bar{\gamma}^T \end{array}\right] .$$

The matrix blocks Φ_{FN}, $\hat{\Phi}_{FN}$, Φ_{RN} and $\hat{\Phi}_{RN}$ are composed of PMF's of signals of the form $[f(t)]^j$, $[r(t)]^j$. Such powers of $f(t)$ and $r(t)$ will have to be obtained from the data by suitable means.

We have discussed a case of nonlinear models which is, of course, not general. A universal description for nonlinear models is impossible. We have to consider a class of models and apply the PMF method systematically to each class of models.

Illustrative development in a specific case

Consider a system modelled as shown in Fig. 8.5. We have,

$$r^*(t) = N(r).$$

Consider the case where G(s) is of the form $\frac{1}{s+b}$ and let

$$N(x) = a_1 x + a_2 x^2 + a_3 x^3.$$

The differential equation of the process is

$$\frac{df(t)}{dt} + bf(t) = a_1\, r(t) + a_2[r(t)]^2 + a_3[r(t)]^3.$$

k-th PMF transformation gives

$$(f_{k-1} - \lambda f_k) + bf_k = a_1\, r_k + a_2\{r^2(t)\}_k + a_3\{r^3(t)\}_k.$$

Now, varying k from 1 to 4, the resulting set of equations may be written as

$$\begin{bmatrix} r_1 & \{r^2(t)\}_1 & \{r^3(t)\}_1 & -f_1 \\ r_2 & \{r^2(t)\}_2 & \{r^3(t)\}_2 & -f_2 \\ r_3 & \{r^2(t)\}_3 & \{r^3(t)\}_3 & -f_3 \\ r_4 & \{r^2(t)\}_4 & \{r^3(t)\}_4 & -f_4 \end{bmatrix} \begin{bmatrix} a_1 \\ a_2 \\ a_3 \\ b \end{bmatrix} = \begin{bmatrix} (f_o - \lambda f_1) \\ (f_1 - \lambda f_2) \\ (f_2 - \lambda f_3) \\ (f_3 - \lambda f_4) \end{bmatrix}. \qquad (8.19)$$

Fig. 8.6 shows a scheme to realize the above identification method.

8.4. Piecewise linear system identification

In this section we will consider the problem of parameter identification in piecewise linear models. Piecewise linear models, in general, have fewer parameters than the corresponding analytic models.

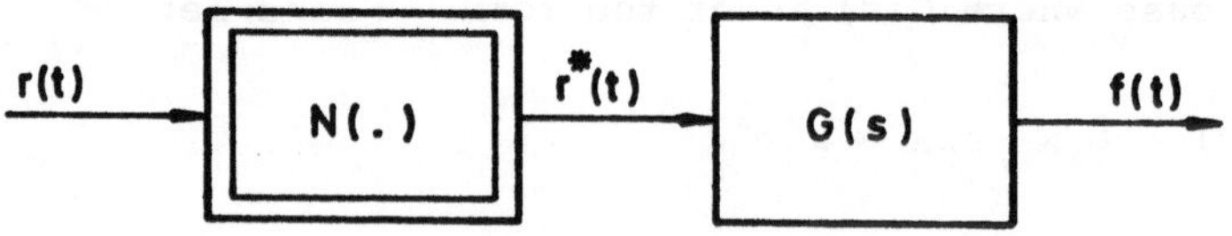

Fig. 8.5. A separable nonlinear model

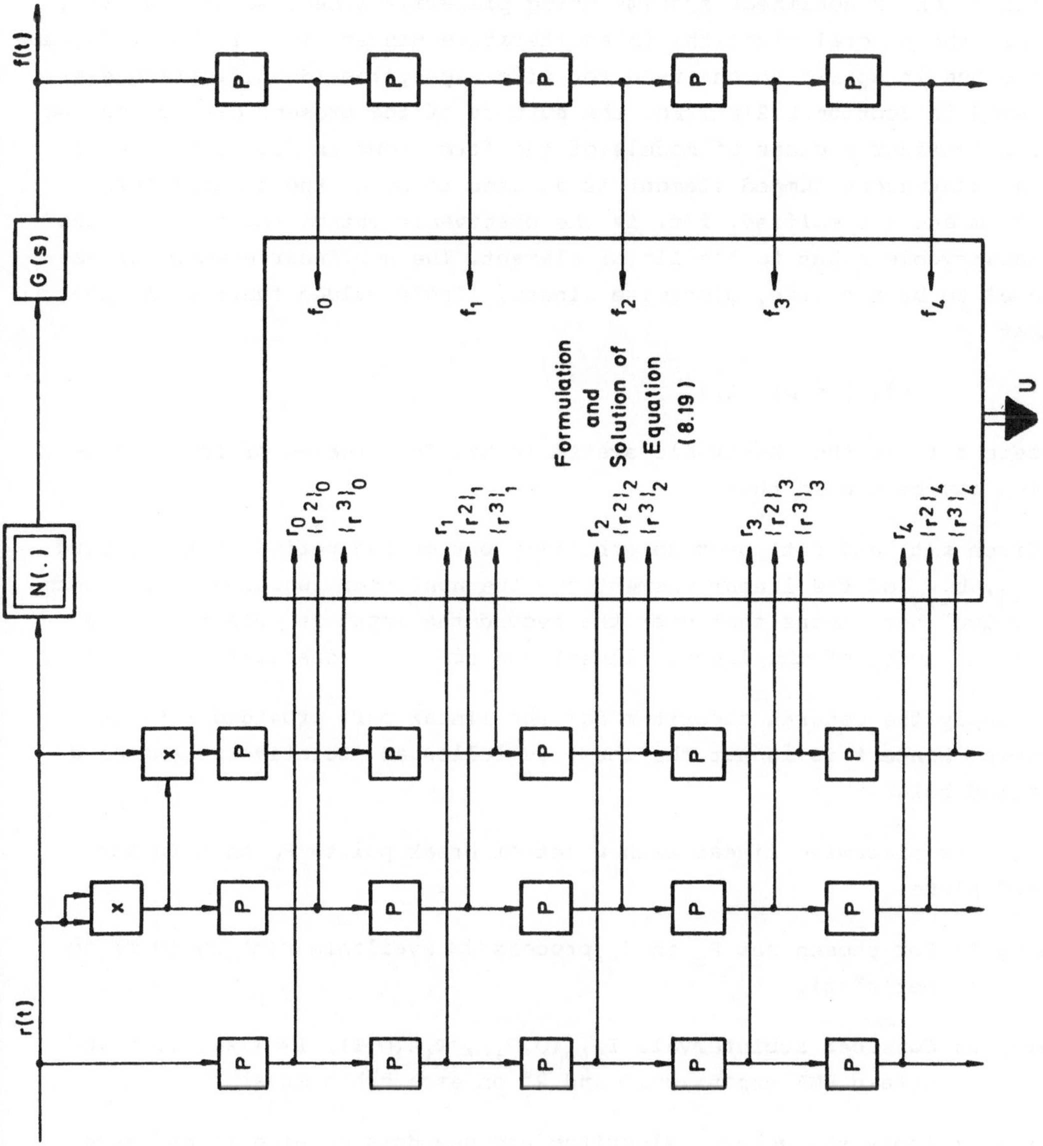

Fig. 8.6. PMF scheme for parameter identification in analytic nonlinear systems

In view of this situation, we will discuss a method of parameter identification of nonlinear systems using piecewise linear models. We will apply the general algorithm in an iterative manner. This iterative scheme is close in spirit to one used for time lag system identification discussed in Section 8.2(a). For the purpose of the present discussion, we will consider a class of models of the form shown in Fig. 8.5. The linear continuous lumped element is assumed to be of the general form with m and n specified. f(t) is the observable output and $r^*(t)$ is the unobservable input to the linear element. The nonlinear element is assumed to be a static, piecewise linear, single valued function N such that

$$r^*(t) = N\{r(t)\},$$

where r(t) is the observable system input. The problem of identification may be stated thus:

'Given r(t) and f(t) over an arbitrary but active period of time, find $a_{i,j}$, $b_{i,j}$ of the linear element and the nonlinear function N. The term "active" here means that over the record the input is able to excite all the modes of the linear element and scan the essential domain of N.

We apply the general algorithm for the linear part provided r(t) is known. Since this is not the case, we follow an iterative scheme as detailed below.

Let N be piecewise linear with a set of break points P_b on N in the r-r^* plane.

Step 1: For chosen set P_b on N, process the available r(t) on (O,T) to get $r^*(t)$.

Step 2: Consider subintervals I_i, (O,T_i), $T_i \varepsilon (O,T)$, $i = 1,2,\ldots, L$ and obtain PMF expansions F and R^* on each subinterval I_i.

Step 3: Apply the general algorithm and use data on each I_i and determine the corresponding vector of unknowns U_i.

Step 4: Compute the error function in any of the following forms:

$$\text{(i)}\quad H(P_b) = \sum_{i=1}^{L-1} \|U_{i+1} - U_i\|$$

(ii) $H(P_b) = \sum_{i=1}^{L-1} ||U_{i+1} - U_i|| / ||U_i||$

(iii) The variance form in noisy situations.

Step 5: Minimise H with respect to P_b. Let P_b^o be the optimum set of break points on N. The dynamic plant parameters corresponding to P_b^o are simultaneously available.

CHAPTER IX

PMF METHOD IN THE PRESENCE OF NOISE

9.1. Introduction

The performance of the PMF method in the presence or additive zero mean noise in the process signals has been studied. Although, the process signals are corrupted with noise, the related PMF's and consequently, the evaluated parameters are found to be naturally immune to such noise to some extent.

9.2. The use of unfiltered PMF's

In order to see this feature, consider a signal f(t) in the presence of a zero mean additive noise $\rho(t)$. The k-th PMF of the noise-contaminated signal about t_o, is given by

$$M_k\{f(t)+\rho(t)\} = \int_0^{t_o} [f(t)+\rho(t)]p_k(t_o-t)\,dt = f_k^o + \rho_k^o \,. \qquad (9.1)$$

For sufficiently large t_o and small λ, $\rho_k^o \to 0$ and consequently its influence on the PMF's of f(t) becomes negligible. Seif et.al [P22] have discussed how repeated integration ($\lambda=0$) naturally reduces the effect of noise in the process signals in real time least square estimation problems.

To illustrate this feature, fifteen hundred measurements, at equal intervals, each of f(t) and r(t) over the interval (0, 1.5 sec) are considered in the processes described by the models

$$\frac{df(t)}{dt} + a_1 f(t) = b_1 r(t) \,, \qquad (9.2a)$$

and

$$\frac{d^2f(t)}{dt^2} + a_1 \frac{df(t)}{dt} + a_2 f(t) = b_1 r(t) \,. \qquad (9.2b)$$

Zero-mean gaussian noise is added to the simulated data. The PMF's with $\lambda=1$ are obtained by numerical integration using Simpson's rule. Tables 9.1 and 9.2 show the results of identification with different degrees of noise level by the two methods described.

Table 9.1. Parameter estimation in equation (9.2a)

Noise to signal ratio in f(t) and r(t)	Method 1: PMF's taken at a single instant of time		Method 2: PMF's taken at several instants of time	
	a_1	b_1	a_1	b_1
0.05	4.04672065	4.03170557	4.04232938	4.02817818
0.10	4.06575760	4.04463527	4.05958649	4.03967886
0.15	4.08014553	4.05441153	4.07263283	4.04837755
0.20	4.09209871	4.06253613	4.08347378	4.05560880
0.25	4.10248199	4.06959563	4.09289263	4.06189366

The true values of the parameters are $a_1 = 4$ and $b_1 = 4$.

9.3. The use of Kalman-filtered PMF's [P23]

Despite their natural immunity to zero-mean additive noise, it is desirable to optimally filter the PMF's before using them in the identification algorithms. Here we show how Kalman filtering may be applied to the situation in order to obtain optimally filtered PMF's and that the method is superior to the conventional least squares approach.

Consider for the sake of an illustrative development, a system modelled by

$$\frac{df(t)}{dt} + af(t) = br(t), \tag{9.3}$$

where r(t) and f(t) are the input and output functions respectively. 'a' and 'b' are the two parameters to be determined. Taking the first PMF transformation of (9.3) about $t=t_k$, $k=1,2,...z$, we get

$$af_1^k - br_1^k = -\lambda f_1^k + f_o^k, \quad k=1,2,\dots,z. \tag{9.4a}$$

f_1^k and r_1^k are the first PMF's about $t=t_k$ of f(t) and r(t) respectively. Equation (9.4a) may be cast into the general format

$$\Phi\, U = C\,. \tag{9.4b}$$

In this particular case

Table 9.2. Parameter estimation in equation (9.2b)

Noise to signal ratio in f(t) and r(t)	Method 1: PMF's taken at a single instant of time			Method 2: PMF's taken at several instants of time		
	a_1	a_2	b_1	a_1	a_2	b_1
0.05	4.26691210	3.03127377	1.03850091	4.65650818	2.80365128	1.08188582
0.10	4.38019940	3.04524610	1.05489830	4.91922270	2.73606653	1.11520163
0.15	4.46764606	3.05630380	1.06757729	5.11588291	2.68970102	1.14035249
0.20	4.54152382	3.06582586	1.07830334	5.27800295	2.65424507	1.16122494

The true values of a_1, a_2 and b_1 are 4,3 and 1 respectively.

The results in Table 9.2 show the superiority of Method 1 over Method 2 in the noisy environment. This is due to the fact that in Method 2 PMF's at distributed instants of time are employed while the PMF's employed in Method 1 are filtered better as they correspond to the terminal instant of the record.

$$\Phi = \begin{bmatrix} f_1^1 & -r_1^1 \\ f_1^2 & -r_1^2 \\ \vdots & \vdots \\ f_1^z & -r_1^z \end{bmatrix} \tag{9.5a}$$

$$C = -[(\lambda f_1^1 - f_o^1),\ (\lambda f_1^2 - f_o^2),\ldots,(\lambda f_1^z - f_o^z)]^T, \tag{9.5b}$$

and

$$U = [a,b]^T\ . \tag{9.5c}$$

When z>2, equation (9.4b) may be normalized and solved by the least square method.

Referring to the PMF scheme of Fig. 9.1 which illustrates the situation in which the PFC's are connected to the system under identification, we note the following:

i) The presence of noise elements α and β is natural in the observed input-output data. α influences the observed input signal but not the main system.
ii) Additional noise elements ξ and η may appear due to the physical operation of the PFC. In a carefully designed set-up, however, this noise in the measurement of PMF's may be negligible.

We include the effects of ξ and η for the sake of completeness and generality in our present treatment although assumption of their absence would simplify the situation. Placing the symbol '*' on the labels of noisy quantities, equation (9.4b) may be written as:

$$\overset{*}{\Phi}\ \overset{*}{U} = \overset{*}{C}\ , \tag{9.4c}$$

whose least squares solution gives

$$\overset{*}{U} = [\overset{*}{\Phi}{}^T\ \overset{*}{\Phi}]^{-1}\overset{*}{\Phi}{}^T\ \overset{*}{C}\ . \tag{9.6a}$$

It is reported in the literature that $\overset{*}{U}$ gives only biased estimates of 'a' and 'b'.

9.3. Optimal filtering of PMF's

A close look at the identification scheme of Fig. 9.1 suggests that the outputs of the various stages of the PFC's are alone of interest to us in the identification algorithm. We assume that all the noise parameters are known. The PFC's may be described in state variable form as follows:

i) Input side PFC

$$\dot{R} = AR + B[r(t)+\alpha]\,, \qquad \overset{*}{R} = R + \xi\,. \tag{9.7a}$$

ii) Output side PFC

$$\dot{F} = AF + B[f(t)+\beta]\,, \qquad \overset{*}{F} = F + \eta\,, \tag{9.7b}$$

where

$$A = \begin{bmatrix} -\lambda & 0 \\ 1 & -\lambda \end{bmatrix}, \quad B = \begin{bmatrix} 1 \\ 0 \end{bmatrix}, \quad R = \begin{bmatrix} r_0 \\ r_1 \end{bmatrix}, \quad F = \begin{bmatrix} f_0 \\ f_1 \end{bmatrix}.$$

r_0, r_1, f_0 and f_1 are continuous functions of time and denote the states of the PFC's.

Let the environment be characterised as:

$$\varepsilon(\alpha) = 0, \varepsilon(\beta) = 0, \varepsilon(\xi_1) = 0, \varepsilon(\xi_2) = 0$$

$$\varepsilon(\eta_1) = 0, \varepsilon(\eta_2) = 0,$$

$$\varepsilon(\xi_i \xi_j)^T = R_r \delta_{ij} = \begin{bmatrix} R_{r_{11}} & 0 \\ 0 & R_{r_{22}} \end{bmatrix},$$

$$\varepsilon(\eta_i \eta_j)^T = R_f \delta_{ij} = \begin{bmatrix} R_{f_{11}} & 0 \\ 0 & R_{f_{22}} \end{bmatrix},$$

$\varepsilon(\alpha.\alpha) = Q_r$ a scalar, and $\varepsilon(\beta.\beta) = Q_f$ a scalar.

To minimise the effect of noise on the parameter estimates, our problem can now be stated in the following manner: Given $\overset{*}{F}$ and $\overset{*}{R}$ find estimates F and R of these for use in the identification algorithm. This is the standard problem of state estimation for systems described by equations (9.7a and 9.7b). The PFC's are identical and well defined. Therefore the Kalman filter problem is well posed. The appropriate estimation model equations are as follows:

<u>Input side PFC</u>

$$\dot{\hat{R}} = A\hat{R} + Br(t) + K_r[\hat{R} - \overset{*}{R}],$$

$$K_r(t) = -P_r(t)R_r^{-1},$$

$$\dot{P}_r(t) = A\,P_r + P_rA^T - P_rR_r^{-1}P_r + BQ_rB^T, \text{ where}$$

$P_r(O)$ is the initial state covariance matrix of input side PFC.

<u>Output side PFC</u>

$$\dot{\hat{F}} = A\hat{F} + Bf(t) + K_f[\hat{F} - \overset{*}{F}],$$

$$K_f(t) = -P_f(t)R_f^{-1},$$

$$\dot{P}_f(t) = AP_f + P_fA^T - P_fR_f^{-1}P_f + BQ_fB^T, \text{ where}$$

$P_f(O)$ is the initial state covariance matrix of output side PFC. With the Kalman-filtered PMF's we now have

$$\hat{\Phi}\hat{U} = \hat{C}\,, \tag{9.4d}$$

where the symbol '^' on the matrices signifies that their elements are Kalman-filtered versions of the noisy ones. The minimum variance estimates are then given by

$$\hat{U} = [\hat{\Phi}^T\hat{\Phi}]^{-1}\hat{\Phi}^T\hat{C}. \tag{9.6b}$$

Optimal filter set up for a general scheme of PFC's is shown in Fig. 9.2. The matrix H in these figures is an identity matrix.

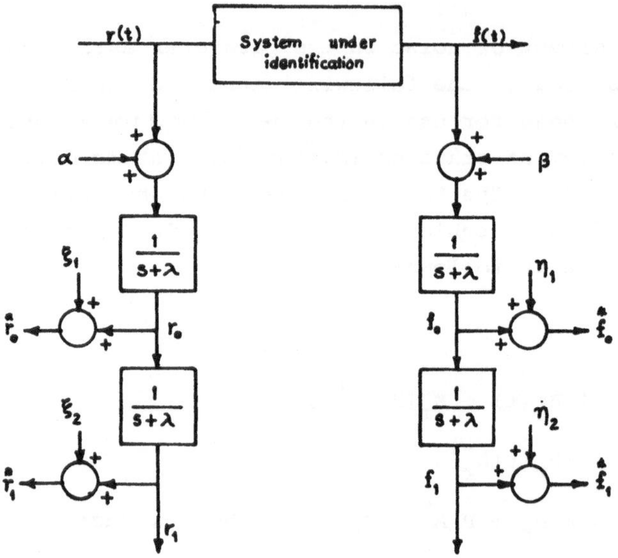

Fig.9.1: PFC in a noisy environment

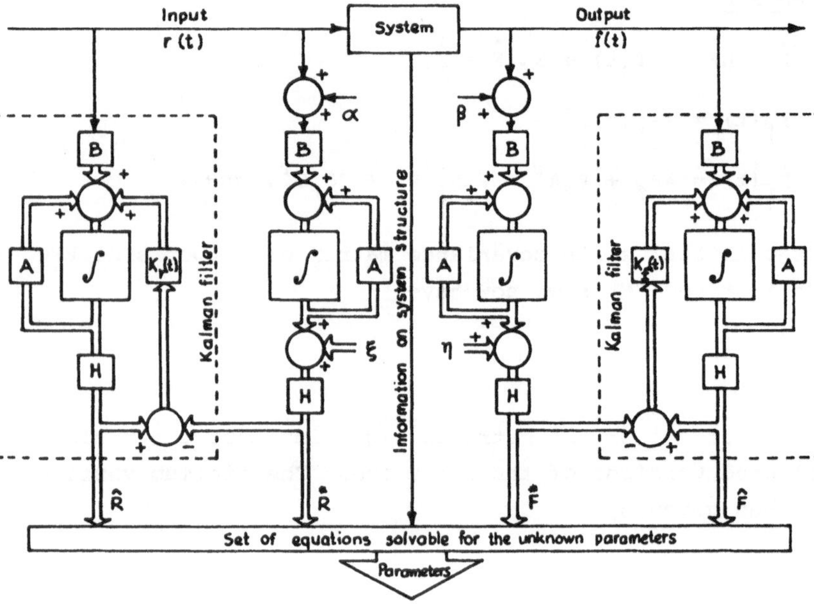

Fig.9.2: PFC's augmented with Kalman filters

9.4. Illustrative example

A system modelled by equation (9.3) is considered.
Noisy environment as in Fig.9.1 is simulated. Parameter estimation has been carried out by (9.6a) and (9.6b) separately. Noise to signal ratios are defined as follows:

$$NSR1 = cov(\alpha)/cov(r)$$

$$NSR2 = cov(\xi_1)/cov(r_o)$$

$$NSR3 = cov(\xi_2)/cov(r_1)$$

$$NSR4 = cov(\beta)/cov(f)$$

$$NSR5 = cov(\eta_1/cov(f_o)$$

$$NSR6 = cov(\eta_2)/cov(f_1)$$

With a=1, b=1 and r(t)=t, the process is simulated for a specified set of NRS's over the interval [0,1] with a sampling interval of 0.005 sec. Table 9.3 lists the various situations simulated in the numerical experiment. The results of identification by the direct least squares approach and those by the Kalman filtered PMF technique are shown together in figures (9.3-9.7). Figures (9.7b-9.7d) show the true PMF's, the noise-corrupted ones, and the Kalman-filtered ones, for instance in case 5. The superiority of the Kalman-filtered PMF technique is noteworthy.

Additional noise terms ξ and η have been included here for the sake of completeness and generality representing possible noise due to measurement of PMF's thenselves. In many cases, however, there may be no such measurement noise. Then, a limiting form of Kalman filter could be used (R^{-1} does not exist). Possibilities of developing a state estimator for measurement noise free cases with considerably less complexity than the usual Kalman filter, are discussed by Anderson and Moore [G1] and Sage and White III [G23].

Table 9.3. Details of stochastic simulation

Case	Percentage						
	NSR1	NSR2	NSR3	NSR4	NSR5	NSR6	Fig. No.
1	5	5	5	5	5	5	9.3
2	5	10	10	5	10	10	9.4
3	5	15	15	5	15	15	9.5
4	10	15	15	10	15	15	9.6
5	10	20	20	10	20	20	9.7a-9.7d

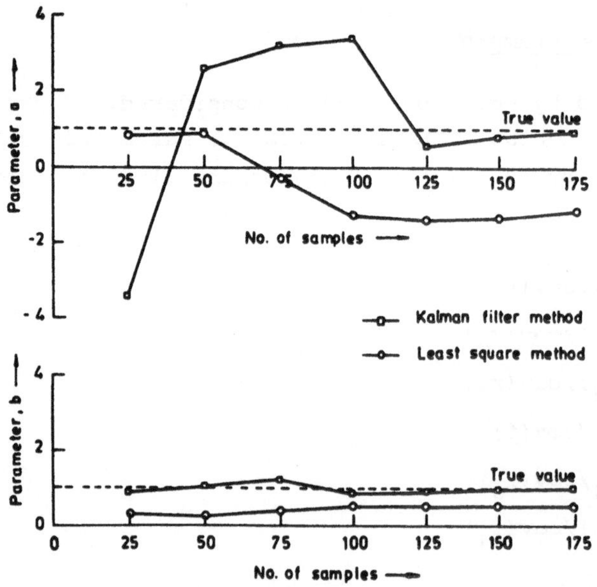

Fig.9.3: Convergence pattern of parameters(case 1)

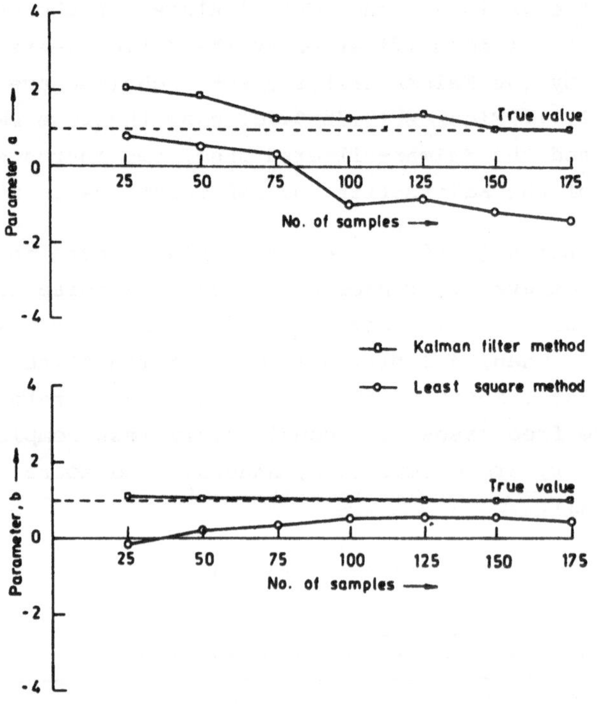

Fig.9.4: Convergence pattern of parameters(case 2)

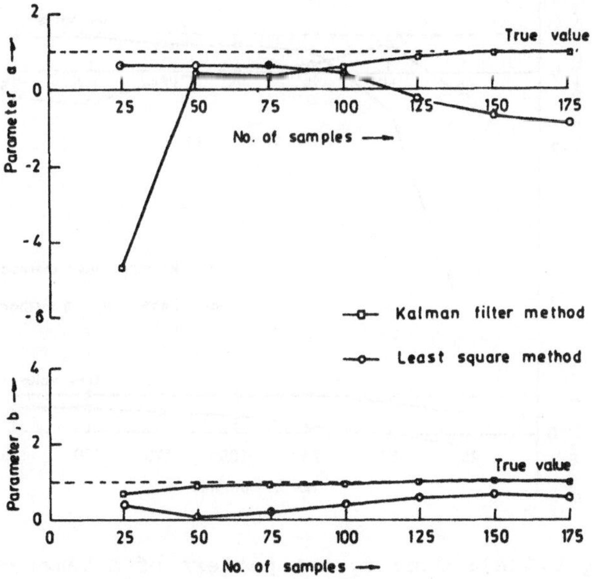

Fig.9.5: Convergence pattern of parameters(case 3)

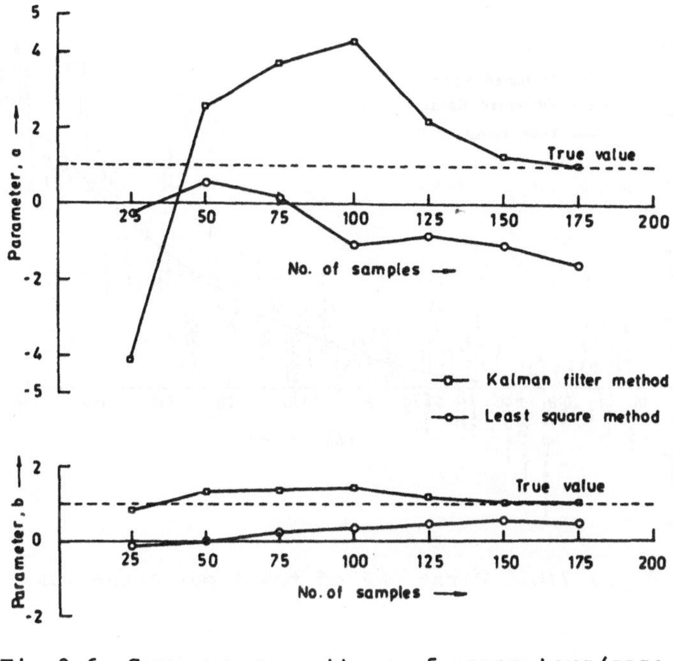

Fig.9.6: Convergence pattern of parameters(case 4)

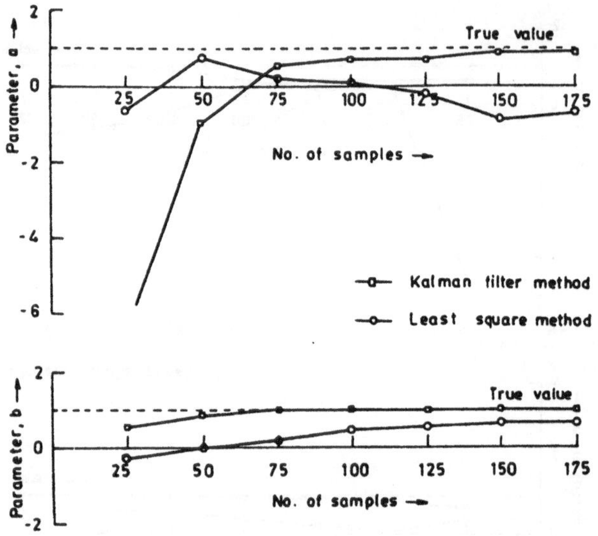

Fig.9.7(a): Convergence pattern of parameters(case 5)

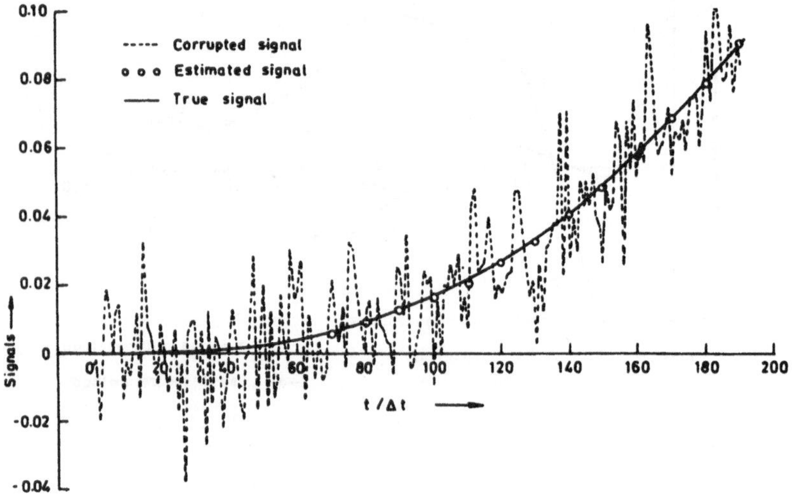

Fig.9.7(b): First PMF of the input signal(case 5)

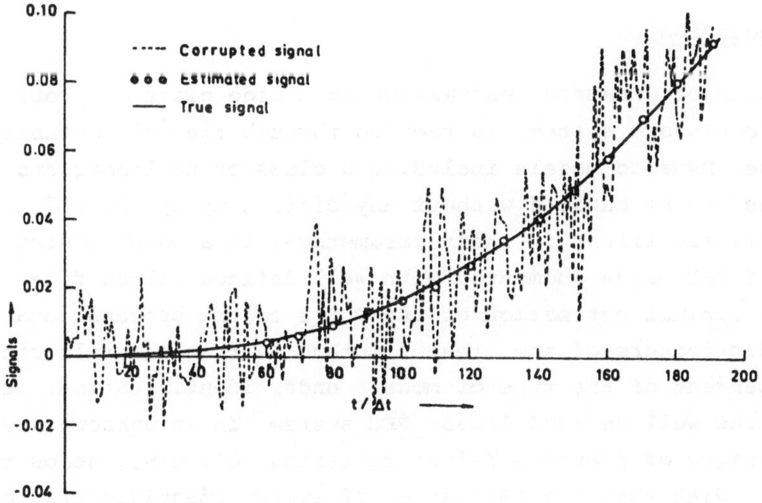

Fig.9.7(c): Zero-th PMF of the output signal(case 5)

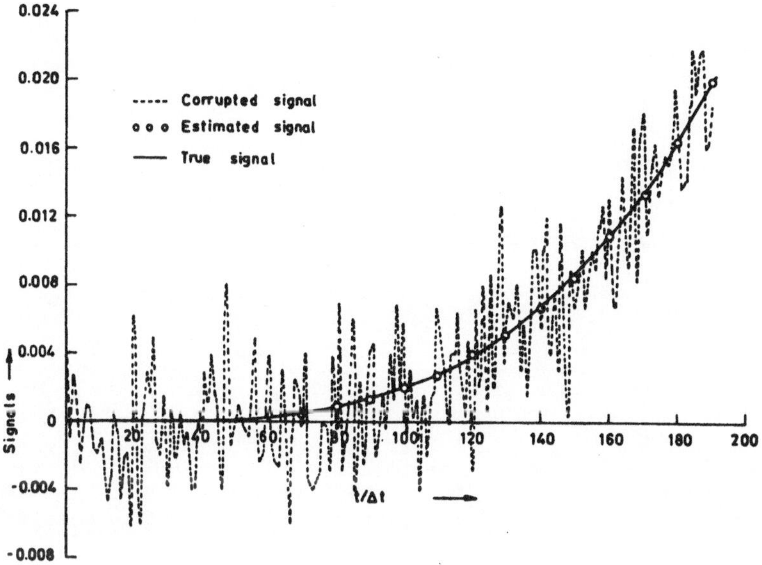

Fig.9.7(d): First PMF of the output signal(case 5)

9.5. Conclusion

The problem of parameter estimation in a wide class of problems of lumped continuous systems is tackled through the well established PMF technique. Dynamic models including a class of nonlinear and time-varying cases can be handled without any difficulty by the PMF method if the models are linear in their parameters. In a noisy environment, the system of PFC may be augmented with well defined Kalman filters for optimal estimation of the PMF's of the process data. An advantageous feature of the present method is that the filtering problem is independent of the type of model under identification. It depends only on the well defined linear PFC system. In an unknown environment the technique of adaptive Kalman filtering [G1, G19], seems to be applicable. With this the PMF method of system identification appears to achieve the desirable generality, thereby becoming a very dependable approach to continuous system identification.

CHAPTER X

MULTIDIMENSIONAL PMF'S AND THEIR USE IN THE IDENTIFICATION OF DISTRIBUTED PARAMETER SYSTEMS [P14]

10.1. Introduction

Identification of distributed parameter systems is of considerable interest to control engineers. Recently Kubrusly [G15] surveyed the various techniques available in the area. Almost all the existing techniques treat the process signals as functions in the ordinary sense, although differentiability in such a characterization is limited. A characterization which permits unlimited differentiability is to treat the process signals as distributions [P6, P20] or generalized functions in the manner conceived and established by Dirac and Schwartz respectively. The use of one dimensional distributions, termed as Poisson moment functional expansions (in time alone), has been demonstrated in the identification of systems described by ordinary differential equations. The problem of identifying distributed parameter systems has been handled by Fairman and Shen [P4] with a hybrid technique employing one-dimensional time distributions combined with the method of lines in space (approximating the partial derivative terms by finite spatial measurements). Here we discuss a technique in which multivariable functions are treated as multidimensional distributions, particularly termed here as multidimensional moment functional expansions as an elegant and straightforward extension of the one-dimensional treatment.

The careful reader will notice the following important features of the present technique making it superior to certain existing ones:

(i) Noise-accentuating numerical differentation is totally avoided in all dimensions.

(ii) The technique involves only well behaved multiple integral operations on problem data and with its natural filtering properties, is successful in handling noisy data.

(iii) The multidimensional distribution expansions have coefficients that stem from integrals in the spirit of modulating function method of Perdreauville and Goodson [P8]. While their arbitrary set of modulating functions is unable to suggest a regular pattern of relations between successive partial derivative terms, the present treatment lends itself to a more systematic approach in a simple and easy-to-remember form.

10.2. Problem formulation

The dynamics of a distributed parameter system (DPS) is usually described by a partial differential equation (PDE) of the form:

$$D\left(\frac{\partial^m u}{\partial x^{m_x}\partial y^{m_y}\partial z^{m_z}\partial t^{m_t}}, \ldots, u, x, y, z, t, \Theta\right)$$

$$= f(x,y,z,t) , \qquad (10.1)$$

where $\Theta = \theta_i$; $i=1,2,\ldots,q$, is a set of parameters, $m=m_x+m_y+m_z+m_t$, $u(x,y,z,t)$ is the state variable, t denotes time, x,y,z are spatial variables in cartesian system. D is a function linear in Θ. The problem of identification is to determine Θ, given measurements of u and the distributed control input f. Since D is linear in Θ, we write (10.1) in the form:

$$\theta_1 h_{i1} + \theta_2 h_{i2} + \ldots + \theta_q h_{iq} = f_i , \qquad (10.2)$$

where the h_{ij}; $i=1,2,\ldots,q$, $j=1,2,\ldots,q$ depend on u,x,y,z,t and the derivatives of u, and the set f_i; $i=1,2,\ldots,q$ depends on the control input and certain terms of D free from the unknown parameters Θ. The q-set of linearly independent equations may be concisely written as

$$\Phi\, \Theta = F, \qquad (10.2a)$$

where

$$\Phi = \begin{bmatrix} h_{i1} & \cdots\cdots & h_{iq} \\ \vdots & & \vdots \\ h_{q1} & \cdots\cdots & h_{qq} \end{bmatrix}, \qquad (10.2b)$$

$$\Theta = [\theta_1 \;\; \theta_2 \;\; \cdots\cdots \;\; \theta_q]^T,$$

$$F = [f_1 \;\; f_2 \;\; \cdots\cdots \;\; f_q]^T,$$

giving

$$\Theta = \Phi^{-1} F . \qquad (10.2c)$$

The basis of most of the techniques of identification of DPS is the formation of (10.2a) where the elements of Φ are functions of u,x,y,z,t and derivatives of u in the ordinary sense. Equation (10.2c) then gives Θ. In the present method the elements of Φ are derived from expansions of u and f in multivariable generalised functions. That is, u and f are first expanded in an exponentially weighted series of the generalised partial derivatives of the multi-variable Dirac delta function in which the coeffcients play an important role in expressing the partial derivative terms in (10.1) in terms of the coefficients in the expansions of u and f themselves leading to equation (10.2a).

10.3. Mathematical basis for the proposed method of solution

The use of higher order time derivatives of Dirac delta function $\delta(t)$ in series expansions of functions of a single variable is by now clear. We now look into such expansions for multivariable functions. We consider an exponentially weighted series of the partial derivatives of the multidimensional Dirac delta function $\delta(x,y,z,t)$ in treating a function u(x,y,z,t) as a multidimensional distribution.

The multidimensional moment functional transformation converts a function u(x,y,z,t) over the region:

$[0 \leq x \leq x_o;\ 0 \leq y \leq y_o;\ 0 \leq z \leq z_o;\ 0 \leq t \leq t_o]$ into a set of real numbers:

$$M_{i,j,k,l}\{u(x,y,z,t)\};\quad i=0,1,2,...;\ j=0,1,2,...;\ k=0,1,2,...,\ l=0,1,2,... .$$

The multidimensional Poisson moment functionals are given by

$$M_{i,j,k,l}\{u(x,y,z,t)\}\Big|_{x_o,y_o,z_o,t_o} = \int_0^{x_o}\int_0^{y_o}\int_0^{z_o}\int_0^{t_o} u(x,y,z,t)$$

$$Q_{i,j,k,l}(x_o-x,\ y_o-y,\ z_y-z,\ t_o-t)dx\ dy\ dz\ dt, \qquad (10.3a)$$

where

$$Q_{i,j,k,l}(x,y,z,t) = \frac{x^i}{i!}\frac{y^j}{j!}\frac{z^k}{k!}\frac{t^l}{l!}\exp\{-[\lambda_x x+\lambda_y y+\lambda_z z+\lambda_t t]\} \tag{10.3b}$$

= Poisson pulse function of order (i,j,k,l) in (x,y,z,t) respectively.

λ_x, λ_y, λ_z and λ_t are positive real numbers.

The Poisson pulse function of order (i,j,k,l) in x,y,z,t respectively is the impulse response at the i+1, j+1, k+1, l+1 stages of a 'multidimensional Poisson filter grid' in which each element in x,y,z,t coordinates has a transfer function $(s_x+\lambda_x)^{-1}$, $(s_y+\lambda_y)^{-1}$, $(s_z+\lambda_z)^{-1}$ and $(s_t+\lambda_t)^{-1}$ respectively, where s_x, s_y, s_z and s_t are the Laplace transform variables corresponding to x, y, z and t respectively.

The MDPMF transformation converts a function in n variables $u(x_1,x_2,\ldots x_n)$ over the region $0\leq x_j \leq X_j$, j=1,2,...,n into a multidimensional array of real numbers about the point $(X_1, X_2,\ldots,X_n)$.

$$M_{i_1,i_2,\ldots,i_n}\{u(x_1, x_2,\ldots,x_n)\}\Big|_{X_1, X_2,\ldots,X_n} \quad i_k=0,1,2,\ldots, \quad k=1,2,\ldots,n$$

$$= \int_0^{X_1}\int_0^{X_2}\ldots\int_0^{X_n} u(x_1, x_2,\ldots,x_n)P_{i_1,i_2\ldots i_n}(X_1-x_1,X_2-x_2\ldots X_n-x_n)dx_1dx_2\ldots dx_n \tag{10.4c}$$

where

$$P_{i_1,i_2,\ldots,i_n}(x_1,x_2,\ldots,x_n) = \sum_{k=1}^{n}\frac{x_k^{i_k}}{i_k!}\exp\{-\lambda_{x_k}x_k\} \tag{10.4d}$$

is a Poisson pulse function of order $(i_1, i_2, \ldots, i_n)$ in $(x_1,x_2,\ldots x_n)$ respectively and λ_{x_k}, k=1,2,...,n are positive real numbers.

For instance, in the case of two-dimensions, the 'two-diemnsional Poisson filter grid' is shown in Fig. 10.1. A two-dimensional signal u(x,t) whose two-dimensional Laplace transform in the sense of present definition is $U(s_x,s_t)$, enters into the filter grid as shown in Fig. 10.1. The Laplace inverse of the output of the (i+1), j+1)-th stages is $M_{i,j}\{u\}$.

In the case of 4 dimensions, the set $M_{i,j,k,l}\{u\}$: i=0,1,2,...; j=0,1,2,...; k=0,1,2,... and l=0,1,2,... comprises of exponentially weighted moments of u, referred to as the multidimensional moment functionals of u.

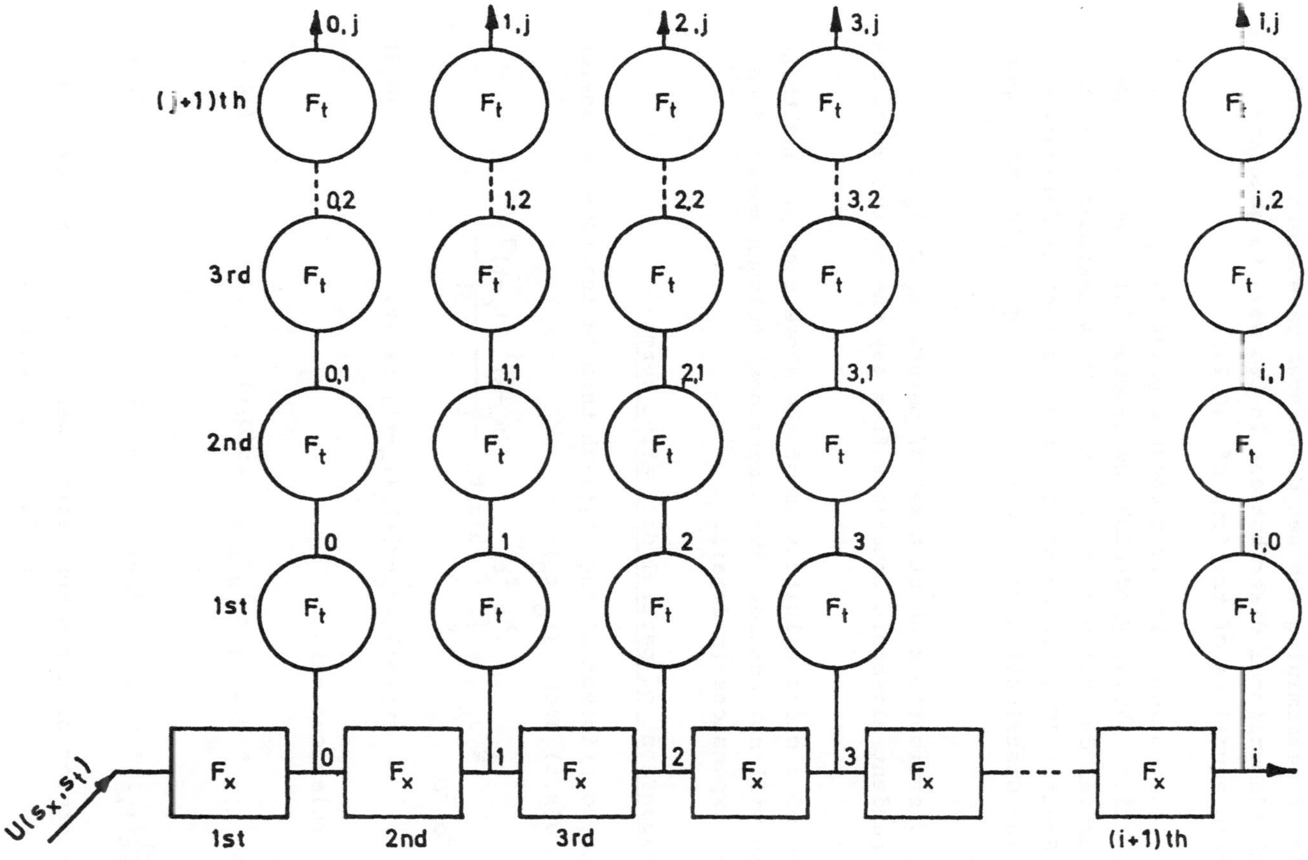

$$F_x = \frac{1}{s_x + \lambda_x} \text{ and } F_t = \frac{1}{s_t + \lambda_t}$$

Fig.10.1: Two-dimensional Poisson filter grid

In the process of determining the set of unknown parameters in a DPS, we can use multidimensional distributions in two ways to generate linear algebraic equations of the form of (10.2a):

i) We employ distribution expansions about a point (x_o,y_o,z_o,t_o) of u and f in equations (10.1) producing new exponentially weighted series of the partial derivatives of (x,y,z,t). This treatment will be explained in Section 10.4. Equating like ordered partial derivatives of the resulting distribution,we form (10.2a) using sufficient number of equations.

ii) We employ distributions about a set of points (x_I,y_J,z_K,t_L) to generate independent algebraic equations from any one of the equations chosen in (i).

For the pupose of a clear illustration of the above concepts and their application we will now consider two dimensional Poisson moment functional (TDPMF) expansions in detail.

10.4. TDPMF expansions of partial derivative terms

If $u_{i,j}$ is the coefficient of the (i,j)-th term in the TDPMF expansion of a function u(x,t) about (x_o,t_o):

$$M_{i,j}\{u(x,t)\}\Big|_{x_o,t_o} \triangleq u_{i,j} = \int_0^{x_o}\int_0^{t_o} u(x,t)\,\frac{(x_o-x)^i}{i!}\,\frac{(t_o-t)^j}{j!}\,\exp\{-[\lambda_x(x_o-x)+\lambda_t(t_o-t)]\}dx\,dt, \tag{10.5}$$

the following relations exist:

$$M_{i,j}\{\frac{\partial u}{\partial x}\} \triangleq \{\frac{\partial u}{\partial x}\}_{i,j} = u_{i-1,j} - \lambda_x u_{i,j} - \{u(0,t)\}_{i,j}\ , \tag{10.6}$$

$$M_{i,j}\{\frac{\partial u}{\partial t}\} \triangleq \{\frac{\partial u}{\partial t}\}_{i,j} = u_{i,j-1} - \lambda_t u_{i,j} - \{u(x,0)\}_{i,j}\ . \tag{10.7}$$

Similar relationsfor higher order partial derivative terms may be generated from (10.6) and (10.7), by following methods, analogous to those of finite difference discussed in the Appendix 10.9. It can be shown, for instance, that:

$$\{\frac{\partial^2 u}{\partial x^2}\}_{i,j} = \lambda_x^2 u_{i,j} - 2\lambda_x u_{i-1,j} + u_{i-2,j} - \{u(0,t)\}_{i-1,j} +$$

$$\lambda_x \{u(0,t)\}_{i,j} - \{u_x(0,t)\}_{i,j} , \qquad (10.8)$$

$$\{\frac{\partial^2 u}{\partial t^2}\}_{i,j} = \lambda_t^2 u_{i,j} - 2\lambda_t u_{i,j-1} + u_{i,j-2} - \{u(x,0)\}_{i,j-1} +$$

$$\lambda_t \{u(x,0)\}_{i,j} - \{u_t(x,0)\}_{i,j}, \qquad (10.9)$$

$$\{\frac{\partial^2 u}{\partial x \partial t}\}_{i,j} = \lambda_x \lambda_t u_{i,j} - \lambda_x u_{i,j-1} - \lambda_t u_{i-1,j} + u_{i-1,j-1} +$$

$$\lambda_x \{u(x,0)\}_{i,j} + \lambda_t \{u(0,t)\}_{i,j} -$$

$$\{u(x,0)\}_{i-1,j} - \{u(0,t)\}_{i,j-1} + \{u(0,0)\}_{i,j} , \qquad (10.10)$$

where u_x and u_t denote $\frac{\partial u}{\partial x}$ and $\frac{\partial u}{\partial t}$ respectively.

Example 10.1. Consider a process modelled by the PDE

$$\frac{\partial u(x,t)}{\partial x} = c\,\frac{\partial u(x,t)}{\partial t} + u(x,t) , \qquad (10.11)$$

whose solution in the region: $[0 \leq x \leq 1,\ 0 \leq t \leq 1]$ is given as shown in Fig. 10.2. Here c is an unknown parameter to be determined. We choose $\lambda_x=1$ and $\lambda_t=1$ and obtain the TDPMF's about $x_0=1$ and $t_0=1$ as the definite double integrals given by equation (10.5a). Depending upon the form of the given data, an appropriate numerical integration routine may be used in this connection. The TDPMF's for the function u(x,t) of Fig. 10.2 are computed from (10.5a) as:

$$u_{0,1} = \int_0^1 \int_0^1 u(x,t)(1-t)\exp[-(1-x)-(1-t)]dx\,dt = 0.1291474$$

$$u_{1,0} = \int_0^1 \int_0^1 u(x,t)(1-x)\exp[-(1-x)-(1-t)]dx\,dt = 0.1456883$$

$$u_{1,1} = \int_0^1 \int_0^1 u(x,t)(1-x)(1-t)\exp[-(1-x)-(1-t)]dx\,dt = 0.0847875$$

$$\{u(0,t)\}_{1,1} = \int_0^1 \int_0^1 u(0,t)(1-t)\exp[-(1-t)](1-x)\exp[-(1-x)]\delta(x)dxdt$$

$$= \exp(-1) \int_0^1 u(0,t)(1-t)\exp[-(1-t)]dt = 0.2987226$$

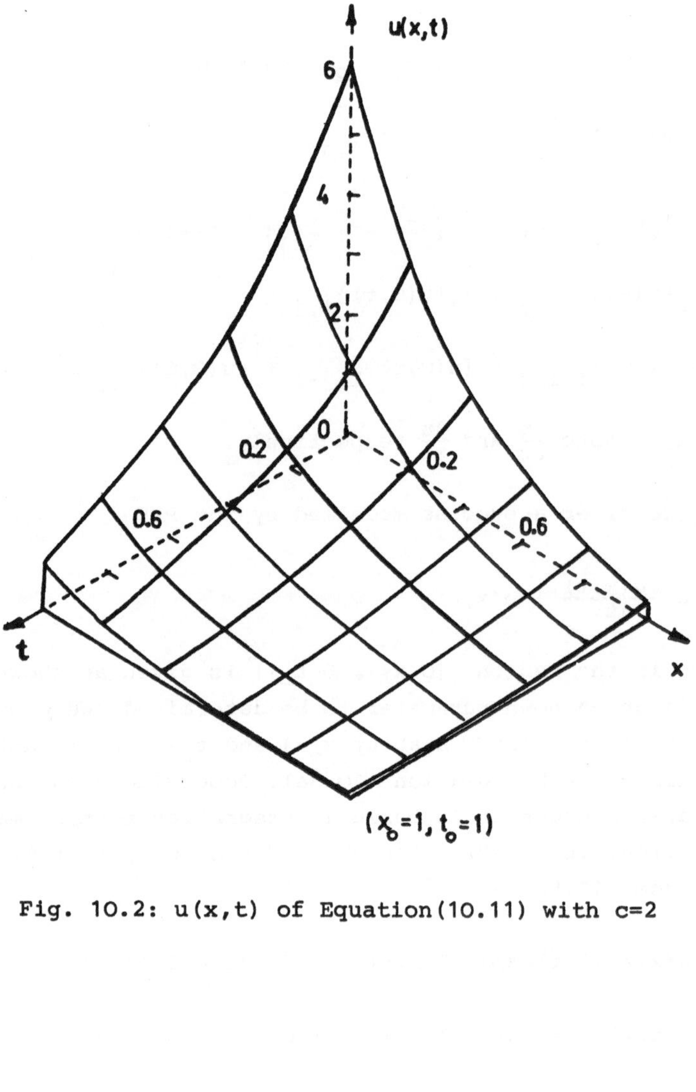

Fig. 10.2: u(x,t) of Equation(10.11) with c=2

and

$$\{u(x,0)\}_{1,1} = \int_0^1 \int_0^1 u(x,0)(1-x)\exp[-(1-x)](1-t)\exp[-(1-t)]\delta(t)\,dxdt$$

$$= \exp(-1) \int_0^1 u(x,0)(1-x)\exp[-(1-x)]dx = 0.2304759 \qquad (10.12)$$

The boundary functions $u(0,t)$ and $u(x,0)$ are, in fact, functions of one-variable and as such are treated as two dimensional functions, without loss of generality, by multiplying with $\delta(x)$ and $\delta(t)$ respectively, in the evaluation of their TDPMF's. Using equations (10.6) and (10.7) with $i=1$, and $j=1$ in (10.11), we get,

$$u_{0,1} - u_{1,1} - \{u(0,t)\}_{1,1} = c[u_{1,0} - u_{1,1} - \{u(x,0)\}_{1,1}] + u_{1,1}. \qquad (10.13)$$

Substituting the TDPMF values of (10.12) in equation (10.13), we obtain $c=1.9988966$.

The TDPMF's in (10.12) are obtained from a $u(x,t)$ which happenes to be the solution of the equation.

$$\frac{\partial u(x,t)}{\partial x} = 2\,\frac{\partial u(x,t)}{\partial t} + u(x,t).$$

<u>Example 10.2.</u> Consider the model of the heat diffusion in a semiinfinite solid, in which the temperature on face is given as a sinusoidal function of time, described by

$$\frac{\partial u(x,t)}{\partial t} = h^2\,\frac{\partial^2 u(x,t)}{\partial x^2}\,, \qquad (10.14)$$

whose solution in the region: $[0\leq x\leq 1,\ 0\leq t\leq 1]$ is given as shown in Fig. 10.3. Here h^2, the unknown diffusivity constant is to be determined. Choosing $\lambda_x=1$, $\lambda_t=1$, $x_0=1$ and $t_0=1$, we compute the following TDPMF's using equation (10.5a):

$u_{2,0} = 0.0119931$, $u_{2,1} = 2.18865\text{x}10^{-3}$, $u_{1,1} = 2.71729\text{x}10^{-3}$,

$u_{1,0} = 0.0270075$, $u_{0,1} = -9.7926\text{x}10^{-3}$, $u_{-1,1} = -0.0538774$,

$\{u(x,0)\}_{2,1} = -5.4542\text{x}10^{-3}$, $\{u(x,0)\}_{1,1} = -0.0214544$,

$\{u(0,t)\}_{1,1} = 0.035952$, $\{u(0,t)\}_{0,1} = 0.035952$,

$\{u(0,t)\}_{2,1} = 0.017956$.

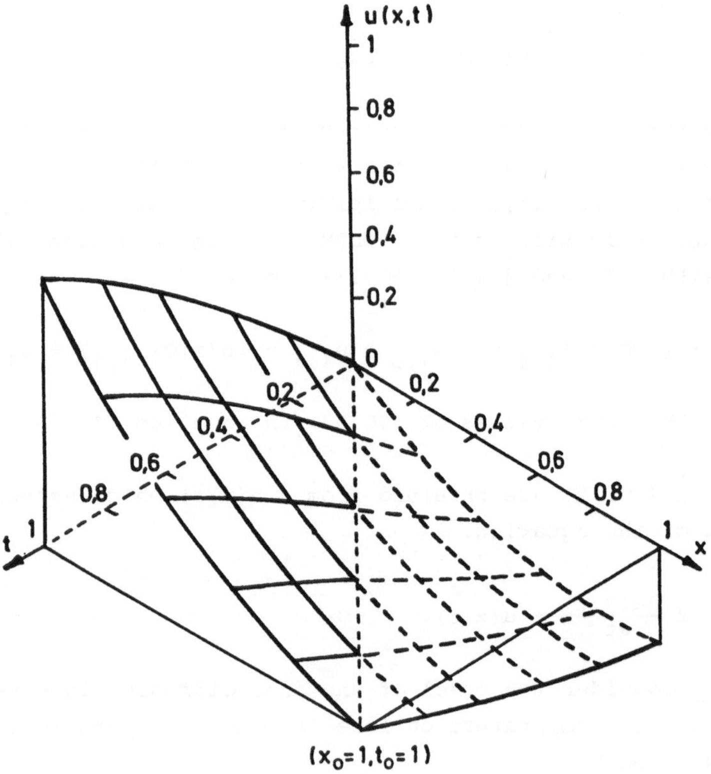

<u>Fig.10.3</u>: u(x,t) of Equation(10.14) with h^2=0.5

In addition, to treat the boundary functions and their derivatives at the boundaries we compute

$$Q_{i,-}(x_o) = \int_o^{x_o} \frac{(x_o-x)^i}{i!} \exp[-\lambda_x(x_o-x)]\delta(x)dx$$

$$= \frac{x_o}{i!} \exp[-\lambda_x x_o], \qquad (10.15a)$$

giving

$$Q_{1,-}(1) = 0.367879 \quad \text{and} \quad Q_{2,-}(1) = 0.1839395. \qquad (10.15b)$$

Using (10.8) and (10.9) with i=2 and j=1, (10.14) may be written as:

$$u_{2,o} - u_{2,1} - \{u(x,0)\}_{2,1} = h^2[u_{2,1} - 2u_{1,1} + u_{0,1} - \{u(0,t)\}_{1,1} +$$

$$\{u(0,t)\}_{2,1}] - h^2\{u_x(0,t)\}_{2,1}. \qquad (10.16)$$

The last term in R.H.S. of (10.16), namely, $h^2\{u_x(0,t)\}_{2,1}$ can be expressed as $h^2 \; Q_{2,-}(x_o)\{u_x(0,t)\}_{-,1}$. Since the derivative type boundary condition $u_x(0,t)$ is usually not available in an actual situation, it is treated as an unknown and elimated using another moment functional equation with i=1, j=1.

$$u_{1,o} - u_{1,1} - \{u(x,0)\}_{1,1} = h^2[u_{1,1} - 2u_{0,1} + u_{-1,1} - u\{(0,t)\}_{0,1} +$$

$$\{u(0,t)\}_{1,1}] - h^2\{u_x(0,t)\}_{1,1} \qquad (10.17)$$

The last term in R.H.S. of (10.17) can be written as $h^2 \; Q_{1,-}(x_o)$ $\{u_x(0,t)\}_{-,1}$. The Q's are, however, known leaving $\{u_x(0,t)\}_{-,1}$ as the only unknown that could be easily eliminated from (10.16) and (10.17) leading to

$$h^2 = \frac{\gamma_1 - \gamma_2}{\gamma_3 - \gamma_4} \qquad (10.18)$$

where

$$\gamma_1 = Q_{1,-}(x_o)[u_{2,o} - u_{2,1} - \{u(x,0)\}_{2,1}] \; ,$$

$$\gamma_2 = Q_{2,-}(x_o)[u_{1,o} - u_{1,1} - \{u(x,0)\}_{1,1}]$$

$$\gamma_3 = Q_{1,-}(x_o)[u_{2,1} - 2u_{1,1} + u_{0,1} - \{u(0,t)\}_{1,1} + \{u(0,t)\}_{2,1}],$$

$$\gamma_4 = Q_{2,-}(x_o)[u_{1,1} - 2u_{0,1} + u_{-1,1} - \{u(0,t)\}_{0,1} + \{u(0,t)\}_{1,1}]. \quad (10.19)$$

Substituting the numerical values from (10.15) in (10.19) and (10.18), we get $h^2 = 0.5000047$.

The TDPMF's in (10.15) are actually obtained from a u(x,t) which happens to be the solution of (10.14) with $h^2 = 0.5$.

One important remark is in order at this stage regarding negative values of i,j. Although these are not defined in the basic development, the TDPMF's with index -1 corresponds to the values of u(x,t) at (x_o,t_o) in the appropriate direction, and satisfy the partial derivative formulae (10.10).

<u>Example 10.3:</u> Consider a process modelled by the wave equation

$$\frac{\partial^2 u(x,t)}{\partial t^2} = c^2 \frac{\partial^2 u(x,t)}{\partial x^2}, \quad (10.20)$$

in which the following TDPMF's with $\lambda_x=1$, $\lambda_t=1$ about $x_o=1$ and $t_o=1$ are obtained and the constant, c^2, is to be determined.

$u_{2,2} = 3.22989\text{x}10^{-4}$, $u_{2,1} = -1.9286\text{x}10^{-3}$, $u_{2,0} = 1.26152\text{x}10^{-3}$
$u_{2,-1} = 0.7862149$, $u_{1,2} = 4.97855\text{x}10^{-4}$, $u_{1,1} = -3.0307\text{x}10^{-3}$
$u_{1,0} = 2.00203\text{x}10^{-3}$, $u_{1,-1} = 1.2853596$, $u_{0,2} = -1.0448\text{x}10^{-3}$
$u_{0,1} = 5.09811\text{x}10^{-3}$, $u_{-1,2} = u_{-1,1} = 0$, $\{u(x,0)\}_{2,2} = 0.1022859$
$\{u(x,0)\}_{2,1} = 0.2045718$, $\{u(x,0)\}_{2,0} = 0.2045718$, (10.21)
$\{u(x,0)\}_{1,2} = 0.1480436$, $\{u(x,0)\}_{1,1} = 0.2960873$,
$\{u(x,0)\}_{1,0} = 0.2960873$, $\{u(0,t)\}_{2,2} = \{u(0,t)\}_{2,1} = 0$.
$\{u(0,t)\}_{1,2} = \{u(0,t)\}_{1,1} = \{u(0,t)\}_{0,2} = \{u(0,t)\}_{0,1} = 0$.

Proceeding in the same manner as in Example 10.2, we eliminate $u_x(0,t)$ and $u_t(x,0)$, taking four moment functional equations for $\{(i,j);\ i=1,2,\ j=1,2\}$, and get

$$c^2 = \frac{\alpha_1 - 2\alpha_2 + 4\alpha_3 - 2\alpha_4}{\beta_1 - 2\beta_2 + 4\beta_3 - 2\beta_4}, \quad (10.22)$$

where

$$
\begin{aligned}
\alpha_1 &= u_{1,1} - 2u_{1,0} + u_{1,-1} - \{u(x,0)\}_{1,0} + \{u(x,0)\}_{1,1}\ ,\\
\alpha_2 &= u_{1,2} - 2u_{1,1} + u_{1,0} - \{u(x,0)\}_{1,1} + \{u(x,0)\}_{1,2}\ ,\\
\alpha_3 &= u_{2,2} - 2u_{2,1} + u_{2,0} - \{u(x,0)\}_{2,1} + \{u(x,0)\}_{2,2},\\
\alpha_4 &= u_{2,1} - 2u_{2,0} + u_{2,-1} - \{u(x,0)\}_{2,0} + \{u(x,0)\}_{2,1},\\
\beta_1 &= u_{1,1} - 2u_{0,1} + u_{-1,1} - \{u(0,t)\}_{0,1} + \{u(0,t)\}_{1,1},\\
\beta_2 &= u_{1,2} - 2u_{0,2} + u_{-1,2} - \{u(0,t)\}_{0,2} + \{u(0,t)\}_{1,2},\\
\beta_3 &= u_{2,2} - 2u_{1,2} + u_{0,2} - \{u(0,t)\}_{1,2} + \{u(0,t)\}_{2,2}\ ,\\
\beta_4 &= u_{2,1} - 2u_{1,1} + u_{0,1} - \{u(0,t)\}_{1,1} + \{u(0,t)\}_{2,1}\ .
\end{aligned}
\qquad (10.23)
$$

Employing moment functional values from (10.21) in (10.23) and (10.22), we get $c^2 = 9.0002469$.

The TDPMF's in (10.21) are obtained from a $u(x,t)$, which happens to be the solution of equation (10.20) with $c^2 = 9$.

Example 10.4.

Consider a third order model

$$
\frac{\partial^3 u}{\partial x^3} + \theta_1 \frac{\partial^2}{\partial x^2}\left(\frac{\partial u}{\partial t}\right) - \theta_2 \frac{\partial}{\partial x}\left(\frac{\partial^2 u}{\partial t^2}\right) - \theta_3 \frac{\partial^3 u}{\partial t^3} = 0 \qquad (10.24)
$$

whose solution $u(x,t)$ is given in the region $0 \le x \le 1$, $0 \le t \le 1$. The parameters θ_1, θ_2 and θ_3 are to be determined.

The authors carried out the necessary steps to eleminate the unknown boundary derivative function effects. The resulting algebra is too unwieldy to be reproduced here. It is the heavy mathematical burden of this example which motivated the authors towards a possible simplification as will be presented in Section 10.7.

10.5. Noisy data

The presence of noise in the data of a practical problem of system identification is natural. An investigation of the performance of the present method under such conditions is in order. For the purpose of this study, let us consider the process modelled by equation (10.11) as in Example 10.1. Measurements of $u(x,t)$ over the region $0 \le x \le 1$, $0 \le t \le 1$ at intervals of $\Delta x = 0.1$ and $\Delta t = 0.1$ are considered. Zero-mean gaussian noise is added to simulate cases of chosen signal-to-noise ratio. The moment functionals required for identifying c are $u_{0,1}$, $u_{1,1}$, $u_{1,0}$ $\{u(0,t)\}_{1,1}$ and $\{u(x,0)\}_{1,1}$. The double integrals involved in the determination of these are approximated by trapezoidal rule and the TDPMF's are systematically computed at points $(i\Delta x, j\Delta t)$, $i=1,2,\ldots,10$; $j=1,2,\ldots,10$ with $\lambda_x=0$ and $\lambda_t=0$. Using the TDPMF's so computed the parameter c is evaluated at each of these points. Interestingly enough, the parameter evaluated at $x_0=1$, $t_0=1$ is quite immune to the noise present in the employed data. Table 10.1 shows the results of identification by the method of TDPMF's, with different degrees of noise level. Alongside these are shown the results of identification by the method [G 7] in which the derivatives are approximated by finite difference formulae.

In the first place, the parameter c is evaluated from the noisy data at 100 grid points obtained in a single run. Next, an ensemble of 20 runs each with 100 data points is considered and the results of parameter estimation using least squares estimated TDPMF's and partial derivatives are presented. The value of the parameter c evaluated at various grid points in the x-t plane becomes random in presence of noise. The means and variances in different cases are also presented in Table 10.1, showing the superiority of the TDPMF method in every case of noisy data.

The TDPMF method illustrated here and the simple minded approach of finite difference approximation of derivatives yield nearly the same results in the absence of noise. With increasing level of noise in problem data, the performance of the derivative method rapidly deteriorates, while TDPMF method shows remarkable immunity.

10.6. Discussion

An elegant method of identifying distributed parameter systems, with its mathematical basis in the theory of distributions, is presented. The resulting technique, a multi-dimensional generalisation of the one-dimensional PMF method is applicable to nonlinear and time-space varying systems provided the related terms in such systems are described as finite polynomials in u, and (x,y,z,t) respectively with unknown coefficients represented as Θ leading to an equation in the form (10.2a) which is linear in the unknown parameters.

The set of definite multiple integrals in the space-time continuum, of the available data modulated by a set of known functions in the parti-

<u>Table 10.1.</u> Parameter estimation in equation (10.11): True value of c = 2.

	Noise to signal ratio in u(x,t)	Value of c obtained at $x_o=1$, $t_o=1$ by		Mean of the parameter values obtained at the 100 grid points by		Variance of the parameter values obtained at the 100 grid points by	
		TDPMF method	Finite difference approximation of derivatives	TDPMF method	Finite difference approximation of derivatives	TDMPF method	Finite difference approximation of derivatives
With data	0.0	1.9952	1.9815	1.9938	1.9815	-	-
over 100	0.05	1.9523	-2.1404	1.8695	10.1185	0.0316	5114.3008
grid points	0.10	1.9355	-3.1785	1.8290	8.2476	0.0488	2237.6692
in a single	0.15	1.9229	-3.5275	1.8016	0.1430	0.0641	263.9890
run	0.20	1.9126	3.3857	1.7806	0.9348	0.0784	123.4424
With an	0.05	2.0197	0.7839	1.9632	1.2097	0.0136	0.3056
ensemble	0.10	2.0257	0.6554	1.9318	1.0640	0.0204	0.3171
of 20 runs	0.15	2.0289	0.5976	1.9031	0.9838	0.0280	0.3079
each with	0.20	2.0307	0.5633	1.8768	0.9296	0.0359	0.2942
100 points							

cular form, termed as the multidimensional Poisson moment functionals, transforms the original PDE into a computationally convenient algebraic form from which the set of unknown parameters of the PDE may be directly obtained. Elimination of the noise accentuating direct derivative operations on problem data is the main virtue of the technique. Choice of the positive real Poisson parameters λ_x, λ_y, λ_z and λ_t is, in theory, arbitrary in the identification scheme. In actual practice, however, one should choose a good numerical integration routine to compute the PMF's bearing in mind that the chosen λ's should not result in severely varying integrands. The multidimensional Poisson moment functionals $\{u(x,y,z,t)\}_{i,j,k,l}$ for l=0,1,2,... may be obtained by physical measurement as the outputs of a time-Poisson filter system excited by u(x,y,z,t). Of much practical importance is the case of noisy measurements of u that produce correlated errors in $u_{i,j,k,l}$. The method of multidimensional Poisson moment functionals possesses natural immunity to noise to some extent as illustrated in Section 10.5. The present treatment further indicates some possibility of removing these errors by the application of certain generalised concepts of Kalman filtering of multidimensional functions, presently under investigation by the authors.

10.7. Simplification with estimated TDPMF's of the boundary derivative functions

For instance, if the data $u(x_i,t_j)$, i=1,2,...,5, j=1,2,...,5 is given at equal intervals of Δx and Δt, then we have the 5-point estimator [G17]

$$u_x(x_i,t_j) = \frac{1}{12\Delta x}[-25u(x_i,t_j) + 48u(x_{i+1},t_j) - 36u(x_{i+2},t_j) + 16u(x_{i+3},t_j - 3u(x_{i+4},t_j)] \quad (10.25)$$

and

$$u_t(x_i,t_j) = \frac{1}{12\Delta x}[-25u(x_i,t_j) + 48u(x_i,t_{j+1}) - 36u(x_i,t_{j+2}) + 16u(x_i,t_{j+3}) - 3u(x_i,t_{j+4})] \quad (10.26)$$

Similar multipoint formulae are possible. Such formulae with their error implications are listed in McCormick and Salvdori [G17]. This estimation may be made sufficiently general by standard least squares fitting procedures if so desired.

In Example 10.2 the data is as shown in Table 10.2(a). Using formula (10.25) $u_x(0,t)$ is estimated and shown in Table 10.2(b).

The $\{u_x(0,t)\}_{2,1} = -61.6441\times10^{-3}$ by Simpson's rule.

The other TDPMF's are obtained and listed in Table 10.2(c). These values when inserted in equation (10.14) give $h^2 = 0.5000709$. The earlier elimination method gave $h^2 = 0.5000047$ [P 14].

Notice that in the present estimation method the number of TDPMF computed from data u(x,t) became much less than in the case of the elimination method.

Next consider Example 10.4 in which simulated data with $\theta_1=2$, $\theta_2=1$ and $\theta_3=2$ is shown in Table 10.2(a) over a region $0\leq x\leq 1$, $0\leq t\leq 1$.

The (i,j)-th TDPMF transformation of the model equation (10.24) with $\lambda_x=\lambda_t=0$ leads to

$$u_{i-3,j} - \{u(0,t)\}_{i-2,j} - \{u_x(0,t)\}_{i-1,j} - \{u_{xx}(0,t)\}_{i,j}$$

$$+ \theta_1[u_{i-2,j-1} - \{u(x,0)\}_{i-2,j} - \{u(0,t)\}_{i-1,j-1} + \{u(0,0)\}_{i-1,j}$$

$$- \{u_x(0,t)\}_{i,j-1} + \{u_x(0,0)\}_{i,j}]$$

$$+ \theta_2[-u_{i-1,j-2} - \{u(x,0)\}_{i-1,j-1} + \{u_t(x,0)\}_{i-1,j}$$

$$+ \{u(0,t)\}_{i,j-2} - \{u(0,0)\}_{i,j-1} - \{u_t(0,0)\}_{i,j}]$$

$$+ \theta_3[-u_{i,j-3} + \{u(x,0)\}_{i,j-2} + \{u_t(x,0)\}_{i,j-1} + \{u_{tt}(x,0)\}_{i,j}] = 0 \quad (10.27)$$

Taking three sets, i.e., (i=3, j=4), (i=4, j=3) and (i=3, j=3) and inserting the TDPMF's from Tables 10.3(d)-10.3(f) we generate the following to reveal the essential system parameters:

$$\begin{bmatrix} 1.9938 & 0.4501 & -1.0043 \\ 2.1430 & 0.5531 & -1.0117 \\ 10.4456 & -1.7225 & -5.4243 \end{bmatrix} \begin{bmatrix} \theta_1 \\ \theta_2 \\ \theta_3 \end{bmatrix} = \begin{bmatrix} 2.4060 \\ 2.7946 \\ 8.4571 \end{bmatrix} \quad (10.28)$$

Solving equation (10.28) we get

$$[\theta_1 \quad \theta_2 \quad \theta_3]^T = [2.0667 \quad 0.9318 \quad 2.1248]^T \quad (10.29)$$

The actual parameter vector is $[2 \quad 1 \quad 2]^T$.

Table 10.2(a). u(x,t) in Example 10.2

t↓ \ x→	0	0.25	0.50	0.75	1.0
0	0	-0.1926783	-0.2907862	-0.3219833	-0.3095598
0.25	0.2474039	0	-0.1500580	-0.2264645	-0.2507608
0.50	0.4794255	0.1926783	0	-0.1168653	-0.1763707
0.75	0.6816387	0.3733769	0.1500580	0	-0.0910148
1.00	0.8414709	0.5308607	0.2907862	0.1168653	0

Table 10.2(b). Estimated $u_x(0,t)$ in Example 10.2

t→	0.	0.25	0.50	0.75	1.0
$u_x(0,t)$	-1.0011028	-1.218053	-1.3592706	-1.4159733	-1.3846391

Table 10.2(c). TDPMF's used in Example 10.2 ($\lambda_x=\lambda_t=1$, $x_o=t_o=1$)

TDPMF of	Order (i,j)	Value
u(x,t)	(0,1)	-9.7926×10^{-3}
	(1,1)	2.71729×10^{-3}
	(2,0)	0.0119931
	(2,1)	2.18865×10^{-3}
u(x,0)	(2,1)	-5.4542×10^{-3}
u(0,t)	(1,1)	0.035952
	(2,1)	0.017956
$u_x(0,t)$	(2,1)	-61.6441×10^{-3}
		Computed from Table 10.2(b)

Table 10.3(a). u(x,t) in Example 10.4

t↓ \ x→	0	0.25	0.50	0.75	1.0
0	3.0	2.6693568	2.6231314	2.8124967	3.2214965
0.25	3.8520762	3.4275219	3.3681673	3.6113172	4.1364833
0.50	4.9461639	4.4010254	4.3248126	4.6370232	5.3113198
0.75	6.351	5.6510283	5.5531691	5.9540555	6.819908
1.0	8.1548454	7.256064	7.1304103	7.6451585	8.759353

Table 10.3(b). Estimated boundary partial derivatives in Example 10.4

x→	0	0.25	0.50	0.75	1.0
$u_t(x,0)$	2.996407	2.6661582	2.6199888	2.8091284	3.2176384
$u_{tt}(x,0)$	3.0587456	2.7216336	2.6745065	2.867568	3.2845757

Table 10.3(c). Estimated boundary partial derivatives in Example 10.4

t→	0	0.25	0.50	0.75	1.0
$u_x(0,t)$	-1.9893821	-2.5544171	-3.2799367	-4.2115217	-5.4077012
$u_{xx}(0,t)$	5.8140249	7.4653529	9.5857065	12.308285	15.804158

Table 10.3(d). $\{u(x,t)\}_{i,j}$ in Example 10.4

j↓ \ i→	0	1	2	3	4
0	-	-	-	0.1983808	0.399611
1	-	-	0.3293216	0.0829277	-
2	-	0.2990449	0.100085	-	-
3	0.1436312	0.0707124	-	-	-
4	0.0276839	-	-	-	-

Table 10.3(e). $\{u(0,t)\}_{i,j}$ in Example 10.4

j↓ \ i→	1	2	3	4
1	-	-	0.35513921	0.08978480
2	-	0.3272910	0.10914303	-
3	0.15483989	0.07741995	-	-
4	0.02984539	-	-	-

Table 10.3(f). $\{u(x,0)\}_{i,j}$ in Example 10.4

j↓ \ i→	1	2	3	4
1	-	-	0.11546191	0.02326159
2	-	0.22925218	0.05773095	-
3	0.22833390	0.07641739	-	-
4	0.05708348	-	-	-

10.8. Conclusion

In the MDPMF approach to distributed parameter system identifcation, two significant simplifications, helpful particularly in large scale situations, can be suggested. The first one is due to separation of variables in the development of relations among the MDPMF's of functions and their partial derivatives as shown in Appendix 10.9. The resulting relations are expressible systematically in terms of single dimensional PMF's of the functions in the separated variables. These relations reduce the partial calculus of distributed parameter systems to an elegant algebra without involving any approximation.

Next, the technique of estimated partial derivatives of functions along the boundaries suggested in this chapter uses a suitable finite difference formula for the estimation. This does not mean that we are falling back on the finite difference technique [G7]. The identification algorithm ultimately uses the MDPMF's of these estimated partial derivatives along boundaries and not the functions. Thus the spirit of MDPMF approach and its several advantages are maintained here. To sum up, the advantages achieved are:

(a) the size of the identification problem is reduced, and

(b) the variety of MDPMF's required in the resulting algorithm is enormously reduced implying a corresponding saving of the computational effort.

The inherent approximation in the derivative estimation procedure is the only price, which should be marginal, paid towards this simplification. In conclusion we suggest the original derivative elimination technique [P14] for models of order and dimension two and the present derivative estimation method for models of higher order and dimension.

10.9. Appendix: Moment functional formulae for higher order partial derivative terms

With equations (10.6) and (10.7) as the basis, it is possible to develop moment functional formulae for higher order partial derivative terms as illustrated in the following. We make use of a representation in the form of grids analogous to those employed in developing finite difference partial derivative operators. In the present development the moment functional indices are used as node coordinates unlike the finite difference grid which has pivotal point indices as the coordinates. Consider at first, equation (10.6), that gives$\{\frac{\partial u(x,t)}{\partial x}\}_{i,j}$. The terms in it may be classified into two groups: (i) MF's of u(x,t), and (ii) MF's of the boundary function u(0,t). The MF formula (10.6) for $\{\frac{\partial u(x,t)}{\partial x}\}_{i,j}$ is a superposition of the MF grids of the signals u(x,t) and u(0,t) as shown in Fig. 10.4.

Similarly it is possible to represent $\{\frac{\partial u(x,t)}{\partial t}\}_{i,j}$ as in Fig. 10.5.

If we wish to obtain MF expansions for higher order parial derivative terms we take Figs. 10.4 and 10.5 as the operators to suitably expand each term of the lower order operators with the appropriate grid. For instance, if we wish to get $\{\frac{\partial^2 u(x,t)}{\partial x \partial t}\}_{i,j}$, we may take the grid of Fig. 10.4 in which each node is operated upon by the grid of Fig.10.5 or vice versa. The result is shown in Fig.10.6.

Similarly, the grid-node representations of the other higher order partial derivative terms are given in Fig. 10.7 to Fig. 10.12.

The development of these formulae through integration by parts and the diagramatic representations become increasingly unwieldy. The complexitiy in the case of higher order and higher dimensional terms cannot be overemphasized. We will have an alternative look at these formulae through separated variables.

MDPMF's via separated variables

We will assume here within the framework of the MDPMF approach, that, the variables are separable. That is,

$$u(x_1,x_2,\ldots,x_n) = g_1(x_1)\ g_2(x_2)\ \ldots\ g_n(x_n)$$

$$\{u(x_1,x_2,\ldots,x_n)\}\Big|_{i_1,i_2,\ldots,i_n} = \{g_1(x_1)\}_{i_1}\ \{g_2(x_2)\}_{i_2}\ \ldots\{(g_n(x_n)\}_{i_n},$$

where $g_k(x_k)$, $\{g_k(x_k)\}_{i_k}$; k=1,2,...,n are functions and their i_k-th PMF's in respective single dimensions.

For example, it we consider two dimensional problems,

$$u(x,t) = g(x)\ h(t)\ ,$$

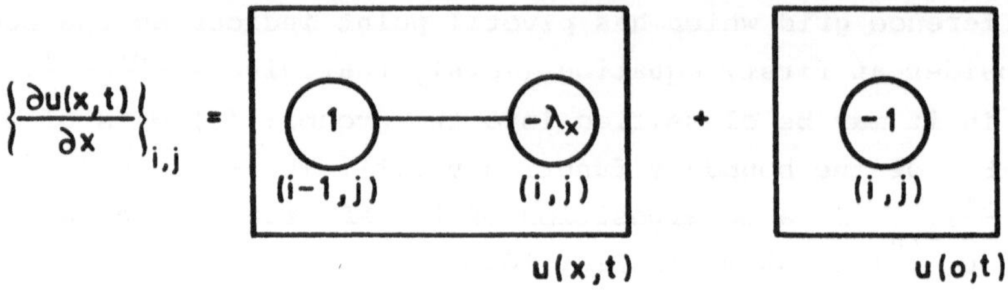

Fig. 10.4. Grid-node representation of $\{\frac{\partial u(x,t)}{\partial x}\}_{i,j}$

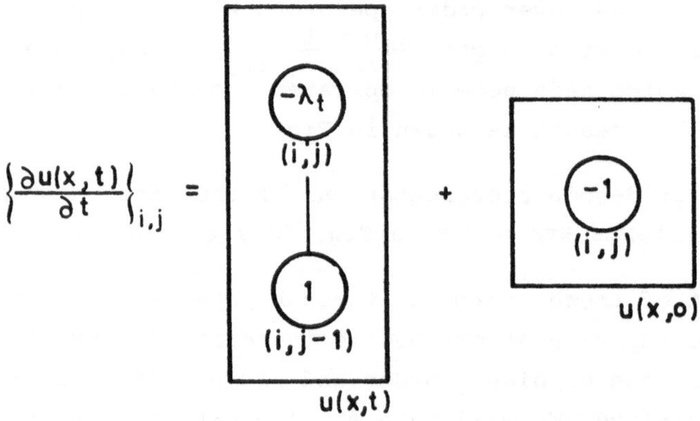

Fig. 10.5. Grid-node representation of $\{\frac{\partial u(x,t)}{\partial x}\}_{i,j}$

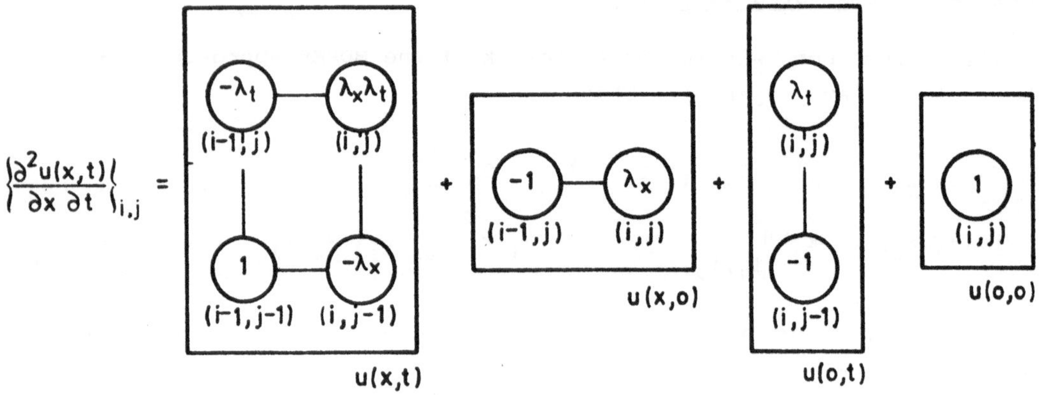

Fig. 10.6. Grid-node representation of $\{\frac{\partial^2 u(x,t)}{\partial x \partial t}\}_{i,j}$

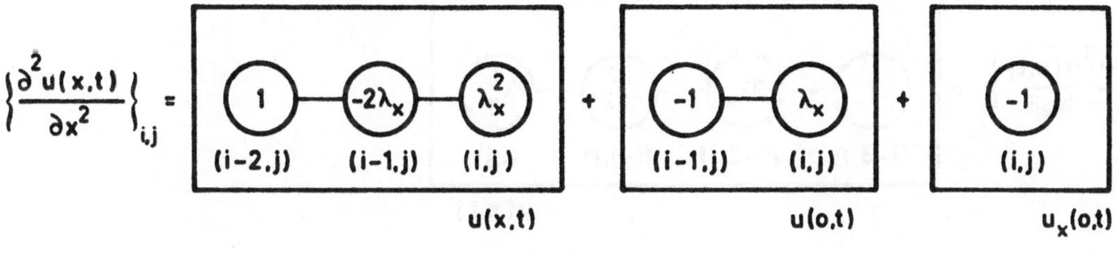

<u>Fig. 10.7.</u> Grid-node representation of $\{\frac{\partial^2 u(x,t)}{\partial x^2}\}_{i,j}$

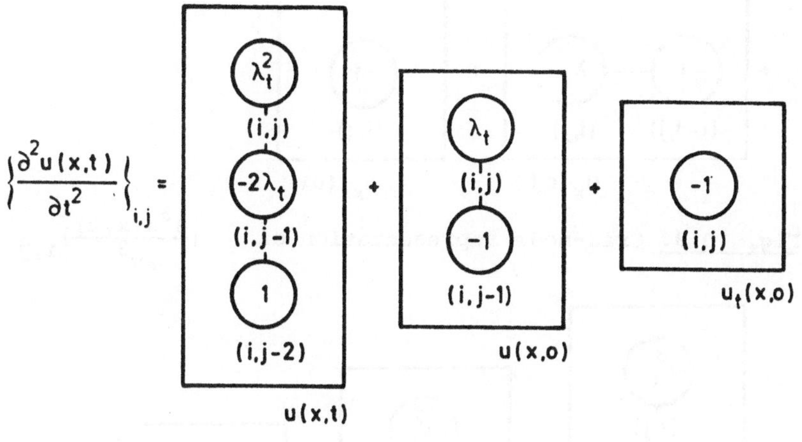

<u>Fig. 10.8.</u> Gird-node representation of $\{\frac{\partial^2 u(x,t)}{\partial t^2}\}_{i,j}$

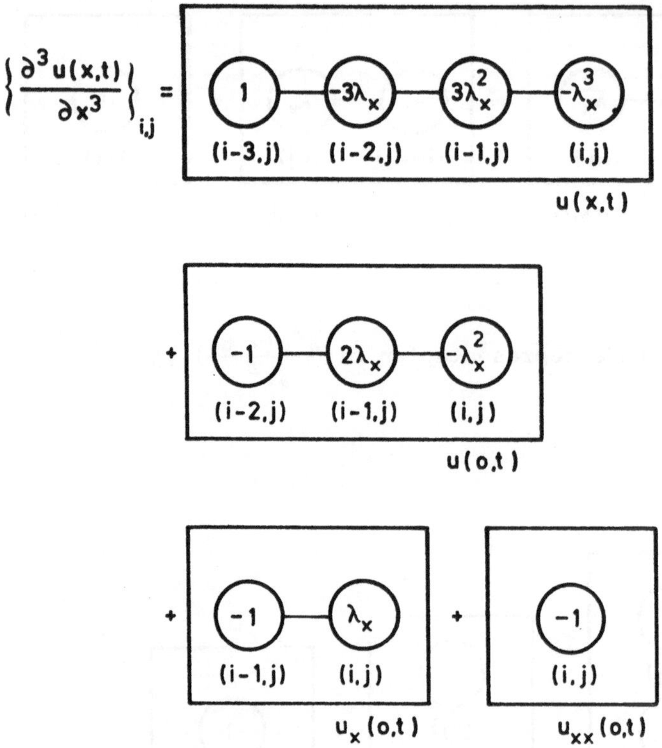

Fig. 10.9. Grid-node representation of $\left\{\frac{\partial^3 u(x,t)}{\partial x^3}\right\}_{i,j}$

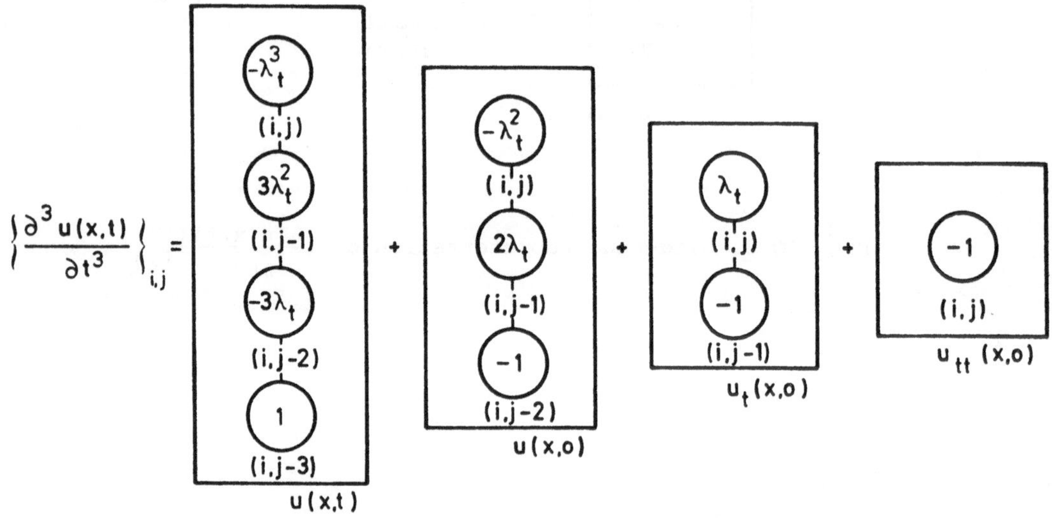

Fig. 10.10. Grid-node representation of $\left\{\frac{\partial^3 u(x,t)}{\partial t^3}\right\}_{i,j}$

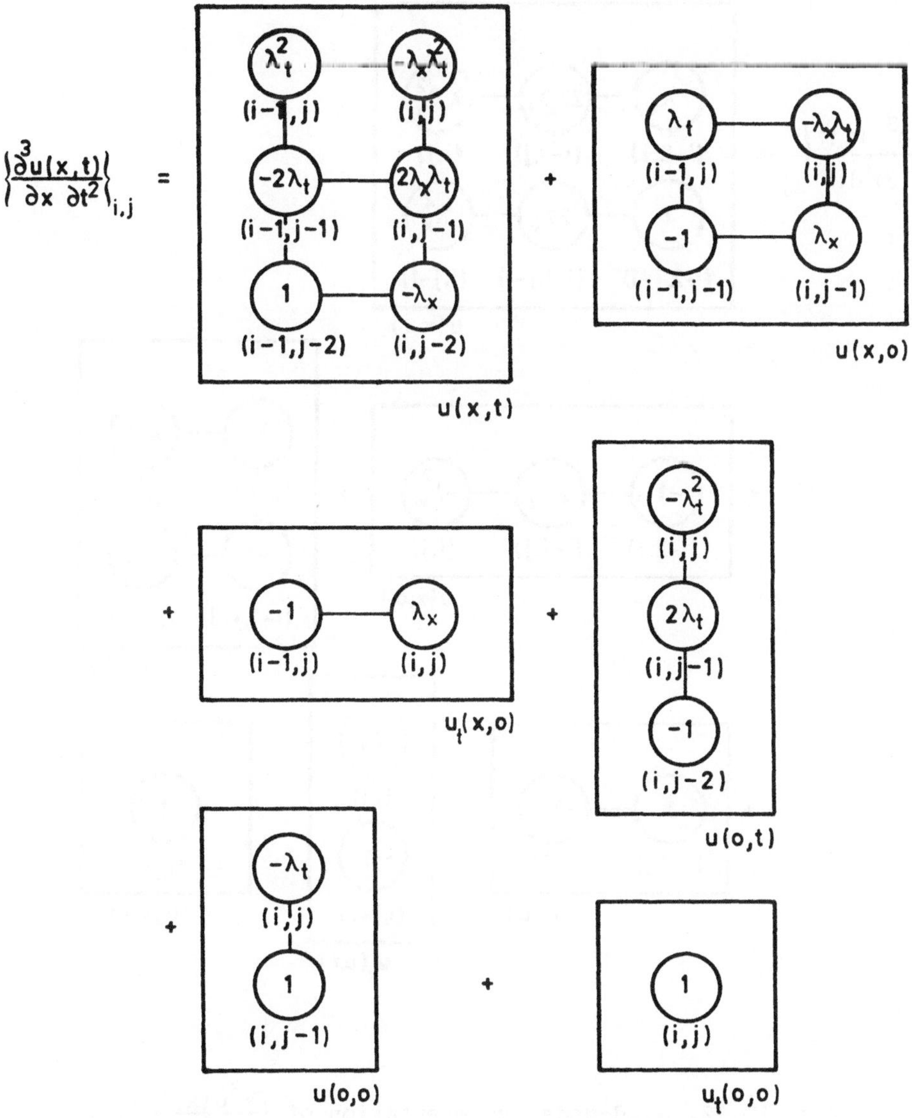

<u>Fig. 10.11.</u> Grid-node representation of $\left\{\frac{\partial^3 u(x,t)}{\partial x \partial t^2}\right\}_{i,j}$

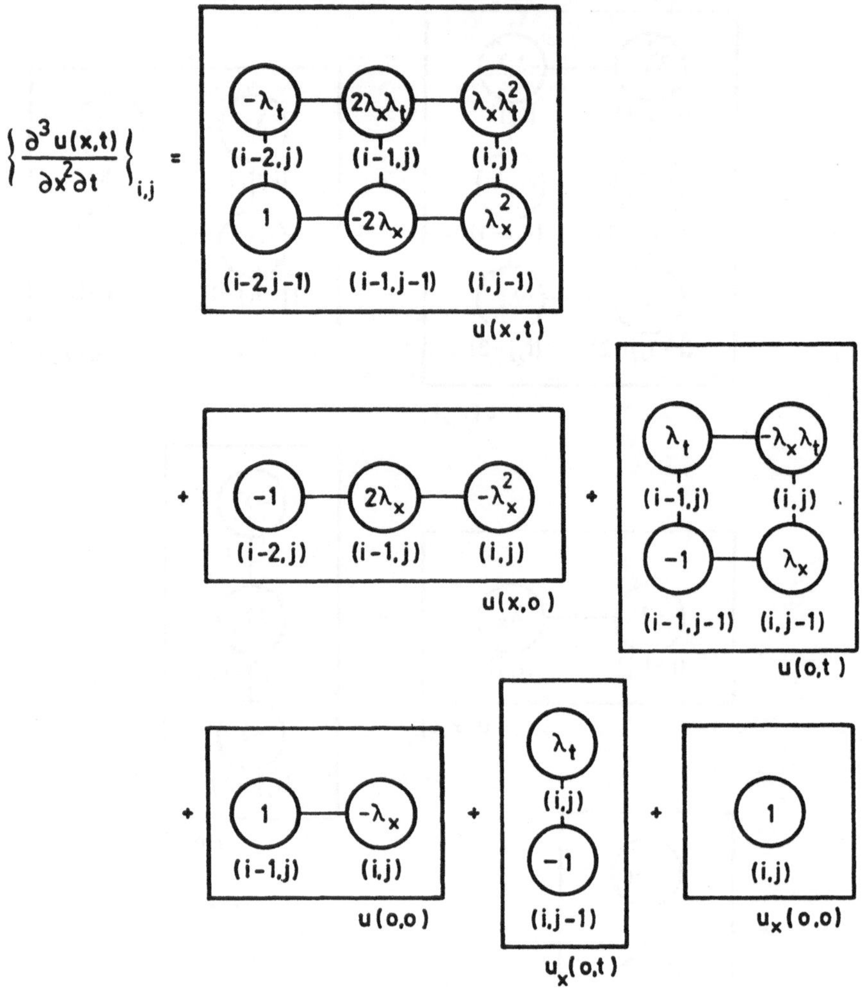

<u>Fig. 10.12.</u> Grid-node representation of $\{\frac{\partial^3 u(x,t)}{\partial x^2 \partial t}\}_{i,j}$

where g(x) and h(t) are separated functions, each of a single variable and if $\{.\}_{i,j}$ denotes (i,j)th PMF transformation,

$$\{u(x,t)\}_{i,j} = g_i h_j ,$$

where $g_i = \{g(x)\}_i$ and $h_j = \{h(t)\}_j$ about x_o and t_o respectively.

As a result of the above separation

i) $\{u(0,t)\}_{i,j} = g(0)\ p_i h_j$,

ii) $\{u(x,0)\}_{i,j} = g_i q_j\, h(0)$,

where p_i and q_j are the i-th and j-th order Poisson pulse functions each in single dimension at x_o and t_o respectively. g(0) and h(0) are the initial values of g(x) and h(t) respectively.

iii) $\{\frac{\partial u}{\partial x}\}_{i,j} = \{\frac{dg}{dx}\ h(t)\}_{i,j} = [g_{i-1} - \lambda_x g_i - p_i g(0)]h_j$

$$= g_{i-1}h_j - \lambda_x g_i h_j - p_i g(0) h_j .$$

Recognizing that

$$g_{i-1}h_j = u_{i-1,j},$$

$$g_i h_j = u_{i,j}, \text{ and}$$

$$p_i g(0) h_j = \{u(0,t)\}_{i,j},$$

we obtain the relation in (10.6).
Similarly

iv) $\{\frac{\partial u}{\partial t}\}_{i,j} = \{g(x)\ \frac{dh}{dt}\}_{i,j} = g_i [h_{j-1} - \lambda_t h_j - q\ h(0)] \doteq$ RHS of (10.7).

v) $\{\frac{\partial^2 u}{\partial x^2}\}_{i,j} = \{\frac{d^2 g}{dx^2}\ h(t)\}_{i,j}$

$$= [g_{i-2} - 2\lambda_x g_{i-1} + \lambda_x^2 g_i - p_{i-1} g(0) + \lambda_x p_i g(0)]h_j$$

$$- p_i g'(0) h_j$$

$$= u_{i-2,j} - 2\lambda_x u_{i-1,j} + \lambda_x^2 u_{i,j} - \{u(0,t)\}_{i-1,j}$$

$$+ \lambda_x \{u(0,t)\}_{i,j} - \{u_x(0,t)\}_{i,j}$$

In a similar way, relations for higher order terms can be easily obtained.

BIBLIOGRAPHY

WALSH AND BLOCK-PULSE FUNCTION METHODS OF SYSTEM IDENTIFICATION

W.1 Bohn, E.V.: Estimation of continuous time linear system parameters from periodic data, Automatica, 1982, Vol. 18, No. 1, pp 27-36.

W.2 Chen, C.F. and Hsiao, C.H.: Time-domain synthesis via Walsh functions, Proceedings IEE, 1975, Vol. 122, No. 5, pp 565-570.

W.3 Jan, Y.G. and Wong, K.M.: Bilinear system identification by block-pulse functions, Jou. Frantlin Inst., 1981, Vol. 12, No. 5, pp 349-359.

W.4 Karanam, V.R., Frick, P.A. and Mohler, R.R.: Bilinear system identification by Walsh function, IEEE Trans. on Aut. Control, 1978, Vol. AC-23, No. 4, pp 709-713.

W.5 Palanisamy, K.R. and Bhattacharya, D.K.: System identification via block pulse functions, Int. Jou. Systems Science, 1981, Vol. 12, No. 5, pp 643-647.

W.6 Paraskevopoulos, P.N. and Bounas, A.C.: Distributed parameter system identification via Walsh functions, Int. Jou. of systems Sci., 1978, Vol. 9, No. 1, pp75-83.

W.7 Prasada Rao Ganti: Piecewise constant orthogonal functions and their application to systems and control, Monograph , LNCIS Series, 1983, Springer Verlag Berlin Heidelberg New York.

W.8 Prasada Rao Ganti and Palanisamy, K.R.: Improved algorithms for parameter identification in continuous systems via Walsh functions, Proccedings IEE, 1983, Pt-D, CTA, Vol. 130, No. 1, pp 9-16.

W.9 Prasada Rao Ganti and Sivakumar, L.: System identification via Walsh functions. Proceedings IEE, 1975, Vol. 122, No. 10, pp 1160-1161.

W.10 Prasada Rao Ganti and Sivakumar, L.: Identification of time-lag systems via Walsh functions, IEEE Trans. on Aut. Control, 1979, Vol. AC-24, No. 5, pp 806-808.

W.11 Prasada Rao Ganti and Sivakumar, L.: Transfer function matrix identification in MIMO systems via Walsh functions, Proceedings of the IEEE, 1981, Vol 69, No. 4, pp 465-466.

W.12 Prasada Rao Ganti and Sivakumar, L.: Order and parameter identification in continuous linear systems via Walsh functions, Proceedings of the IEEE, 1982, Vol. 70, No. 7, pp 764-766.

W.13 Prasada Rao Ganti and Sivakumar, L.: Piecewiese linear system identification via Walsh functions, Int. Jou. of systems Science, 1982, Vol. 13, No. 5, pp 525-530.

W.14 Sinha, M.S.P., Rajamani, V.S. and Sinha, A.K.: Identification of nonlinear distributed systems using Walsh functions, Int. Jou. Control, 1980, Vol 32, No. 4, pp 669-676.

W.15 Tzafestas, S.: Walsh series approach to lumped and distributed system identification, Jou. of Franklin Inst., 1978, Vol 305, No. 4, pp 199-220.

POISSON MOMENT FUNCTIONAL METHOD AND RELATED TOPICS

P.1 Diamessis, J.E.: A new method of determining the parameters of a physical system, Proc. IEEE, 1965, Vol 53, pp 205-206.

P.2 Diamessis, J.E.: On the determination of the parameters of certain nonlinear systems, Proc. IEEE, 1965, Vol. 53, pp 319-320.

P.3 Eisenfeld, J.: Remarks on the modulating function method for impulse response identification, IEEE Trans. on Auto. Cont., Vol. AC-24, No. 3, June 1979, pp 498-499.

P.4 Fairman, F.W. and Shen, D.W.C.: Parameter identification for a class of distributed systems, Int. Jou. Control, 1970, Vol. 11, No. 6, pp 929-940.

P.5 Fairman, F.W. and Shen, D.W.C.: Parameter identification for linear time varying dynamic processes, Proc. IEE, 1970, Vol. 117, No. 10, pp 2025-2029.

P.6 Green, H.S. and Messel, H.: On the expansion of functions in terms of their moments, Quart. Appl. Math., 1954, Vol. 11, pp 403-409.

P.7 Mathew, A.V. and Fairman, F.W.: Transfer function matrix identification, IEEE Trans. on Circuits and Systems, Vol. CAS-21, Sept. 1974, pp 584-588.

P.8 Perdreauville, F.J. and Goodson, R.E.: Identification of systems described by partial differential equations. Jou. of. Basic, Engg. Trans. ASME, June 1966, Vol. 88, Series-D, No. 2, pp 463-468.

P.9 Prasada Rao, G. and Sivakumar, L.: A general framework for a class of identification methods, International Conf. on Systems and Control, Aug.30-Sept. 1, 1973, PSG College of Technology, Coimbatore, India, paper No. A-21.

P.10 Prasada Rao, G. and Sivakumar, L.: Identification of deterministic time lag systems, IEEE Trans. on Aut. Cont. Vol. AC-21, Aug. 1976, pp. 527-529.

P.11 Prasada Rao, G., Saha, D.C., Rao, T.M., Bhaya, A. and Aghoramurthy, K.: A microprocessor based system for online parameter identification in continuous dynamical systems, IEEE Trans. on IE, 1982, Vol. IE-29, No. 3, pp 197-201.

P.12 Saha, D.C. and Prasada Rao, G.: Time domain synthesis via Poisson moment functionals, Int. Jou. Control, 1979, Vol 30, No. 3, pp 417-426.

P.13 Saha, D.C. and Prasada Rao, G.: Identification of lumped linear systems in the presence of unknown initial conditions via Poisson moment functionals, Int. Jou. Control, 1980, Vol 31, No. 4, pp 637-644.

P.14 Saha, D.C. and Prasada Rao, G.: Identification of distributed parameter systems via multidimensional distributions, Proc. IEE, 1980, Vol 127, Pt-D, CTA, pp 45-50.

P.15 Saha, D.C.and Prasada Rao, G.: Identification of lumped linear timevarying parameter systems via Poisson moment functionals, Int. Jou. Control, 1980, Vol 32, No. 4, pp 709-721.

P.16 Saha, D.C. and Prasada Rao, G.: Identification of lumped linear systems in the presence of small unknown time delays via Poisson moment functionals, Int. Jou. Control, 1981, Vol. 33, pp 945-951.

P.17 Saha, D.C. and Prasada Rao, G.: A general algorithm for parameter identification in lumped continuous systems - the Poisson moment functional approach, IEEE Trans. on Aut. Cont. , Feb. 1982, Vol. AC-27, No. 1, pp 223-225.

P.18 Saha, D.C. and Prasada Rao, G.: Transfer function matrix identification in MIMO systems via Poisson moment functionals, Int. Jou. Control, 1982, Vol. 35, pp 747-738.

P.19 Saha, D.C., Rao, B.B.P. and Prasada Rao, G.: Structure and parameter identification in linear continuous lumped systems - the Poisson moment functional approach, Int. Jou. of Control, 1982, Vol. 36, No. 3, pp 477-491.

P.20 Schwartz, L.: Mathematics for physical sciences, 1966, Addison Wesley.

P.21 Seif, A.A., Hanafy, A.A. and Sakr, M.F.: Real time least squares estimation using successive integration, Information and Control, 1978, Vol. 36, pp 42-55.

P.22 Shinbrot, M.: On the analysis of linear and nonlinear systems, Trans. ASME, Vol. 79, April 1957, pp 547-552.

P.23 Sivakumar, L. and Prasada Rao, G.: Parameter identification in lumped linear continuous systems in a noisy environment via Kalman-filtered Poisson moment functionals, Int. Jou. of Control, March 1982, Vol 35, No. 3, pp 509-519.

P.24 Mukherjee, A.K., Saha, D.C. and Prasada Rao, G.: Identification of large scale distributed parameter systems - Some simplifications in the multidimensional Poisson moment functional (MDPMF) approach, Int. Jou. Systems Science, 1983, (to appear).

GENERAL SYSTEM IDENTIFICATION AND RELATED TOPICS

G.1 Anderson, B.D.O. and Moore, J.B.: 1979, optimal filtering, Prentice Hall, Englewood Cliffs, NJ.

G.2 Aström, K.J. and Eykhoff, P.: System identification - a survey, 1971, Automatica, Vol. 7, p 123.

G.3 Balakrishnan, A.V. and Peterka, V.: Identification in automatic control systems - a survey, Proceedings of the 4th IFAC Congress, 1969.

G.4 Bellman, R. and Roth, R.S.: A scanning technique for system identification, Jou. Math. Anal. Appl., 1979, Vol. 71, pp 403-411.

G.5 Billings, S.A.: Identification of nonlinear systems - a survey, Proceedings. IEE, 1980, Vol 127, Pt-D, CTA, No. 6, pp 272-285.

G.6 Bolch, G.: Identifikation Linearer Systeme durch Anwendung von Momentenmethoden. Dr. Ing. Dissertation, Department of Electrical Engineering, University of Karlsruhe, 1973.

G.7 Collins, P.L. and Khatri, H.C.: Identification of distributed parameter systems using finite differences, Jou. of Basic Engg., Trans. ASME, June 1969, Vol. 91-D, No. 2, pp 239-245.

G.8 Cuenod, M. and Sage, A.P.: Comparison of some methods used for process identification, IFAC Symposium, Identification in Automatic Control Systems, Prague, Paper 1, 1967.

G.9 Desai, V.K. and Fairman, F.W.: On determining the order of a linear system, Mathematical Biosciences, Vol. 12, 1971 pp 217-224.

G.10 Diekmann, K. and Unbehauen, H.: Tests for determining the order of canonical models of multivariable systems, IFAC Symposium on Theory and Application of Digital Control, Jan. 5-7, 1982, New Delhi, India.

G.11 Eykhoff, P.: System identification, John Wiley, London, 1974.

G.12 Halfon, E., Unbehauen, H. and Schmid, Chr.: Model order estimation and system identification theory and application to the modelling of ^{32}P kinetics within the trophogenic zone of a small lake, Ecological Modelling, Vol. 6, 1979, pp 1-22.

G.13 Hsia, T.C.: On a sampled data approach to parameter identification of continuous linear systems, IEEE Trans. on Aut. Control, Vol. AC-17, No. 2, 1971, pp 247-249.

G.14 Hsia, T.C.: A discrete method for parameter identification in linear systems with transportation lags, IEEE Trans. on Aerosp. Electron. Systems, Vol AES-5, 1969, pp 236-239.

G.15 Kubrusly, C.S.: Distributed parameter system identification - a survey, Int. Jou. of Control, Vol 26, 1977, pp 509-535.

G.16 Lee, R.C.K.: Optimal estimation, identification and control, MIT Press, Cambridge, MA, USA, 1964.

G.17 Ljung, L. and Glover, K.: Frequency domain versus time domain methods in system identifiation, Automatica, Vol. 17, No. 1, 1981, pp 71-86.

G.18 McCormick, J.M. and Salvadori, M.G.: 1971, Numerical methods in FORTRAN, Prentice Hall of India, New Delhi.

G.19 Mehra, R.K.: On the identification of variances and adaptive Kalman filtering, IEEE Trans. on Aut. Contrl, 1970, Vol.AC-15, pp 175-184.

G.20 Rake, H.: Step response and frequency response methods, Automatica, Vol 16, 1980, pp 519-526.

G.21 Roberto P. Guidorzi: Invariants and Canonical forms for systems structural and parametric identification, Automatica, Vol. 17, 1981, pp 117-133.

G.22 Rucker, R.A.: Real time system identification on the presence of noise, IEEE Wescon Convention, Record, Preprint 23, 1963.

G.23 Sage, A.P. and Melsa, J.L.: System identification, Academic Press, NY, 1971.

G.24 Sage, A.P. and White III, C.C.: 1977, Optimum systems control, Prentice Hall, Englewood Cliffs, NJ.

G.25 Sinha, N.K.: Estimation of transfer function of continuous system from sampled data, Proc. IEE, May 1972, Vol 119, No. 5, pp 612-614.

G.26 Smith, F.W.: System Laplace transform estimation from sampled data, IEEE Trans. on Aut. Control, Feb. 1968, Vol. AC-13, pp 37-44.

G.27 Temple, G.: The theory pf generalised functions. Proc. Roy, Soc. (Lond.) 1955, Vol 228, pp 175-190.

G.28 Unbehauen, H. and Bauer, B.: Aspects of selection of parameter estimation methods for identification of industrial processes, 4th IFAC Symposium, Tbilisi, 1976.

G.29 Unbehauen, H., Bauer, B., Göhring, B. and Schmid, Chr.:"On-line" Identifikationverfahren. Literaturauswertung und Einschätzung der Verfahren. PDV-Bericht KFK-PDV 14, Gesellschaft für Kernforschung mbH, Karlsruhe, 1973.

G.30 Unbehauen, H. and Göhring, B.: Tests for determining model order in parameter estimation, 1974, Automatica, Vol. 10, pp 233-244.

G.31 Wellstead, P.E.: An instrumental product moment test for model order estimation, Automatica, 1978, Vol 14, pp 89-91.

G.32 Young, P.: Parameter estimation for continuous.time models - a survey, Automatica, Vol 17, No. 1, pp 23-29.

G.33 Young, P., Jakeman, A. and McMurtrie, R.: An instrumental variable method for model order identification, Automatica, Vol 16, 1980, pp 281-291.

INDEX

K

L

M

P

R

S

Lecture Notes in Control and Information Sciences

Edited by A. V. Balakrishnan and M. Thoma

Vol. 22: Optimization Techniques
Proceedings of the 9th IFIP Conference on Optimization Techniques,
Warsaw, September 4–8, 1979
Part 1
Edited by K. Iracki, K. Malanowski, S. Walukiewicz
XVI, 569 pages. 1980

Vol. 23: Optimization Techniques
Proceedings of the 9th IFIP Conference on Optimization Techniques,
Warsaw, September 4-8, 1979
Part 2
Edited by K. Iracki, K. Malanowski, S. Walukiewicz
XV, 621 pages. 1980

Vol. 24: Methods and Applications in Adaptive Control
Proceedings of an International Symposium
Bochum, 1980
Edited by H. Unbehauen
VI, 309 pages. 1980

Vol. 25: Stochastic Differential Systems – Filtering and Control
Proceedings of the IFIP-WG7/1 Working Conference
Vilnius, Lithuania, USSR, Aug. 28 – Sept. 2, 1978
Edited by B. Grigelionis
X, 362 pages. 1980

Vol. 26: D. L. Iglehart, G. S. Shedler
Regenerative Simulation of Response Times in Networks of Queues
XII, 204 pages. 1980

Vol. 27: D. H. Jacobson, D. H. Martin, M. Pachter, T. Geveci
Extensions of Linear-Quadratic Control Theory
XI, 288 pages. 1980

Vol. 28: Analysis and Optimization of Systems
Proceedings of the Fourth International Conference on Analysis and Optimization of Systems
Versailles, December 16–19, 1980
Edited by A. Bensoussan and J. L. Lions
XIV, 999 pages. 1980

Vol. 29: M. Vidyasagar,
Input-Output Analysis of Large-Scale Interconnected Systems – Decomposition, Well-Posedness and Stability
VI, 221 pages. 1981

Vol. 30: Optimization and Optimal Control
Proceedings of a Conference Held at Oberwolfach, March 16–22, 1980
Edited by A. Auslender, W. Oettli, and J. Stoer
VIII, 254 pages. 1981

Vol. 31: Berc Rustem
Projection Methods in Constrained Optimisation and Applications to Optimal Policy Decisions
XV, 315 pages. 1981

Vol. 32: Tsuyoshi Matsuo,
Realization Theory of Continuous-Time Dynamical Systems
VI, 329 pages, 1981

Vol. 33: Peter Dransfield
Hydraulic Control Systems – Design and Analysis of Their Dynamics
VII, 227 pages, 1981

Vol. 34: H.W. Knobloch
Higher Order Necessary Conditions in Optimal Control Theory
V, 173 pages, 1981

Vol. 35: Global Modelling
Proceedings of the IFIP-WG 7/1 Working Conference Dubrovnik, Yugoslavia,
Sept. 1–5, 1980
Edited by S. Krčevinac
VIII, 232 pages, 1981

Vol. 36: Stochastic Differential Systems
Proceedings of the 3rd IFIP-WG 7/1 Working Conference
Visegrád, Hungary, Sept. 15–20, 1980
Edited by M. Arató, D. Vermes, A.V. Balakrishnan
VI, 238 pages, 1981

Vol. 37: Rüdiger Schmidt
Advances in Nonlinear Parameter Optimization
VI, 159 pages, 1982

Vol. 38: System Modeling and Optimization
Proceedings of the 10th IFIP Conference
New York City, USA, Aug. 31 – Sept. 4, 1981
Edited by R.F. Drenick and F. Kozin
XI, 894 pages. 1982

Vol. 39: Feedback Control of Linear and Nonlinear Systems
Proceedings of the Joint Workshop on Feedback and Synthesis of Linear and Nonlinear Systems
Bielefeld/Rom
XIII, 284 pages. 1982

Vol. 40: Y.S. Hung, A.G.J. MacFarlane
Multivariable Feedback: A Quasi-Classical Approach
X, 182 pages. 1982

Vol. 41: M. Gössel
Nonlinear Time-Discrete Systems – A General Approach by Nonlinear Superposition
VIII, 112 pages. 1982

Vol. 42: Advances in Filtering and Optimal Stochastic Control
Proceedings of the IFIP-WG 7/1 Working Conference
Cocoyoc, Mexico, February 1–6, 1982
VIII, 391 pages. 1982

Lecture Notes in Control and Information Sciences

Edited by A. V. Balakrishnan and M. Thoma

Vol. 43: Stochastic Differential Systems
Proceedings of the 2nd Bad Honnef Conference
of the SFB 72 of the DFG at the University of Bonn
June 28 – July 2, 1982
Edited by M. Kohlmann and N. Christopeit
XII, 377 pages. 1982.

Vol. 44: Analysis and Optimization of Systems
Proceedings of the Fifth International
Conference on Analysis and Optimization of Systems
Versailles. December 14–17, 1982
Edited by A. Bensoussan and J. L. Lions
XV, 987 pages, 1982

Vol. 45: M. Arató
Linear Stochastic Systems
with Constant Coefficients
A Statistical Approach
IX, 309 pages. 1982

Vol. 46: Time-Scale Modeling of Dynamic Networks
with Applications to Power Systems
Edited by J. H. Chow
X, 218 pages. 1982

Vol. 47: P. A. Ioannou, P. V. Kokotovic
Adaptive Systems with Reduced Models
V, 162 pages. 1983

Vol. 48: Yaakov Yavin
Feedback Strategies for Partially
Observable Stochastic Systems
VI, 233 pages, 1983

Vol. 49: Theory and Application of Random Fields
Proceedings of the IFIP-WG 7/1
Working Conference
held under the joint auspices of the
Indian Statistical Institute
Bangalore, India, January 1982
Edited by G. Kallianpur
VI. 290 pages. 1983

Vol. 50: M. Papageorgiou
Applications of Automatic Control Concepts
to Traffic Flow Modeling and Control
IX, 186 pages. 1983

Vol. 51: Z. Nahorski, H.F. Ravn, R.V.V. Vidal
Optimization of Discrete Time Systems
The Upper Boundary Approach
V, 137 pages 1983

Vol. 52: A. L. Dontchev
Perturbations, Approximations and Sensitivity Analysis
of Optimal Control Systems
IV, 158 pages. 1983

Vol. 53: Liu Chen Hui
General Decoupling Theory of Multivariable
Process Control Systems
XI, 474 pages. 1983

Vol. 54: Control Theory for Distributed
Parameter Systems and Applications
Edited by F. Kappel, K. Kunisch,
W. Schappacher
VII, 245 pages. 1983.

Vol. 55: Ganti Prasada Rao
Piecewise Constant Orthogonal Functions
and Their Application to Systems and Control
VII, 254 pages. 1983.

Vol. 56: Dines Chandra Saha, Ganti Prasada Rao
Identification of Continuous
Dynamical Systems
The Poisson Moment Functional
(PMF) Approach
IX, 158 pages. 1983.